PRAISE FOR

The Firm

"Thought-provoking. . . . A fascinating look behind the company's success. . . . [*The Firm*] chronicles McKinsey's rise but also raises an important question about it that is applicable to the entire netherworld of consultants, advisers, and other corporate hangers-on: Are they worth it or not?"

—Andrew Ross Sorkin, *The New York Times DealBook*

"There have been other books about this American icon, but *The Firm* is an up-to-date, full-blown history, told with wit and clarity."

—*The Wall Street Journal*

"Through an expert accretion of damning detail, McDonald builds a convincing case that, for better and (mostly) worse, McKinsey became the quintessential American business of the twentieth century."

—*Bloomberg Businessweek*

"[An] admiring book that nevertheless asks hard questions about the organization's future."

—*The Economist*

"[*The Firm*] is a book that fits one McKinsey colleague's description of former managing director Ron Daniel—'so smooth he could skate on your face and not leave a mark.' . . . Very readable."

—*Financial Times*

"Duff McDonald's book on McKinsey, one of the world's biggest consulting firms, should be made mandatory reading for every management education aspirant around the globe."

—*Business Standard*

"[A] highly readable and thoughtful history. . . . Duff McDonald offers a lucid and engrossing narrative as he considers the question of the effects and value of McKinsey."

—Blogcritics.com

"Duff McDonald has written a breezy, entertaining book about McKinsey's glorious past. . . . Refreshingly light on buzz words and heavy on personalities. . . . A fascinating tale, deftly told."

—*The Globe and Mail* (Toronto)

"A fascinating account of the rise of McKinsey. If you want to know what it is about the culture of the firm that sets it apart and has made it so successful, read this book."

—Liaquat Ahamed, Pulitzer Prize–winning author of *Lords of Finance*

"In this highly readable history, Duff McDonald brings us deep inside one of the smartest and most important firms doing business today—a place where no other journalist has taken us before. With his straightforward storytelling and thoughtful analysis, McDonald demystifies the secrets behind McKinsey's successes and offers concrete lessons on changing companies and practices for the better."

—Jamie Dimon

"In his superb examination of one of the most powerful, secretive, and least understood organizations on the planet, Duff McDonald finally solves the mystery, in elegant prose, of how McKinsey can be well known without anyone knowing anything about it. Thanks to McDonald, now we do."

—William D. Cohan, bestselling author of *The Last Tycoons*, *House of Cards*, and *Money and Power*

"I read it. It's a good book."

—Dominic Barton

"Duff McDonald's new book about the people who built McKinsey, the consulting firm that has quietly influenced American business for decades, explains the firm's tremendous accomplishments—and its equally stunning failures. As McDonald shows, the firm's greatest success may well be itself. This is critical reading for anyone who wants to understand how the world of business really works."

—Bethany McLean, coauthor of the *New York Times* bestseller *All the Devils Are Here*

"McDonald has written the definitive history of McKinsey, and through McKinsey of the entire multibillion-dollar industry that is management consulting. It's a heartbreaking tale of wasted talent."

—Felix Salmon, finance blogger, Reuters

"Timely. . . . A fast-paced account of a key business institution, its deeds and misdeeds."

—*Kirkus Reviews*

"Revealing. . . . McDonald combines a lucid chronicle of McKinsey's growth and boardroom melodramas."

—*Publishers Weekly*

ALSO BY DUFF McDONALD

Last Man Standing

THE FIRM

THE STORY OF McKINSEY AND ITS SECRET INFLUENCE ON AMERICAN BUSINESS

DUFF McDONALD

SIMON & SCHUSTER PAPERBACKS
New York London Toronto Sydney New Delhi

Simon & Schuster Paperbacks
A Division of Simon & Schuster, Inc.
1230 Avenue of the Americas
New York, NY 10020

First Simon & Schuster paperback edition September 2014

SIMON & SCHUSTER PAPERBACKS and colophon are registered trademarks of Simon & Schuster, Inc.

Designed by Akasha Archer

Manufactured in the United States of America

10 9 8 7 6 5 4 3 2 1

The Library of Congress has cataloged the hardcover edition as follows:

McDonald, Duff.
The firm : the story of McKinsey and its secret influence on American business / Duff McDonald.
p. cm.
Includes bibliographical references and index.
1. McKinsey and Company. 2. Business consultants. I. Title.
HD69.C6M386 2013
338.7'61001—dc23 2013002023

ISBN 978-1-4391-9097-5
ISBN 978-1-4391-9098-2 (pbk)
ISBN 978-1-4391-9099-9 (ebook)

For the most wonderful gift any man can receive: a daughter.

Thank you, Marguerite, for being mine.

NEW YORK, MARCH 2013

CONTENTS

INTRODUCTION: THE McKINSEY MYSTIQUE

Two minutes out of business school, Jamie Dimon decided to become a consultant. The experience left him unimpressed, and he has looked down on it since. "It's substitute management," he told me when I was deep into writing his biography. "A *Good Housekeeping* seal of approval. It's political, so if you make a decision, you can say, 'It's not my fault, it's their fault.' . . . I think consultants can become a disease for corporations." Dimon, who went on to become the chairman and CEO of JPMorgan Chase and was hailed as an Olympian financier for steering the bank above Wall Street's 2008 humbling—only to be somewhat humbled himself four years later when its own trading caused more than $5 billion in losses—made one exception to his consultant rule. Most consulting engagements weren't worth the price paid, he said, but McKinsey—well, it was the real thing.

Four years later, the Republican candidate for president, once a consultant himself, was asked how he would reduce the size of government. "So I would have . . . at least some structure that McKinsey would guide me to put in place," Mitt Romney told the editorial board of the *Wall Street Journal*. When his audience seemed surprised, he added, "I'm not kidding. I probably would bring in McKinsey."

After almost a century in business, McKinsey can lay claim to the following incomplete list of accomplishments: Once before, well before Romney was running for the presidency, it remapped the power structure within the White House; it guided postwar Europe through a massive corporate reorganization; it helped invent the bar code; it revolutionized business schools; it even created the idea of budgeting as a management tool.

Above all, McKinsey consultants have helped companies and governments create and maintain many of the corporate behaviors that have shaped the world in which we live. And in becoming an indispensable part of decision making at the highest levels, they have not only emerged as one of the great business success stories of our time but also helped invent what we think of as American capitalism and spread it to every corner of the world. The abstract, white-collar nature of modern business—the fact that the greatest value in our economy is now created by people sitting in air-conditioned skyscrapers and corporate parks who manipulate information—is a reality that McKinsey was instrumental in establishing, championing, and profiting from. The best evidence for McKinsey's expertise is the firm itself. It has followed its own advice into an enviable position of power and prestige.

At the same time, however, the company can also be saddled with a list of striking failures, missteps that would have doomed lesser firms. McKinsey consultants were on the scene when General Motors drove itself into the ground. They were Kmart's advisers when the retailer tumbled into disarray. They pushed Swissair in a direction that led to its collapse. They played a critical role in building the bomb known as Enron and collected massive fees right up until the moment of its spectacular explosion. And these are just the clients unlucky enough to have had their woes splashed across headlines. Many more have paid handsomely for guidance that shortchanged shareholders, led to unnecessary layoffs, and even prompted bankruptcies. And yet the consultants are rarely blamed for their bad advice—at least not publicly so.

Remarkably, that pervasive influence has come even though McKinsey contains more contradictions than the Bible. The firm is well known, but there is almost nothing known about it. Precious few McKinsey employees have ever become acclaimed in the outside world. The employees are trusted and distrusted—and loved and despised—in equal measure. They are a collection of huge egos that are yet content to stay behind the scenes. They are confident but also paranoid. And they are helpful yet manipulative with their clientele—and even their own people.

What do they actually do? They are managerial experts, cost cutters, scapegoats, and catalysts for corporate change. They are the businessman's businessmen. They are the corporate Mandarin elite, a private corps, far from prying eyes, doing behind-the-scenes work for the most powerful people in the world. How do they do it? Well, their methods have been compared (by others and by themselves) to the Jesuits, the U.S. Marines, and the Catholic Church. They feel so strongly about themselves that they have insisted on a proper noun where one need not exist. To an outsider, they are a consulting firm. To themselves, simply, The Firm.

• • •

But the McKinsey story is even more than all of that. It's also about the rise and reach of American business in the twentieth century—and its remarkable adaptability to changing times. American capitalism may be under stress now, but modern American management technique—which McKinsey has played a part in both creating and disseminating—has distinguished itself as much by its innovative ability as by its sheer might. Today McKinsey is a global success story. But first it was a distinctly American one.

One of the secrets of McKinsey is its very similarity to America—it has a solid foundation with an adaptive overlay, all topped off with a bit of old-fashioned luck. Make no mistake: McKinsey is not an enduring institution by accident. It has been built with much purpose. Still, could it be an accident of history, founded in the right place at the right time? Yes, but only in the same way that Google, LEGO, and Toyota are accidents. Other companies stumble into extinction.

McKinsey started in typically American fashion: with self-invention. Although it was technically founded in 1926 by a University of Chicago accounting professor named James O. McKinsey, the mythical leader of the firm is a successor, Marvin Bower, a man whose abiding goal was to invent a new profession committed to preparing clients for the challenges and uncertainties of the onrushing future. Plenty of other firms had the same idea at the same time, some even earlier, but none could match Bower's discipline and focus. He distinguished McKinsey not just for what it did but for *how* it went about it, starting with the physical appearance of its employees and moving right on through hiring, training, and the culling of their ranks through a merciless system known as "up-or-out."

Consultants of one kind or another have existed for centuries. Han Fei Tzu, founder of the so-called legalist school of ancient Chinese philosophy and adviser to the emperor, has been called the first consultant.[1] But McKinsey can nevertheless claim a remarkable number of firsts: It was the first consulting firm to realistically apply scientific approaches to management, solving business problems with a method of hypothesis, data, and proof. It was the first to gamble on youth over experience, and the first to take on the challenge of becoming truly global.

McKinsey was a major player in the efficiency boom of the 1920s, the postwar gigantism of the 1940s, the rationalization of government and rise of marketing in the 1950s, the age of corporate influence in the 1960s, the restructuring of America and rise of strategy in the 1970s, the massive growth in information technology in the 1980s, the globalization of the 1990s, and the boom-bust-and-cleanup of the 2000s and beyond. So pervasive is the firm's influence today that it is hard to imagine the place of business in the world without McKinsey.

• • •

So what is the net effect of McKinsey consultants in the world? What has been gained and lost as this relatively small group of like-minded people has consolidated power and spread the gospel of American capitalism? It's best to take that question from a few different perspectives.

McKinsey's clients, specifically those in the executive suite and the boardroom, have gotten an extremely intelligent if high-priced sounding board, a beacon in the night of managerial uncertainty. McKinsey offers a kind of industrial espionage couched in the language of "best practices." Want to know what the competition is up to? Hire McKinsey. After all, it's working with everyone else as well. The flip side of that argument is that your competitors find out about you too. But most clients have found the tradeoff rewarding.

When IBM wanted to expand into Europe in the 1950s, whom did it call for some hand-holding? McKinsey. So too did scores of other companies, from Heinz to Hoover. And then when Europe started recovering its own confidence? Why, McKinsey was there to tell the likes of Volkswagen and Dunlop Rubber that they could surely bounce back from near devastation with the consultants' help. With McKinsey's army of hardworking and youthful overachievers—what one reporter called "a SWAT team of business philosopher-kings"[2]—clients have surely gotten more effort per dollar spent than you might find anywhere else in the corporate milieu.

They have a remarkable ability to be in the right place at the right time—so many times, in fact, that you have to wonder whether they really can see the future. But the truth is subtler than that. They have created one of the most flexible business models in the history of Western capitalism: They sell what their clients are buying, and where the clients are buying it.

So powerful is the McKinsey name that merely hiring the firm can bring the desired effect—as in 2009, when publishing giant Condé Nast brought in McKinsey to demonstrate its seriousness about reducing expenses by 30 percent. The rank and file got the message. The act of hiring McKinsey can be as symbolic as it is practical.

Of course, criticisms of McKinsey's contributions to client welfare are not hard to find. For one, once McKinsey is inside a client, its consultants are adept at artfully creating a feedback loop through their work that purports to ease executive anxiety but actually creates more of it, offering and then obscuring what one author has referred to as "an illusion of a sure path to the future."[3] Executives can get so accustomed to McKinsey's presence that they can't function without it, leading to situations like the one at AT&T in the early 1990s, when the company paid the firm $96 million over five years for ongoing work.

In situations like this, there is a potential anticlient bias to the consultants' business, where the long-term result is dependence on, not independence from, the consultants. In other words, once they get the wedge end of a relationship into a company in the form of one engagement, they usually manage to hammer in the rest—becoming the so-called Men Who Came to Dinner. (To wit: They never leave.) McKinsey isn't actually embarrassed by this notion—the firm calls it the "transformational relationship," arguing that true change comes only from long-term relationships. But over the years, many McKinsey clients have paid for exorbitant, lengthy engagements with little to show for it.

• • •

What the McKinsey consultant himself has gained is a far simpler question to answer. He has gained money, power, and prestige, as well as the pretense of an intellectually minded pursuit within the corporate sphere. He is not a banker, accountant, or lawyer. He is a thinker. He has had the chance to whisper into the ears of power, to exercise influence while being insulated from responsibility. McKinsey was Enron CEO Jeff Skilling's most favored outside adviser during the Houston natural gas company's rise and fall. Skilling went to jail for his transgressions; McKinsey emerged from the scandal largely unscathed.

Perhaps best of all, a job at McKinsey is a ticket to almost anywhere in the world. The firm is the best finishing school in business, a launching pad, and a matchless résumé line. A job at McKinsey, regardless of duration, can serve as an enviable listening post for plum corporate roles, particularly at McKinsey's own clients. The firm has an astonishingly successful network of alumni, occupying corner offices and boardrooms all over the world. Lou Gerstner, the man famous for turning IBM around, worked at McKinsey before decamping for one of his clients, American Express. Morgan Stanley CEO James Gorman spent a decade at McKinsey before jumping ship to his client, Merrill Lynch. It literally happens about once a week.

Of course, not everyone goes on to a distinguished career. Enron's Skilling came from McKinsey. Two figures convicted in the greatest insider-trading scandal in history—the 2009–12 investigation of convicted hedge fund manager Raj Rajaratnam—are ex–McKinsey: former director Anil Kumar as well as former *managing director* Rajat Gupta.

You rarely see an old McKinsey consultant—like its symbiotic other, the Harvard Business School, the institution favors youth over experience. McKinsey is like Harvard in other ways. To the Harvard grad, there is Harvard and there is nowhere else. Likewise McKinsey. Indeed, McKinsey alumni almost all wear their sense of specialness for the rest of their lives. This is why the Rajaratnam scandal has shaken the firm to its roots. Even though Anil Kumar sold client secrets and Rajat Gupta trashed the firm's long-cherished value system in a public and mortifying way, neither event really affected the firm's business. The damage to its self-image has been much more severe.

• • •

Finally, what of society? There is little doubt that McKinsey has made the corporate world more efficient, more rational, more objective, and more fact based. But to what extent have its contributions gone beyond the bottom line?

McKinsey would have the world believe that its consultants are missionaries of the best in business thinking; that by pushing companies fearlessly into the future they are not just boosting profits but aiding the cause of human progress itself. There is more than some merit to this point of view. And if the smartest, most successful companies in the world continue to hire them, that in and of itself is evidence of the value they create.

But as with many of the world's big firms, it is also hard to overlook the mounting number of instances in which McKinsey advisers have behaved no better than mercenaries, collecting huge fees for work of dubious worth. At their most craven, they can be recruited to provide a high-gloss imprimatur of objectivity that is in reality mere cover for executives. They are, without question, the go-to consultants for managers seeking justification for savage cost cutting as well as a convenient scapegoat on whom to blame it. While this is surely impossible to measure, there is a distinct possibility that McKinsey may be the single greatest legitimizer of mass layoffs than anyone, anywhere, at any time in modern history.

In a sense, McKinsey is the Goldman Sachs of the consulting world. Both occupy the top rung of their respective professions, but both have come to symbolize something else as well—a nagging question of whether all the brainpower and energy devoted to them have truly been worth the opportunity cost. Is this really where America's best and brightest can make their most meaningful contributions? McKinsey itself has answered that question in part by shifting its sights to a more global clientele, as the U.S. economy faces its starkest challenges in more than fifty years. The country has been thoroughly McKinseyed, and there's nothing left to do but rebuild it from the bottom up, a task for which McKinsey may be ill suited.

In that, a question for McKinsey is the same one we might pose to American business itself: Is it still coming up with new ways of thinking, or is it merely relying on past accomplishments to stay ahead of the competition? It is surely doing both, but in what measure of each?

• • •

Consulting in general—and McKinsey in specific—has always been a difficult phenomenon to pin down. On the one hand, that's because the ideal client-consultant relationship is one in which the consultant fades into the background almost immediately after the work is done and the checks are cashed. But there's another reason, and that's the elusiveness of what is actually being bought and sold in the first place.

In a word, McKinsey sells its own enlightenment, the firm's ability to see things more clearly than its clients. Doing that once is no great accomplishment—a fresh perspective is the way out of many problems, in business or otherwise. Doing it for nearly a century is a tall order indeed, but it is one that McKinsey has apparently met.

When a CEO hires McKinsey, he knows he is hiring some of the smartest and hardest-working people worth opening the corporate checkbook for. Insight can—and often does—come from extreme analysis, and there is no better army of analysts in the world than McKinsey's. And they do always seem to be where the action is: In 2012, McKinsey's China-based business was one of the most rapidly growing areas of the firm.

But the CEO who hires McKinsey is also hiring it for its influence and its power, for the fact that the firm is woven tightly into the fabric of decision making at the very highest levels—corporate, political, or otherwise. It really is no surprise that Rajat Gupta, the former McKinsey managing director, was dealing in inside information from his seat in the boardroom of Goldman Sachs. Sometimes it really is simply about whom you know. And McKinsey knows everybody.

For better or for worse, McKinsey just might be the most influential collection of talent in the world. How the firm managed to gain and hold on to that influence without most of us noticing is only one part of its story. What it has done with that influence since its founding in the 1920s is what this book is about.

1. THE OZARK FARM BOY

From Gamma to Lake Shore Drive

The history of American business is the story of men who came along with a healthy dose of self-confidence. Henry Ford knew he had found a way to mass-produce cars. Steve Jobs knew there was huge opportunity in taking the computer out of the office and into the home. Jeff Bezos of Amazon.com saw the promise of the Internet early, and he took retailing into the ether.

James O. McKinsey's confidence wasn't about something so tangible. Did you have a problem in your business? Let him have a look at it, and he was confident he could help you figure out what to do about it. Not only that, he promised to tell the rich and powerful what they were doing *wrong*. It was on these two convictions that he founded the company that eventually became the most powerful consulting firm in the world. It was nervy, and it was new, and in that way it was a distinctly American business that helped shape the history of business itself.

"I have spent a considerable amount of my time during the last fifteen years in saying and doing things which should have been said and done by others, but which they hesitated to say and do," McKinsey wrote in a 1936 letter. "I assume this is due to the fact that because of my philosophical inclinations I have developed some tendency to think in a logical manner and when this thinking indicates a conclusion I think it difficult to resist the temptation of stating it. Furthermore, when such a conclusion indicates definitely the need for action I feel I am rendering a service by trying to secure such action. I suppose I am doomed, therefore, to go through life doing things which make people think I am aggressive and hardboiled."[1]

Yes, people thought both those things. But they also thought he was the man to call when the problem seemed insoluble, the one who could set a wayward billion-dollar operation back on the right track. Even though McKinsey's death at a relatively young age deprived him of the chance to properly reflect on his own career, he had already made it a long way from his days as a barefoot farm boy in the Ozarks,[2] and he died as one of the most respected businessmen and innovators of his era. He didn't just understand the needs of the giant corporations that were reshaping American society in their own image—he anticipated those needs and helped companies solve problems they didn't even know they had.

It all started with accounting, which McKinsey rescued from the dismal routines of bookkeeping and reimagined as a tool of strategic management. He was a straight talker whose air of assurance inspired others to follow his lead. He defined corporate management away from managing the routines of a bureaucracy and toward imagining the future and preparing a workforce for it. He was an early advocate of downsizing and other means of cost cutting as a way to save struggling firms. And he used all these ideas, and many more, to build what in time became the most powerful consulting firm, and one of the strongest business franchises, on the planet.

McKinsey was born in 1889 to James Madison and Mary Elizabeth McKinsey in Gamma, Missouri, and was raised in a three-room farmhouse. At a young age, he distinguished himself as a wizard with numbers. One early biographer claimed that McKinsey's high school principal hired him to teach algebra to his own teachers,[3] though another said that he merely taught other students, not teachers.[4] Whatever the version of the story, teaching was clearly his early passion, and it looked as if it would become his lifelong profession. He graduated from the state teachers college in Warrensburg, Missouri, in 1912 with a bachelor's degree in pedagogy. He saw himself first—and above all—as a man who had lessons to give.

Those who met him remarked on his "presence"—he was tall, at six feet four—and forthright mien. He was also quite stubborn: Despite suffering temporary blindness while in college, he later ignored his doctor's advice to quit smoking cigars or risk another loss of eyesight.[5] Whether or not the doctor knew what he was talking about is beside the point; McKinsey refused to change his behavior.

Teachers college was just the start of an education odyssey that included a bachelor of law degree from the University of Arkansas at Fayetteville, a stint studying and teaching bookkeeping in St. Louis, and a bachelor of philosophy degree from the University of Chicago. As it did for most of the young men of his era, World War I took him on a detour. In 1917 he was drafted into the army; starting as a private, he was promoted to lieutenant in the Ordnance Department the next year and traveled across the United States, working with suppliers of war matériel.[6] He was shocked by what he found: The inefficient and disorganized supply system offended his orderly accountant's inclinations. Here was a problem that cried out for expert management, but where could it be found?

Following his discharge at the age of twenty-nine, McKinsey continued to add to his list of credentials. In the span of a single decade, he managed to obtain a master's in accounting from the University of Chicago, was appointed an assistant professor of accounting at the university, and joined fellow professor George Frazer's accountancy firm of Frazer and Torbet. But that was not all. In 1923 he was named vice president of the American Association of University Instructors in Accounting, and in 1926 he became a professor of business policy at the University of Chicago.

This last appointment was the first hint that the man knew accounting could be more than mere bookkeeping—that numbers could reveal not just profit and loss, assets and liabilities, but the whole story of a business and what it could accomplish. To that point, accounting had been viewed as a record of the past. McKinsey spun it around and aimed it at the future, turning it into a tool of effective management.

Mac met Alice "Polly" Louise Anderson of Sioux City, Iowa, when she took an accounting class taught by McKinsey at the University of Chicago. In just the second session she told him that she was dropping the class, as she had decided there was nothing more she could learn from him.[7] With her boldness, she won his heart, and the two were married in 1920. In 1921 she gave birth to twin sons, Robert and Richard.

But McKinsey's life was defined by ambition more than by family. His son Robert remembers him as an absentee father who bore the scars of his threadbare upbringing. Although he became very rich by his late thirties—he once rented a summer farm that had its own polo fields and eventually moved to one of Chicago's elite addresses on the 1500 block of Lake Shore Drive—he refused his children toys because he considered them "inessential" purchases.[8]

He was a workaholic who was rarely at home. He once claimed that he ate all his lunches, half of his breakfasts, and a third of his dinners with prospective clients.[9] When he was around, his children were not allowed to bother him while he was "working." While he had the ability to be warm and affable, he deployed those qualities only for work. He had no interest in literature or culture. While he joined many local clubs, he did it for professional contacts, not for the social or extracurricular pleasures of the clubs themselves.

That's pretty much all that is known about Mac McKinsey's personal life. But a few points are worth reinforcing. First, McKinsey saw that a company's secrets could be found in its accounting. He proudly wrote books about the minutiae of budgeting and forecasting, because he believed it was only through rigorous adherence to such "fact-based" analysis that a company could truly reach its potential. His protégé Marvin Bower, however, later distanced McKinsey & Company from this image of accounting, so much so that it came to define itself in opposition to the field. In Bower's mind, accountants were drones bound by rules while consultants were free thinkers whose vision and creativity extended far beyond balance sheets. Bower's McKinsey started with the numbers and then added perspective.

Second: With his own experience as proof of concept, McKinsey attracted a cohort that wanted to achieve in life the same things he did—rising above an often humble upbringing to become rich and important men. McKinsey pursued success by combining an ability to focus relentlessly with a knack for breaking rules. And he decided early on that he would gain power by speaking truth to it. "He was quite poised," wrote William Newman, who worked with McKinsey in the 1930s. "No trace of Ozark poor farm boy, not the least. He'd had poverty in his childhood and I think that left its mark. He wanted to succeed, but he also wanted to have money, the satisfaction that he did have money and that he was free to spend it."

The American Century

In 1941 Time Inc. publisher Henry Luce coined the term "American Century" in a *Life* magazine editorial. He was describing the country's global economic and political dominance leading up to World War II. But Luce was also correct in the literal sense: The American Century had actually started several decades before.

The building of the railroads and coincident spread of the telegraph in the United States in the middle and second half of the nineteenth century helped create the world's first truly "mass" markets. If an executive had ambition, his company didn't have to serve just local customers. It could serve an entire continent and beyond, if it had the wherewithal to get the organization and logistics right.

The economic historian Alfred Chandler documented the momentous changes in what came to be known as the Second Industrial Revolution in his seminal book *Scale and Scope*—the title of which referred to the simultaneous revolutions in both scale (in manufacture) and scope (in distribution) in American enterprise. Those twin revolutions transformed the United States from an agrarian society to an industrial powerhouse in the span of a single generation. In 1870 the nation accounted for 23 percent of the world's industrial production. By 1913 that proportion had jumped to 36 percent, exceeding that of Great Britain.[10]

By 1920, when only a third of homes in the country had electricity and only one in five had a flush toilet,[11] the country's business establishment was embarking on a course of radical, unprecedented expansion. This brought with it a dilemma that has preoccupied business leaders ever since: how to grow big while maintaining control over the enterprise. Moving from a single-product, owner-run enterprise into a complex and large-scale national one is a difficult task. First, you have to build production facilities massive enough to achieve the desired economies of scale. Second, you have to invest in a national marketing and distribution effort to ensure that sales have a chance of matching that scaled-up production. And third, you have to hire, train, and *trust* people to administer your business. Those people are called managers, and in the first half of the American Century, they were in very short supply.

The benefits to successful first-movers were gigantic. In industries where only one or two companies took the plunge early, they dominated their field for a very long time to come; this group includes well-known names like Heinz, Campbell Soup, and Westinghouse.[12] A ten-year merger mania, from 1895 through 1904, also brought the creation of a number of corporate entities the likes of which the world had never seen—1,800 companies were crunched into 157 megacorporations,[13] including stalwarts like U.S. Steel, American Cotton, National Biscuit, American Tobacco, General Electric, and AT&T.[14]

The key business problem identified during this transition—and one that underwrote McKinsey's success for several decades—was that a single, central office could no longer adequately administer such far-flung empires. Power had to be ceded to the extremities. The question was how. It was a quandary that beguiled some of the great thinkers of the time, including political scientist Max Weber, who argued that a systematic approach to marshaling resources through bureaucracy was a necessary and profound improvement over pure charismatic leadership.

In his book *American Business, 1920–2000: How It Worked,* Harvard professor Thomas McCraw pinpointed the issue: "In the running of a company of whatever size, the hardest thing to manage is usually this: the delicate balance between the necessity for centralized control and the equally strong need for employees to have enough autonomy to make maximum contributions to the company and derive satisfaction from their work. To put it another way, the problem is exactly where within the company to lodge the power to make different kinds of decisions."[15]

Companies such as DuPont, General Motors, and Sears Roebuck were the first to address this problem systematically. According to

Chandler, DuPont sent an emissary to four other companies experiencing similar issues—the meatpackers Armour and Wilson and Company, International Harvester, and Westinghouse Electric—to ask what *they* were doing.[16] And the answers were remarkably similar: The innovators moved from the centralized system to a multidivisional structure with product and geographic breakdowns. The concept left operating division chiefs with total control over everything except funding resources. Top managers took a more universal view of the business, monitoring the divisions and allocating capital accordingly.

The most successful companies of the era, such as General Electric, Standard Oil, and U.S. Steel, all employed some variant of this model. But by and large, they had developed these ideas on their own, a process of trial and error that was costly and time consuming. They would have much preferred hiring outside experts to help them with it, if only such experts existed. This was a huge commercial opportunity that called for an entirely new kind of service.

Stepping into the Breach

Unwittingly, the federal government did its part to create the modern consulting business. Starting in the last part of the nineteenth century, Washington made periodic regulatory efforts to curb the power of big business, including the 1890 Sherman Antitrust Act, the Federal Trade Commission Act and Clayton Act of 1914, and the Glass-Steagall Act of 1933. The intended effect of these measures was to prevent corporations from colluding with one another to fix prices and otherwise manipulate the markets. The unintended effect, according to historian Christopher McKenna, was to accelerate the creation of an informal—but legal—way of sharing information among oligopolists. Who could do that? Consultants.[17]

Regulatory efforts paid another rich benefit to the likes of McKinsey: Restricted from cutting backroom deals with each other, firms were thus obliged to actually compete, which meant they needed to make their operations more efficient. Here again, consultants were the answer.

But perhaps the circumstance that most aided the creation of the consulting industry was the entry of a new, key player into business itself. Empire builders with names like Carnegie, Duke, Ford, and Rockefeller had built huge, vertically integrated companies, but they had neither the time, the talent, nor the inclination to create and carry out management systems for those entities. These were the conquerors of capitalism, not its administrators. And yet, as Chandler pointed out, "their strategies of expansion, consolidation, and integration demanded structural changes and innovations at all levels of administration."[18]

Into the breach stepped a new economic actor who was neither capital nor labor: the professional manager. Gradually, he replaced the robber baron as the steward of American business. Alfred P. Sloan, the legendary president of General Motors, was the first nonowner to become truly famous for his managing skills. His decentralized, multidivisional management structure gave GM the agility to outmaneuver the more plodding Ford Motor Company and snatch the industry lead. Ford may have revolutionized manufacturing, but Sloan realized that the car-buying market had become big enough to be segmented into people who bought Buicks, Cadillacs, Chevrolets, Oldsmobiles, and Pontiacs. By the late 1920s, the car market was maturing, and people wanted *choice*. Sloan also gave them the ability to buy a car on *credit*—a groundbreaking idea at the time. Before the decade was over, GM had surpassed Ford as the market share leader, a position it didn't relinquish until the 1980s.

Sloan and his ilk were perfect customers for McKinsey: Lacking the legitimization of actual ownership, professional managers felt great pressure to show they were using cutting-edge practices. And who better to bring those practices to their attention than consultants who were talking to everyone else? This was the beginning of a decades-long separation of ownership from control in corporate America, and the consultant was an able ally to the professional manager in this tug-of-war—an ally who wasn't gunning for the manager's job. Thus began the era of managerial capitalism.

For more than two centuries, economists had argued that companies operated in some sense at the mercy of Adam Smith's "invisible hand" of the market. But the revolution in management thinking in the United States offered up an alternative idea: the "visible hand" of management, which made things happen, as opposed to merely responding to external market forces.

The academy helped move this ideology along. Before 1900, there was only one undergraduate business school in the country, the University of Pennsylvania's Wharton School of Finance and Economy, founded in 1881 with a $100,000 donation from financier Joseph Wharton. The Tuck School of Business at Dartmouth followed in 1900. Over the next decade, pretty much every major institution started explicitly preparing its students for careers in management.

Although the rise of today's industrial-farm-style MBA programs is really a postwar phenomenon, Harvard founded its Graduate School of Business Administration in 1908, with a second-year business policy course designed to give the student an integrative approach to addressing business problems, including accounting, operations, and finance.[19] The purpose of the course, according to the school, was to give the student an ability to see those problems from the top management point of view. Much of James McKinsey's academic writing centered on this very issue and later informed the practice of his firm.

McKinsey's Oeuvre

As a young academic, McKinsey was a prolific writer, if not an especially engaging one. His first four books were dry tomes on the nitty-gritty of accounting and taxes: *Federal Incomes and Excess Profits Tax Laws* (1918), *Principles of Accounting* (cowritten with A. C. Hodges, 1920), *Bookkeeping and Accounting* (1921), and *Financial Management* (1922). But with his fifth effort, he broadened his horizons significantly. *Budgetary Control* (1922)—the first definitive work on budgeting—turned accounting on its head, promoting it as an essential tool of managerial decision making. "Budgetary control involves the following," McKinsey wrote. "1. The statement of the plans of all the departments of the business for a certain period of time in the form of estimates. 2. The coordination of these estimates into a well-balanced program for the business as a whole. 3. The preparation of reports showing a comparison between the actual and the estimated performance, and the revision of the original plans when these reports show that such a revision is necessary."[20]

It seems commonsensical, but McKinsey's new way of looking at the use of the budgeting process sparked nothing short of a revolution. "No other mechanism of management of similar scope and complexity has ever been introduced so rapidly," wrote one commentator just ten years later. "It is estimated that 80 percent of budgets installed in industry have been put in since 1922."[21]

Up to that point, budgeting was a one-way exercise: Accountants added up all of a firm's expenses and then tossed in a sales projection almost as an afterthought. In McKinsey's view, companies should start by developing their business plan, figure out how to achieve it, and then estimate the costs of doing so. In this new context, budgeting wasn't just a ledger activity; it could also be used to identify excellence in performance (i.e., those who outperform their budget), to spot weaknesses (those who underperform), and to take corrective action. "[While] there are many who do not yet plan scientifically. . . ," he wrote, "there are few who will deny the merits of the system."

Two subsequent books fleshed out McKinsey's ideas: 1924's *Managerial Accounting* and *Business Administration*. The former taught students how accounting data could be used to solve business problems. Using the data of traditional recordkeeping, he suggested the possibility for much greater control over a company's destiny, including the establishment of standard procedures (how things should be done and to whom information should be reported), financial standards (ways to judge operating efficiency), and operating standards (including nonfinancial measures, such as quality). To today's business student, this kind of comprehensiveness seems obvious. But at the time, the idea of planning, directing, controlling, and improving decision making by means of regular and rigorous reporting of company results was novel. The latter book contained the seeds of McKinsey's General Survey Outline—a thirty-page system for understanding a company in its entirety, from finances to organization to competitive positioning. It became part of his consultants' toolkit sometime in the early 1930s.

It is hard to overestimate the impact of the General Survey Outline (GSO). It served as the foundation of his approach to understanding a company and provided novice consultants with a clear road map to do so themselves. The survey also shaped consultants' thinking: The emphasis in the GSO was more on *why* managers did things, as opposed to *how* they did them. Using the GSO, consultants started every engagement by thinking of the outlook for the industry of their client, the place of the client in the industry, the effectiveness of management, the state of its finances, and favorable or unfavorable factors that might affect the future of the firm. No detail was too small to take note of, whether it was a study of all firm policies—including sales, production, purchasing, financial, and personnel—or an analysis of whether the layout of equipment in a company's plant provided for the most efficient flow of the production operations. By the time the young consultant had completed the survey for his client, he knew the company and its business cold.

"You can see McKinsey's intellectual development," says John Neukom, who worked at McKinsey from 1934 to the early 1970s and wrote a brief memoir of his time at the firm. "He had lost interest in the details of accounting. By the time I arrived, he had lost interest in the budgetary procedure and was now excited and interested in analyzing companies and seeing how companies worked. He was clearly diagnosing the total problems of the company."[22] In a 1925 speech at a conference for financial executives in New York, McKinsey offered the kind of pointed insight for which he is remembered: "Usually, I find that the executive who says he does not believe in an organization chart does not want to prepare one because he does not wish other people to know that he had not yet thought through his organization properly. For the same reason many men are opposed to budgets. They are unwilling for anyone to see how little they have thought about what they are going to do in future periods."

Armed with that insight—and the general philosophy that management can shape a company's destiny—he decided to set up shop and sell it.

Bastards Require No Diplomacy

In the mid-1920s, McKinsey began doing business under the banner of James O. McKinsey and Company, Accountants and Management Engineers, the progenitor of the modern-day McKinsey & Company. Strangely for a company that prides itself on getting the details right, the actual date of its founding is unknown—a firm training manual from 1937 suggests 1924,[23] while John Neukom's memoir says 1925.[24] Whichever it was, McKinsey's timing was excellent. The economy was booming, and the need for consulting services was seemingly endless.

It is worth noting that the word "consultant" was not in the name of his firm. Rather, the term "management engineers" reflected the prevailing ethos of the time: that science held the answers to most serious questions, and even human commerce could profit from the rigors of this kind of data-driven analysis. McKinsey's standard working pads have always been crosshatched graph paper, another nod to engineering. The fact that McKinsey himself employed no actual engineers was beside the point.

Intellectual underpinnings aside, the firm's real-world roots were in red meat. McKinsey's first client was Armour & Company, one of the country's largest meatpackers. The treasurer of Armour had read *Budgetary Control* and wanted McKinsey to help rethink the meatpacker's approach to budgeting and planning.

The first partner McKinsey brought on board was A. Tom Kearney, who had been director of research at Swift & Company, another Chicago meatpacker. Kearney was a warmer, more congenial complement to McKinsey's formal and pointed demeanor. Another early partner was William Hemphill, the same treasurer of Armour who had hired McKinsey in the first place.

McKinsey continued to teach at the University of Chicago for a time, but he eventually switched full-time to the firm. One reason he seems to have juggled so many responsibilities is that he didn't waste time with niceties at the office. In Hal Higdon's 1970 history of consulting, *The Business Healers,* one associate recalled him saying: "I have to be diplomatic with our clients. But I don't have to be diplomatic with you bastards."[25] (Marvin Bower later modeled his own approach to constructive criticism after McKinsey's tough love approach.)

McKinsey was blunt, but he was also a quick and agile thinker. He once diagnosed a client's problems just by looking at the company's letterhead. A Midwestern maker of air conditioners had stationery that announced "Industrial Air Conditioning Installations—Coast to Coast from Canada to Mexico." In an era before salespeople traveled by airline, McKinsey observed that travel expenses were probably eating up the majority of the company's profits and that employees should confine themselves to a radius of five hundred miles around Chicago. He was right.[26]

Even the Depression couldn't stop the growth of the firm. By 1930, McKinsey's professional staff totaled fifteen. In 1931 he drafted the General Survey Outline, and the next year he opened a New York outpost in the offices of a defunct investment house at 52 Wall Street—six offices with a reception area. The New York–based consultants busied themselves working not only for local industrial companies but also for investment banks like Kuhn, Loeb & Co. In 1934, the Chicago office moved to the forty-first floor of the new Field Building on 135 South LaSalle. By the mid-1930s, McKinsey's partners were charging $100 a day for their services—a giant figure, though nothing compared with the founder himself, who was billing five times that, the highest rate for a consultant in the country.

Taking the Pianist Out of the Brothel

Before James McKinsey could be successful, he had to clean up the reputation of management as a concept. In *The Management Myth,* philosophy-student-turned-consultant-turned-author Matthew Stewart's highly critical look at the history of management thinking, the author argued that it was flawed from the get-go. And he pinned original sin on Frederick Winslow Taylor, the father of "scientific management."

Taylor's famous time-and-motion studies used stopwatch analyses of manual labor with the goal of shaving seconds off rote, repeated activities, thereby enhancing productivity. There was, Taylor argued, just "one best way" to produce anything, and a manager armed with Taylor's tools could identify it. In Stewart's account, Taylor was a pseudoscientific proselytizer who promoted the spurious notion that "laborers are bodies without minds, managers are minds without bodies."[27]

But Taylor's ideas about improving the efficiency of labor were very popular and influential in his day; in 1911 he published *Principles of Scientific Management,* an instant hit that was eventually translated into eight languages. In 1914 he attracted 16,000 people to a New York speech on his theories.[28] Edwin Gay, who opened the Harvard Business School, was a Taylor disciple. Henry Ford's line production system was a pure distillation of Taylor's thinking. Even Lenin and Trotsky embraced him, envisioning Taylorism as the solution to Russia's problems.[29]

As Taylor rocketed to fame, countless firms sprang up to cash in on similar technical-sounding solutions to business problems. Most have vanished, including Harrington Emerson and Bacon & Davis, though some live on more than a century later: The consultancy Arthur D. Little was founded in 1886. ADL's engineers earned early acclaim for *actually* making a silk purse from a sow's ear in 1921 by spinning gelatin from the sow's ears into artificial silk. Edwin Booz founded his eponymous firm—later Booz Allen Hamilton—in 1914. There was also Charles E. Bedaux, who developed a system called "payment by results" and founded his Bedaux Company in 1919. He was one of the first consultants to expand overseas, planting a flag in Britain, Germany, and France in the 1920s. By 1930 more than a thousand companies were using Bedaux consultants, including Eastman Kodak, DuPont, and General Electric.[30]

The fact that just about anyone could call himself a consultant meant that shysters and scam artists abounded, tarnishing the entire field's reputation. E. N. B. Mitton, a mining engineer who joined the British office of Bedaux in the 1930s, joked at the time that he would rather tell his mother that he was working "as a pianist in the local brothel" than admit that he had joined a consulting firm.[31]

From the very beginning, James McKinsey went to great lengths to distinguish his firm from its less savory predecessors—he and his partners had multiple university degrees and strong connections to the establishment. And just as McKinsey flipped accounting on its head, he and his contemporaries likewise turned Taylorism on its head. Instead of focusing on line workers at the bottom of the organizational chart, they zeroed in on the growing white-collar bureaucracy and top managers.[32] But Taylor's pretensions to scientific rigor were very much part of McKinsey's sales pitch too. By co-opting the rhetoric of engineering, wrote Harvard professor Rakesh Khurana, McKinsey grounded managerial authority in the realm of the "disinterested expert"—instead of just one side in an increasingly violent struggle between capital and labor—and helped provide justification for management's ultimate dominance in the relationship.[33]

As the managerial class grew in size, so too did the demand for consultants. Between 1930 and 1940—while the country was in the grip of the Depression—the number of consulting firms grew from 100 to 400. By 1950 there were more than 1,000 such firms in existence.[34] This kind of growth—far in excess of the overall economy—makes sense for an emerging profession. What's remarkable is that the consulting industry outgrew the economy for pretty much the rest of the twentieth century too.

Critics of the field have long lamented what they consider the fundamental question at the heart of consulting: whether its contributions to corporate growth and innovation justify its own growing piece of the economic pie. Stewart's argument is that it doesn't actually matter whether Taylor and his immediate descendants provided genuine value. Consultants saw demand and sought to satisfy it—what else is there to business?

"Their specialty, at the end of the day, [was] not the management of business, but the business of management," wrote Stewart. "[And] as in any business, what separates the winners from the also-rans isn't independently verifiable expertise; it is the ability to move product."[35] Over the next four decades, no firm moved this product as well as McKinsey & Company.

The First Ex-Consultant

Given that the early years of the James O. McKinsey & Company coincided with the Depression, it makes sense that the firm built its original reputation helping clients deal with financial difficulties. A good portion of the work was pure restructuring and help in analyzing possible merger and takeover scenarios in the hope of finding efficiencies of scale or relieving competitive pricing pressure. But the firm's bread and butter was finding more effective—and profitable—organizational structures, and a lot of the demand for that came from bankers. Because banks were prohibited from selling their own consulting services, they brought in firms like McKinsey to analyze potential deals, like a proposed merger in 1934 of corporate rivals Republic Steel and Corrigan-McKinney.

The firm did so much work for bankers in the 1930s that the General Survey Outline, James McKinsey's proprietary model for analyzing companies, was colloquially termed the Bankers' Survey. But the firm made inroads in other industries too, particularly in steel. Client work took the consultants from coast to coast: John Neukom wrote in his memoir that he spent 179 nights away from home in 1936, covering 31,000 miles, 33 cities, and 112 Pullman sleeper cars.[36] McKinsey himself became chairman of the board of the American Management Association that same year.

James McKinsey's connections fed the firm's business. He claimed to have taken "every important banker in Chicago or New York to lunch," with the result that "nearly every one at one time or another has given me work."[37] But it wasn't long before the firm found out how to survive without him.

James McKinsey's career as a consultant came to an end in 1935, when McKinsey was retained by Marshall Field & Company, the largest department store in the Midwest. The retailer was in critical condition; it had lost $12 million over the previous five years and was faced with an impending $18 million loan repayment. McKinsey attacked the problem with overwhelming force, dispatching a team of 12 consultants to interview 752 retailers in 32 states, as well as paying visits to factories and wholesale outlets.

McKinsey's conclusion was that Marshall Field should specialize: unload its wholesale business, sell its 18 textile mills, focus entirely on retail, and cut, cut, cut. The board members of Marshall Field not only loved this idea but also asked McKinsey if he would carry it out. While many consultants would recoil at such a notion, McKinsey was intrigued—and in October 1935, he accepted the post of chairman and chief executive of Marshall Field.

Over the years, numerous consultants have left the field because they preferred to "do, not tell." As McKinsey himself found out, it's harder than it sounds. The cost-cutting measures that McKinsey had recommended were brutal to implement. In what came to be known as McKinsey's Purge, more than 1,200 employees of Marshall Field were let go,[38] and though the moves restored the retailer to solid financial footing—it survived until its acquisition by Macy's in 2005—management lost the hearts and minds of its employees.

For several years, the retailer grappled with a disenchanted workforce that had suddenly woken up to the fact that their corporate benefactors *didn't* actually care about them beyond their ability to punch a clock. The process revealed a flaw that critics continue to see in a preponderance of consultants: While long on ability to intellectualize their way out of a business situation, they often come up short on the human factor. It's why words like "restructure," "downsize," and "rationalize" have found their way into the modern business lexicon, all elegant euphemisms for laying people off. Management consultants may bring value to a company's bottom line, or to its executives' bank accounts, but they are rarely accused of adding value to the life of the rank and file.

The job took a serious toll on McKinsey himself. Contending with the day-to-day implications of his harsh prescriptions, he became depressed and physically run down. "Never in my whole life before did I know how much more difficult it is to make business decisions myself than merely advising others what to do," he famously told a colleague—a stinging indictment of the nascent field he had helped found.[39] Not only that, but the effects of the Depression were confounding the problems at Marshall Field. McKinsey soon found himself cutting whole divisions, retiring people early, and firing veteran employees.[40] His son Robert later recalled his father receiving between ten and twenty letters threatening his life.[41]

A Temporary Alliance

While off at Marshall Field, James McKinsey did not abandon his own firm. He was far too controlling for that. In the same month he started his career as a retail executive, he orchestrated the merger of McKinsey & Company with Scovell, Wellington & Company, a rival accountancy/consulting outfit founded in 1910. The deal resulted in a company with two arms—the consulting outfit McKinsey, Wellington & Company and the accounting concern Scovell, Wellington & Company. The firms were supposed to work in close concert. At the time, in 1936, McKinsey, Wellington had twenty-two professionals in Chicago, seventeen in New York, and five in Boston.

Horace "Guy" Crockett of Scovell became the manager of the New York office of McKinsey, Wellington—supplanting the young Marvin Bower, who was mollified by being made a partner in the new entity. McKinsey's Tom Kearney and C. Oliver Wellington took charge of the firm's Chicago outpost. Crockett promptly brought in a gigantic consulting project for U.S. Steel—which topped $1.5 million in total billings. (James McKinsey already knew the U.S. Steel people. He had been spending one day a month in Pittsburgh discussing strategy at $500 per diem with U.S. Steel head Myron Taylor.[42] This kind of advice-on-retainer became an increasingly valuable part of the firm's business in the years ahead.)

Despite the hierarchical setback, Marvin Bower's influence in the firm was actually on the rise. He had convinced McKinsey to eliminate auditing work in New York in 1935 because he considered it at odds with consulting work. Bower had foreseen the conflict between a consultant who openly rooted for his client and an auditor who was supposed to lack prejudice.[43] Still, in this regard, Bower's views were not yet fundamental to the direction of the firm. The Chicago office continued selling accounting services, and McKinsey had actually set his sights on taking control of Scovell, Wellington if he could.

Bower proved to be influential in other ways. Primarily, he didn't like Oliver Wellington. Bower would later espouse a "one firm" philosophy—all offices were equal, regardless of geographic location—

but he did not yet feel this way. He didn't, for example, like reporting to a boss not of his own choosing, and he was furious with Wellington's request that Bower provide him with copies of his letters. Perhaps it was because he wrote what can only be described as obsequious letters to McKinsey, such as an excited 1936 missive about his social plans for obtaining new business in New York.

The eventual severing of the union began in an exchange of letters. In July 1936, McKinsey sent a stinging one to Wellington accusing him of trying to control the McKinsey, Wellington partners too much and of stifling their creativity. In August Wellington responded, questioning the commitment of the McKinsey people to mutual cohesion. The differences were apparently smoothed over for a time, but they erupted in full force after a major shock: the death of James McKinsey.

The Adventurous Conservative

McKinsey was just forty-eight years old when he succumbed to pneumonia, leaving behind a firm with just a handful of offices and a few dozen professionals. The task of turning his company into a major fixture of American business fell to Marvin Bower, who is rightly regarded as the real architect and visionary of the firm.

Born in Cincinnati, Ohio, in 1903, to William J. and Carlotta Preston Bower, young Marvin enjoyed an upbringing more comfortable than McKinsey's. Not that he didn't try his hand at the hard stuff: During high school, he held jobs as a grinding-machine operator and an ice deliverer, before gaining admittance to Brown University in 1921. After graduating with a dual degree in economics and psychology in 1925, he worked for a Cleveland-based law firm, Thompson, Hine & Flory, as a summer associate. A large part of his work was collecting debt from hardware retailers on behalf of the firm's wholesale clients.

Unsure of his future, he asked his father, the deputy recorder of Cuyahoga County, Ohio, for advice. His father told him to study law, a remarkably conservative piece of advice considering it was the Roaring Twenties and there were all sorts of exciting new enterprises. But young Bower dutifully complied, enrolling in Harvard Law School in the fall of 1925. When he eventually climbed to the top of McKinsey & Company, he tilted its recruiting toward the kind of bright and ambitious but risk-averse young man he himself had been.

Between his second and third years of law school, Bower married his high school sweetheart, Helen McLaughlin, and after graduating in 1928, he applied for a job at Jones Day—the most prestigious law firm in Cleveland. Bower badly wanted to be part of the Cleveland establishment and Jones Day was the ticket. But his law school grades weren't high enough and he was turned down. Lacking any further inspiration, he went back to school again, enrolling at the nascent Harvard Business School in the fall. The difficulty in landing the job he wanted apparently chastened the young man; he finished his first year at HBS in the top 5 percent of his class and finally succeeded in getting hired at Jones Day.

With the Depression now in full swing, Bower devoted most of his time at the law firm to serving as secretary to committees of bondholders of eleven separate troubled companies. "No one asked why these companies had failed," he later observed. He also admitted that his own understanding of business and management problems had been both "amateurish and superficial."[44] But Bower liked the challenge of devising recapitalization structures for struggling or bankrupt companies; he thought it creative. On the other hand, the drafting of the associated legal documents—bond indentures and the like—he found interminably boring. He dreamed of a company that would enable him to focus just on the creative stuff he enjoyed. As fortune would have it, a professor at Harvard Business School told him about James O. McKinsey, a man who had ideas eerily similar to Bower's.

The younger man wrote to McKinsey in Chicago, asking for a meeting in early 1933, when Bower was needed in the city for a bondholders committee assignment. It was a meeting of minds. McKinsey told Bower of his thirteen-person firm of "accountants and engineers" who were working on the very issues Bower found enjoyable, while leaving the rest to the lawyers. McKinsey suggested that if Bower were to join his firm, he would enjoy himself 100 percent of the time, instead of just half of the time. After discussing it with his wife, Bower returned to Chicago for a round of three more interviews, after which he was offered a job. He took it. "[The] people at Jones Day thought I had lost my mind," he said later.[45]

Bower's first day at work was November 13, 1933. His first assignment was helping the bondholders committee of New York's Savoy-Plaza Hotel come up with ideas to boost sales and reduce costs, thereby easing considerable financial difficulties.[46] Another early study was for Commercial Solvents, a medium-sized chemical company. When Bower had the temerity to tell the company's president that it was unfair to hold his sales manager responsible for profits when he, the president, retained total control over pricing, the client was furious. "Young man," he roared, "I retained your firm to investigate our sales activities, not my activities. I am going to call Mr. McKinsey and ask him to remove you from the study!" The president did as threatened, and McKinsey did as he was asked, removing Bower from the account.[47]

Bower chose to use the experience as a learning opportunity, realizing that it had perhaps been a little brash to expect the client to take such criticism from a man half his age. It wasn't that he thought his thinking was wrong; it was how he had delivered it, and the fact that he hadn't consulted with James McKinsey first. Bower translated the lesson into one taught to every McKinsey consultant to this day: Deliver the bad news if you must, but deliver it properly.

He hadn't lost the confidence of McKinsey, either. When New York office head Walter Vieh left to return to Chicago, Bower was made New York office manager. He hadn't been with the firm a year, but he had impressed his boss. What's more, he was the most senior consultant in New York at the time.

McKinsey himself exercised almost complete authority over the firm he founded until his death four years later; but in the decades that followed, Bower molded McKinsey into just the firm he had envisioned as a young lawyer: an organization that enjoyed the same prestige and influence as prominent law firms but didn't spend time on the boring stuff. In other words, a law firm that didn't practice law.

Death of a Pioneer

James McKinsey, according to Bower, always intended to return from Marshall Field and run the consulting firm with Bower as his right-hand man. But the stress of retail turnaround led to the case of pneumonia, which, in the age before penicillin, proved fatal. He died on November 30, 1937. The *Chicago Tribune* announced it on the front page.

A tribute in the publication *American Business* noted the progress that McKinsey and his ilk had made in legitimizing their profession and in elevating the status of the entire managerial class: "His record with Marshall Field and Company proves, if proof be needed, that the difference between a profit and a loss, is nearly always a matter of management."[48]

This was not a universally held view. The consulting firm's business in Chicago suffered for more than a decade from the fallout of his ruthlessness at Marshall Field. This was a lesson for the future: Association with a failing firm was toxic for a consultancy's business. From this point forth, McKinsey & Company strove to stay well behind the scenes. It henceforth refused to reveal its client list and at the same time insisted that clients show similar discretion.

Only thirty-four at the time, Bower took Mac's passing particularly hard. He'd idolized the man so much that he named his third son after him—James McKinsey Bower. Of his mentor, Bower wrote: "He felt that everyone who sought success wanted criticism, and he really gave it. Most of his criticism was negative. Indeed, his praise was so occasional that it made a deep impression when it was given. This approach appealed to me. (I have found that when praise is evenly balanced with criticism, only the praise is remembered.)"[49]

Throughout his career, Bower constantly paid tribute to the influence of a man with whom he'd worked for only four years. But decades later, he began to occasionally inflate his own role in accounts of the firm's history. Bower's biographer Elizabeth Edersheim documented a conversation he later had with a McKinsey director who asked him why he never changed the name of the company to Bower & Co. "My partners and I had to go out and convince clients to keep us on, even though we had lost our principal partner," he said. "I had to seek out new engagements as the head of the firm, even though my name was not McKinsey. . . . I resolved right then that I would never place my successor in the same position of having to explain why his firm wasn't named after him. So we kept Mac's name on the door, and I've never regretted it."[50] Bower's remarks belie an obvious fact at the time. In the wake of Mac's death, Marvin Bower was *not* the head of the firm; he didn't take on that role for another twelve years. So it was not Marvin Bower's company to do with as he wished. At least not yet.

The Cult of Servitude

Firms don't always survive the death of their founders, and McKinsey could have easily been one of those that didn't. The month before Mac died, the U.S. Steel study, which had accounted for 55 percent of New York billings, came to an end. At its peak, the U.S. Steel study employed over forty people from McKinsey,[51] an early model of the money to be made if you got your hooks into a big client. It would have been hard, under any circumstances, to make up for such a large drop in earnings. The next year, 1938, was no easier. New York and Boston struggled, and Chicago couldn't pick up the slack. The firm lost $57,000, which was a lot more than it sounds like today—especially considering that the firm's total assets were just $256,376, the equivalent of roughly $4 million in 2012.

In April 1938, Bower wrote a memo to Tom Kearney and Guy Crockett in which he suggested they throw Wellington overboard. He envisioned a new firm in which the three men were partners—but in which only Kearney and Crockett contributed significant capital. His senior partners liked him, but they also knew that he didn't have the cash.

By October, Bower had achieved his goal. McKinsey, Wellington & Company "regretted" to announce the withdrawal of C. Oliver Wellington from the consulting firm. What's more, the consultancy was to be split in two: in New York and Boston, McKinsey & Company; in Chicago, McKinsey, Kearney & Company. Tom Kearney had suggested that the two consulting offices consolidate in Chicago, but the New York contingent chose to go their own way. Marvin Bower didn't yet have the power and influence to emerge from the fracas as head of McKinsey & Company, but there is no doubt that he played a critical—if not *the* critical—role in having Wellington banished from the business and in establishing New York's independence.

Bower's own reminiscences of the time are rife with damning critiques of his colleagues. A run-in with partner Walter Vieh on the Savoy-Plaza had resulted in Vieh's being sent back from New York to Chicago. "I soon discovered that he approached problems like an accountant,"[52] Bower later wrote, a damning indictment from the self-styled big thinker. He also stuck a shiv in both Oliver Wellington and Tom Kearney when contemplating just who would take the mantle from James McKinsey: "Oliver could not lead . . . [and] . . . Tom was not a natural leader."[53]

Crockett and another partner, Dick Fletcher, each kicked in $28,000, enabling McKinsey & Company to stand on its own feet; Crockett became the managing partner. "I was too young," explained Bower, as if that were all there was to it. Too young, and too poor: Bower's ante was a mere $3,700, an amount that clearly made him subordinate to Crockett. Ewing "Zip" Reilly, a friend of Bower's from the Harvard Business School Club of New York, loaned the fledgling firm $10,000, a favor that Bower never forgot. The firm restated its purpose as "management consulting" as opposed to "management engineering."

While New York and Chicago were separate legal entities, the plan was for them to be loose affiliates, exchanging pieces of business they might land in the other's backyard (for a 15 percent finder's fee) and jointly maintaining the integrity of the McKinsey brand. In the meantime, the partners of the two firms committed to buy McKinsey's widow out of her 21 percent stake over the next two years, for a total of $141,796—more than $2.2 million in 2012 dollars.

Bower and his contemporaries carried Mac McKinsey's torch in some ways but not in others. With McKinsey gone, Bower was free to act on his distaste for accounting and banish it from the firm's offerings. A profile in *Consulting* magazine after Bower's death summed it up neatly: "It is perhaps an ironic footnote that what may have been

McKinsey's greatest contribution to business is seemingly at odds with the contribution of the man who has most influenced the makeup of the firm that bears the McKinsey name. For while few people did more to unshackle accounting professionals than James O. McKinsey, few people worked harder than Bower in the coming years to put the shackles back on. Or at least, keep the accountants out of the boardroom."[54] James McKinsey was an accountant; Marvin Bower was not. Under Bower's direction, McKinsey & Company employees used accounting tools, but they were no mere accountants. They were *consultants*.

While Guy Crockett nominally led the consultancy over the next decade-plus, it became Marvin Bower's firm. It is said of some things that they refer to someone "in name only." By the time Bower was done at McKinsey, it was just the opposite: While the firm did not bear his name, everything else about it screamed Marvin. First and foremost: Everything was sacrificed at the altar of the client. The client, the client, the client. Bower saw himself as little more than a servant to client interests. In building a firm of like-minded individuals, he also built a paradox of remarkable proportions: Marvin Bower and his colleagues were going to become the most successful and influential servants in history.

2. THE MAKING OF THE FIRM

The Repeater

If James McKinsey invented the idea of strategic planning, his successor, Marvin Bower, perfected it by turning the idea into a profession. Bower was obsessed about making sure he and his peers would not be dismissed as corporate parasites and would enjoy a respect similar to other early twentieth-century professionals like doctors, lawyers, engineers, and ministers. But for that to happen, he needed to come up with the rules, protocols, language, and codes of behavior—the whole culture—of the American consultant. As it happens, this was exactly what Bower was born to do. He had the focus, discipline, and fastidiousness that made it possible for him to give birth to the unique and enduring institution that McKinsey remains today. The military has the Marines; the Catholic Church has the Jesuits. Consulting, thanks to Bower, has McKinsey.

The main reason for his success is a quality often overlooked in the corporate world: a willingness to repeat himself. He spent fifty years of his life saying the same things over and over again. "He never deviated from his message," said Lou Gerstner, a former McKinsey consultant who went on to acclaim at RJR Nabisco and IBM. "Being a great leader is often less a matter of eloquence and more a matter of repetition and consistency." Asked about that very trait in 2011, James Gorman, a former McKinsey consultant and current CEO of Morgan Stanley, was blunt. "What a great quality. I wish I had more of it."[1]

First, Bower had to invent the McKinsey persona: The McKinsey consultant would be selfless, be prepared to sacrifice money and personal glory for the sake of building a stronger firm, never look for public credit, and always be confident and discreet. British foreign secretary William Hague, a former McKinsey consultant, put it this way: "You are encouraged to believe that you belong to a special club of elite people."[2]

When it came to sacrifice, Bower himself set the example. When the firm opened a San Francisco office in 1944 in partnership with Kearney's Chicago contingent, it was Bower and his wife, Helen, who moved to Palo Alto for the summer of 1945 to stand the office on its feet. But it wasn't until 1963 that Bower made a decision that, journalist John Huey correctly concluded, "permanently set him—and McKinsey—apart from its competitors."[3]

Bower and his partners could have sold their firm at market value at the end of their careers as a way of cashing out, thereby personally reaping the rewards of their efforts. After all, at any successful firm, market value exceeds book value by a significant margin. Their contemporaries did it—the founders of George Fry & Associates and Barrington Associates both cashed out in the 1950s. McKinsey's competitor Cresap, McCormick and Paget actually managed to sell itself twice in twelve years—first to Citicorp in 1970, and then to Towers Perrin in 1982 after having bought the firm back from Citi in 1977.

Instead, Bower sold his shares back to the firm at book value. In doing so, he demonstrated precisely the kind of allegiance to the cause he expected of anyone wishing to be successful at McKinsey: He forsook considerable riches for the good of the institution, in the process giving young consultants the ability to buy their way into the partnership without mortgaging their houses to do so. His McKinsey would be self-perpetuating, and he gave up a fortune to make it so. But he also sent the message that working for McKinsey was like joining a special order of men willing to put the higher cause of the firm ahead of self-interest.

Bower's decision came as a surprise to many, including his own family. "Let me just say there was shock on people's faces when he told us that he was selling his shares back to McKinsey at book value," said his son Dick Bower. "It felt unbelievable, to tell you the truth. But that was Marvin for you."[4]

Before Bower came along, any huckster could call himself a consultant, and many did. So Bower came up with a version of the job that drew from other real twentieth-century professions: The consultant would comport himself as a lawyer, with discretion and integrity; he would bring scientific, fact-based rigor and precision to the task, like an engineer or accountant. Like a doctor, he would dispense advice to unhealthy companies on how to get better and to healthy companies on how to stay that way. And, like a priest, he would serve his clients.

Because Bower had a background in law, his desire to be just like a law firm was perhaps the most explicit of all. Historian Christopher McKenna wrote of a 1940 brochure in which the firm explained: "We serve business concerns on management problems in much the same way that the larger law firms serve them on legal problems."[5] Another way of looking at it: It's hard to get any business done in the United States without hiring a lawyer. If Bower could achieve a similar result for McKinsey, the firm could entrench itself in the economy.

What's more, Bower was already trying to move away from the idea of consultants as "business doctors" and to position the firm as a resource used by the best companies more than by the worst. "Those who use us the most, need us the least," he told *Fortune* in 1954.[6]

In his 1997 book *The Will to Lead,* Bower outlined the five primary responsibilities of the professional consultant; some of them overlap, but as we know, Bower was prone to repeating himself. First, the consultant must put his client's interests ahead of the firm's interests. If a McKinsey consultant thinks a study is not in the interests of a client—a waste of money, or a misguided investigation—he must tell the client so. Second, he must adhere to the highest standards of truthfulness, integrity, and trustworthiness. Third, he must keep to himself the client's private and proprietary information. Fourth, he must maintain an independent position and tell the client the truth as he sees it. And fifth, he must provide only services that have real value.

On the surface, there seems nothing controversial about this set of rules. Do your best for your clients, they say, and try not to screw them over in any way. But Bower's idea of the professional was more nuanced than that. Part of the reason for his split in 1947 with Tom Kearney, he wrote, was that his partner was satisfied with "ethical" standards instead of "professional" ones.[7] To act ethically means acting within the bounds of morality, which any honest person should be able to do. To act professionally means to take on a whole additional set of responsibilities. If that seems like an impossibly fine distinction, well, it was clear as day to Bower. To him, the *purpose* of the enterprise was to serve clients; profits were a byproduct.

Gibberish

Can an adviser to a business really claim he's not engaging in a commercial act? It's practically an absurd notion on its face—helping to increase profits as a selfless exercise—but that's the line Bower chose to take, and thousands of McKinseyites have absorbed his view. "I still run to work—figuratively of course," said Ron Daniel, the venerated former managing director of McKinsey, in 2010. "[It] may sound like motherhood, [but this] is a life of service. It's not the same as being a doctor or part of the clergy, but in our own way, we are here because we serve our clients, and that idea of service just happens to be important to me."[8]

Bower carried out this service approach by mandating an all-for-one-and-one-for-all approach to moneymaking. He directed that all consultants share in one big pool of company earnings, not just the earnings of their office. This boosted the entrepreneurial spirit within the firm, spreading risks associated with opening a new office and encouraging talent to move freely throughout the company. The policy also sent a clear signal to potential clients—that when you enlist the services of McKinsey & Company, you have the full resources of the firm at your disposal.

To go along with this philosophy, Bower came up with a new language. McKinsey had *clients,* not customers. Its consultants played a *role* rather than worked at a job. It had a *practice* and *firm members,* not a business and employees. It didn't sell, nor did it have products or markets. The firm did not *negotiate* with clients, that being far too adversarial a term. It merely *made arrangements*. It didn't have rules. It had *values*. And, perhaps most important, McKinsey was not a company; it was *The Firm.*

There were occasions when Bower's McKinsey didn't behave like a secular priesthood. Though he stipulated that the firm never solicit work or advertise its services, McKinsey did produce 2,600 copies of a 42-page booklet titled *Supplementing Successful Management,* the majority of which ended up in the hands of current and prospective clients. In 1966 the company advertised in *Time* magazine under the guise of looking for recruits. "What does it take to succeed at McKinsey?" the headline asked in one ad. The answer: "Outstanding mental equipment finely honed by a first-rate education, coupled with the imagination to solve complex problems; the self-confidence, skill in expression, and sensitivity to other people that lead to high personal effectiveness; and, of course, good character and high standards."

The message was clearly aimed at potential clients as much as potential hires. But the firm denied any advertising motivation once again.[9] McKinsey's insistence that it did not engage in a PR strategy was simply false; in the 1960s, the firm contracted with PR pioneer Pendleton Dudley. It later used the services of Murden and Co., a consulting firm even more behind the scenes than McKinsey. Murden was an early force in the Bilderberg conferences, the secretive annual meeting of Western influencers.

Bower's insistence that the firm avoid traditional advertising for professional reasons also made a virtue of obvious necessity. For what could McKinsey advertise even if it wanted to? Certainly not its client list. "Management consulting is too complex an art to be explained effectively in the limited space of an advertisement," wrote journalist Hal Higdon in *The Business Healers*. "About all a consulting firm can talk about effectively is the extremely high competence of its personnel. The effect might be somewhat similar to the Roman Catholic Church's taking two pages of *Life* to advertise God."[10]

So what made a McKinsey consultant successful? Bower dedicated his life to defining him. First, said Bower, "the successful consultant has a personality that causes most people to like him."[11] And with that likable personality, the McKinsey consultant should make his way into his community's establishment: He was expected to join local boards, get involved in charities, and even attend church. This was community relations as business strategy, another manifestation of Bower's pragmatic idealism. (There was an ugly side to McKinsey's caste system: Henry Golightly, a New York–based consultant, was run out of the firm when it was discovered that he was homosexual. Truman Capote, a friend who at times stayed over at Golightly's

Hamptons beach house, named his *Breakfast at Tiffany's* heroine after the consultant, who was placed on "medical leave" when the details of his private life became known.)

Second, the McKinsey consultant had to inspire confidence with his appearance. Bower's writings are full of physical descriptions of people he hired in part because of how they looked. "I found that [Harrison Roddick] had an attractive appearance and personality," he wrote in one instance;[12] "Walter Vieh . . . was a fine looking and likable man in his late forties"[13] in another. As recently as the 1990s, said one former McKinsey consultant, the notion that one was "clubbable"—the type to be asked to join a high-end social club—remained an explicit characteristic of McKinsey hires.

Bower's obsession with appearances was of the time. When George MacDonald Fraser began writing his multititled chronicle of the cad Harry Plaget Flashman in 1969, he described his antihero in the precise terms one might think Bower looked for in recruits: "His eyes [were] blue and prominent and unwinking—they looked out on the world with that serenity which marks the nobleman whose uttermost ancestor was born a nobleman, too. It is the look that your *parvenu* would give half his fortune for, that unrufflable gaze of the spoiled child of fortune who knows with unshakeable certainty that he is right and that the world is exactly ordered for his satisfaction and pleasure."[14]

And the McKinsey consultant was usually tall too. One (not-so-tall) rival consultant suggests that McKinsey has long hired taller-than-average people for the sole reason that history has shown people pay more attention to them. And he's right: In a recent excavation of the mausoleum of Chinese emperor Qin, the average height of an infantryman was five feet nine, the average height of an honor guard was six feet two, and an infantry general was six feet four.

Bower enforced an unyielding dress code: dark suits, hats, and garters. Long socks were required because Bower abhorred the sight of "raw flesh." Maurice Cunniffe, who worked at the firm from 1963 to 1969, could remember the protocol as if it were yesterday. "Definitely long socks," he said. "And a feather on your hat only if it was barely peeking over your hat band."[15]

"You would wear garters and you would wear a hat," recalled McKinsey consultant Jack Vance. "You didn't wear bow ties and Lord knows you didn't have a mustache." Or argyle socks. In one heralded piece of McKinsey lore, Bower is said to have attended a client meeting in 1966 with a young associate who had the audacity to reveal a flash of argyle under his pants cuff during the meeting. Upon returning to the office, Bower whipped off one of his signature blue memos on appropriate sock wear, and he even held a Saturday clinic on the right way to dress.[16] As recently as the 1990s, consultants were strongly encouraged never to leave their offices without their suit jackets on, although they were allowed to work in shirtsleeves. It wasn't until 1995 that the firm conceded business casual days to its hardworking minions. Competitors and clients still make fun of McKinsey consultants and their cuff links.

Bower once explained the rationale for his sartorial standards. "If your job is to help a client have the courage to follow the trail indicated by the facts, you need to do everything you can to minimize the distractions and deviations the client is likely to take," he told his biographer Elizabeth Edersheim. "If you have revolutionary ideas, they are much more likely to be listened to if you do not have revolutionary dress. . . . If you were an airline passenger, and the pilot came aboard the plane and he wore shorts and a flaming scarf, would you have the same confidence as you did when he came on with his four stripes on the shoulder? Basically, the dress code all has to do with what you want to do, when you want to build confidence and an identity."[17] Whatever the argument, Bower was cooking the individuality of his consultants out of them as soon as possible. In 1962 McKinsey staffers gently mocked their workplace by publishing *The Consultants' Color-*

ing Book, in which every color suggested was black or gray. Longtime partner Warren Cannon compared the dress code to that of "moderately well-to-do morticians."

(Bower wasn't entirely blind to shifts in fashion. Three years after John F. Kennedy shocked the nation in 1961 by forgoing a hat at his inauguration, Bower turned up at the office without one. Bower's consultants consulted with one another: Had the decree been lifted? "I'd wait six weeks," one consultant told another. "It may be a trap."[18] It wasn't: The hat requirement had gone by the wayside.)

Conformity was enforced too in the way the offices looked and how the memos were written. All offices were made to look the same—and they still do, to this day. And the reports that the company produces for such extravagant fees all adhere to a precise formula—blue covers, the same typeface, sparse use of text, and a common language. Most McKinsey reports begin with a page titled "Today's Discussion." It's a brief of what the consultants hope to get across to the client, presented in outline form, and it shows not just how McKinsey presents but how its consultants are taught to think: in logical, well-structured, and easy-to-follow steps. A McKinsey consultant, according to the Bower way, was never supposed to put his personal stamp on anything.

So Bower substituted himself for the firm; he was its embodiment, and thus every detail deserved and received his attention. He took memo writing to an extreme, delivering his thoughts at excessive length on any subject that crossed his mind. It became a McKinsey tradition: To this day, firm leaders will write fifteen-page memos to the entire staff on a whim, discussing their view on the role of a consultant or how to succeed at McKinsey. Bower once concluded that too many ellipses and dashes had found their way into company reports. He issued a memo banning their use.[19]

Bower wrote the firm's first Basic Training Guide in 1937. It included everything from expense protocols to directions on how to write a proper letter to a client. That same year, McKinsey, Wellington inaugurated its reading program for associates, complete with required book reports. Every McKinsey consultant was forced to read what can only have been a page-turner, the two-volume *Air Conditioning,* as well as more compelling titles such as *The Human Problems of an Industrial Civilization, Modern Economic Society,* and *Automotive Giants of America*.

The firm demanded that every consultant read at least fifteen books in the coming year, and submit book reports to partner Harrison Roddick in New York. If that seemed like a lot of reading for already busy consultants, the guide suggested that each man employ what could only be described as a sort of rudimentary speed-reading technique. "It has been well proven that one should practice reading as rapidly as possible, first for short and then for longer periods," the consultants were told. "It will be found that gradually the general reading pace will be quickened. It is best not to read word for word, but to take in at a glance phrases and sentences." And a threat: "The names of men who do not send in reviews will be brought to the attention of the partners."

Bower's exhaustiveness in producing the guide was typical of the man. Did a consultant need a sample engagement letter? There were two samples included for his perusal. Did he need guidance on how to respond to a potential inquiry regarding the relationship between McKinsey, Wellington & Company and Scovell, Wellington & Company? There were several pages on the matter. There were copies of speeches by James McKinsey, rules for when the use of a Pullman car was allowed on a train trip to see a client (when it was more than 100 miles), and five pages on the creation of time sheets for internal use as well as submission to clients. McKinsey later dispensed with giving clients much more than a single sheet of paper that included its fee, but in 1937 the firm was as enamored as all of American industry with the meticulous gathering and analysis of data. They were management *engineers,* after all.

Another example of an early philosophy that has since been jettisoned: The guide included an engagement letter that touted the "considerable experience" that all men working for McKinsey had before joining the firm. Later, McKinsey flip-flopped precisely on that point, having come to consider such experience an obstacle to broad-gauged problem solving, but in 1937 it was one of the firm's most cherished assets.

As with almost everything he wrote about McKinsey to McKinsey people, Bower insisted on an almost ridiculous level of secrecy about the Basic Training Guide, despite the fact that it contained hardly anything of a competitive or proprietary nature. "The Manual should be treated in the strictest confidence," he wrote. "It is recommended that it not be taken away from the office or from your hotel room when away on long engagements. This will avoid its loss." Why did it matter? Because unlike other professions—law, medicine—consulting was obviously built on pretense, where dress, manners, and language were meant to present some notion of capability that wasn't there to see on a diploma.

One reason for his caution might have been that at the end of the guide, Bower let loose with a bit of unbridled ambition that he usually took great pains to keep out of public view. "It is not unreasonable to compare the outlook for the [firm] today with that of the Ford Motor Company at the beginning of the Century," he wrote. "The [firm] has relatively as satisfactory conditions under which to operate as Ford did in the early days of the automobile industry, and our progress during the next thirty years depends entirely upon the extent to which we develop these possibilities." Ambitious, perhaps, but also dead-on.

Such expressions, though, were rare for Bower, who preferred to steer pretty much any conversation back to the topic of professionalism. Doug Ayer, a consultant at the firm from 1962 to 1968, recalled telling Bower of his plans for an upcoming ski trip. "He said he regarded skiing as unprofessional," said Ayer. "I laughed. He didn't. He said, 'You're running the risk of breaking your leg, and having that get in the way of client work.' I told him I was going anyway, but that I appreciated his opinion."[20]

Upgrading the Clientele

As World War II raged in the early 1940s, McKinsey improbably hit its stride. Conflict and corporate confusion proved good for business, as the firm helped American industry convert to war production. It advised ketchup-maker Heinz on making gliders and American Automotive on making tanks. While this wasn't necessarily the kind of work Bower envisioned for his platonic McKinsey, business was nevertheless booming: By 1945, the firm had eighty-nine clients in New York (up from thirty-five five years earlier), twenty-five in Boston (up from nine), and four in San Francisco.

Revenues climbed from $284,000 in fiscal 1940 to $420,000 in 1942. In 1943, when payments to the McKinsey estate ended, the underlying vitality of the business was revealed: a profit of a quarter-million dollars and a net margin in excess of 40 percent. The firm posted losses in the last two years of the war, but the business was growing. The year after the war, the consulting staff numbered sixty-eight, up from twenty-five in 1942. Numbers like that promised a bright future for consulting.

At every pass, the firm expanded its vision of what consulting could be. Bower made speeches all over the country to professional organizations and composed treatises with paint-peeling titles like *Unleashing the Department Store* and *The Management Viewpoint in Credit Extension*. The point was to give the firm the patina of intellectualism, to sell big concepts to big clients.

In 1937 the Boston office hired Paul Cherington, a former marketing professor at Harvard Business School and author of *Consumer Wants and How to Satisfy Them*. The book was one of the first expressions of the product cycle—the idea that, like humans, products had different life stages (birth, growth, maturity, and decline) and that opportunities and problems changed in each stage. After the 1935 Wagner Act, which mandated collective bargaining with unions, McKinsey created its own specialty in the field. It hired Harold Bergen, former labor-relations manager at Procter & Gamble, and began advising clients on how to deal with their growing masses of employees and the rise of labor unions.

Bergen brought with him a client list that upgraded McKinsey's roster in one fell swoop: Cluett-Peabody, H.J. Heinz, Johns Manville, Lukens Steel, United Parcel Service, Upjohn Company, Sylvania Electric, and Sunbeam Electric.[21] McKinsey was never so foolish as to get labeled anti-union, but to its clients—corporate executives—it was clear which side of this growing struggle the consultants were on.

James McKinsey's animating idea was that the firm would operate like an exclusive private club admitting only the most prestigious clients. By 1940, it actually started to look that way: In addition to Bergen's list, the membership included American Airlines, U.S. Steel—and Marshall Field. Despite the serious damage Mac's brutal layoffs had inflicted on the firm's image in Chicago, the retailer remained a client.

A Strategy Around Strategy

The firm specialized in turning problems into profits. With banks holding lots of foreclosed property and corporate assets from the Depression, McKinsey pitched its general surveys as essential tools. When the economy began to recover, McKinsey deftly began to pitch more aggressive methods for making businesses grow, all the way down to unraveling the workflow processes for companies like Four Roses Whiskey. "[It was] the most miserable thing I ever did," recalled Warren Cannon. "[It] involved my traveling with whiskey salesmen to find out how they really sold the stuff which was, by the way, a lot of drinking."[22]

The key, though, was to persuade people that McKinsey's ability to solve problems was just as inspired as the solutions themselves. When the Progressive Era ushered in a cultural acceptance of scientific methods, there was McKinsey, offering scientific evaluation of customer problems. Cutting back because of the Depression? McKinsey offered to help you downsize. When the challenge shifted to managing huge organizations, McKinsey offered advice on the newest thinking in organizational structure.

This was not only satisfying people's desire to better themselves. It was also preying on the insecurity of keeping up with the Joneses. McKinsey offered the former, but the implicit sell was the latter. In organization theory, they call this "mimetic isomorphism"—the tendency to imitate another organization in the belief that, if others are doing something, it must be worthwhile.

In the first half of the century, the nation's industrial giants were mostly preoccupied with maximizing economies of scale. The dominant idea had been to organize themselves around function—purchasing, marketing, sales—while executives overseeing those groups had responsibility for *all* of the company's products. The insight of GM's Sloan and his peers at DuPont and Sears was to invert that structure and put executives in charge of single product lines. This dissemination of responsibility—dubbed "multidivisional" or "M-form"—enabled companies to be more responsive to changes in the marketplace, and it allowed managers to make decisions without sending every single one up the executive chain for approval.

By the mid-1940s, General Motors and a few others had embraced the M-form, to their tremendous benefit. But much of corporate America remained in the dark, and this was a great opportunity for the consulting industry—to spread the new corporate gospel, the secrets of the best companies. At this point, McKinsey was not even the market leader; it faced strong competition from the likes of Robert Heller & Associates; Cresap, McCormick and Paget; and Booz Allen Hamilton. Within the span of a decade, though, the firm not only grabbed the lion's share of organizational work in the United States but also led the way into Europe, where the devastation of World War II had cleared the way for new thinking.

The new corporate structure liberated the people at headquarters from day-to-day problems and allowed them to focus on the big picture. It also created a whole new class of top-tier executives—highly compensated free thinkers with no actual line responsibility. They got to spend their time doing "strategic thinking." Strategy was not new—the word originated with the Greek *strategos,* meaning "army leader." But as Walter Kiechel pointed out in *The Lords of Strategy,* the word didn't really enter the corporate lexicon until the mid-twentieth century. One of the earliest mentions of the word was in New Jersey Bell executive Chester Barnard's 1938 book, *The Functions of the Executive,* in which he mentioned "strategic factors."[23] Most people don't strategize alone, however. And you certainly don't strategize with your competitor. Enter, once again, the disinterested consultant. Consultants didn't merely solve business problems—they helped this new breed of executives rationalize and protect their own existence.

Business historians regard the emergence of strategic thinking as a big breakthrough. "Management is not just passive, adaptive behavior," wrote Peter Drucker in his 1955 book, *The Practice of Management*. "It means taking action to make the desired results come to pass." In other words, companies did not have to be at the mercy of impersonal forces, says Harvard Business School professor Pankaj Ghemawat. Strategic planning enabled them to control their own destinies.[24] As executives of top American firms came to believe this and embrace it, they turned to McKinsey for help. And when those same companies shifted their focus to going abroad in the aftermath of the war to take advantage of momentarily crippled Continental competitors, McKinsey helped them find their way.

One Final Obstacle

Believing he was James McKinsey's chosen heir, Bower wanted full control, which meant wresting the firm away from Tom Kearney, who had been James McKinsey's first partner and was running the Chicago office. The New York operation was dominant, bringing in more than twice as much revenue as Chicago. With Crockett's backing, Bower made plain his desire to bring the firm together under one name—McKinsey & Company—which irked Kearney, who was convinced it was *his* name that brought in business. A split was inevitable, and it came in 1947 when Bower and his partners bought full rights to the name McKinsey & Company and opened their own Chicago office under the leadership of Harrison Roddick. Roddick had joined the firm as a twenty-six-year-old in 1935 and had since risen to the level of director in the New York office.

With Kearney out the door, Bower had just one last obstacle in his path to power—Guy Crockett—who served as McKinsey's managing director from 1939 to 1950 but is largely a forgotten man in the firm's history. Most accounts jump straight from James O. McKinsey to Marvin Bower. That is at least in part because Crockett was a pliable figure who was happy to let Bower, a driven, righteous man, consolidate power. While Bower took pains to acknowledge Crockett in his own writings, others haven't been so kind. "Crockett was the head, but Bower was the drive and the idea person," former managing director Ron Daniel told an interviewer in 2003.[25] Another colleague threw the dreaded pejorative at Crockett: "There was no comparison between [Crockett and Bower]. Crockett was an *accountant*."[26]

The McKinsey Process

McKinsey insisted that it would work only for the chief executives of firms and not be shunted off to their underlings. Anything that wasn't important enough to involve the CEO wasn't important enough for the consultants. This had the added advantage of freeing McKinsey from having to offer specialized, technical advice. CEOs didn't have time for such intricate details, so McKinsey didn't bother with them either. This became a major piece of the firm's identity: Narrow expertise is for chumps; we do vision.

As the firm gained the confidence of its clients, it was able to institute a new and enviable approach to billing. Whereas it had historically billed like a law firm—on a per-diem basis—in the 1940s, McKinsey began what it referred to as "value billing": simply charging clients what McKinsey deemed its services to be worth. It was a stroke of genius. To this day, McKinsey invoices for extensive consulting engagements can run little more than a single page, with a staggering total—say, $10 million—for services rendered. Should a client ever object, the firm can correctly claim that it's been standard practice for more than fifty years.

Another practice instituted fifty years ago was never to reveal the list of its clients. CEOs like this because they don't want competitors, or anyone else, to know they need outside help. McKinsey is content to let credit for any success accrue to the client. As the journalist and biographer Robert Caro once observed: "You can get a lot of good done in this world if you're willing to let someone else take the credit for it."[27]

That's what McKinsey does: It *sells the credit* to its clients. And it's a good idea. What manager would want to hire someone looking to *take credit*? In exchange, though, McKinsey does not take responsibility for what a firm does with the advice it receives. While some clients have broken the compact and tried to pin blame on McKinsey for this outcome or that one over the years, in large part both McKinsey and its clients have remained mum about the work it does. Only in the most extreme circumstances—in the 1990s, the collapses of both Enron and Swissair prompted the firm to publicly defend itself—has the firm ever deigned to engage in open and public debate about the quality of its work.

Among the problems that McKinsey promised to solve for CEOs was the information bottleneck. Top executives are routinely criticized for not understanding what's going on at the front line of their companies. McKinsey created a system for interviewing scores of employees and organizing the information for quick consumption by the chief executive. But the consultants didn't see themselves as mere messengers. They were *advisers*. And they thought so highly of their advice that in the 1940s Bower began pushing the idea that clients *had to act* on the firm's recommendations or McKinsey might reconsider future engagements. (Astonishingly, their clients tolerated it.) The firm's mythology is replete with stories of partners who bravely rejected problematic clients. Consultant Ev Smith is said to have walked away from a study at Chrysler because the CEO wouldn't fire someone who was "corrupt."[28]

In his privately published memoir, Bower tells of personally rebuffing the eccentric billionaire Howard Hughes when he sought McKinsey's help with Paramount Pictures. After flying to Los Angeles to meet Hughes, Bower was led to an apartment by one of Hughes's assistants and told that Hughes would be there when he could. A day and a half later, Bower called Hughes's secretary and told her that if Hughes didn't show by two o'clock the next afternoon, Hughes would not only lose the chance to meet him on this trip but also lose the chance to *ever* meet him. Hughes promptly showed up and, after some original discussions, convinced Bower to at least speak to some of his executive team. The results were disastrous: Bower concluded that a paranoid kook like Hughes was never going to listen to anyone, and the fees, high as they surely would've been, weren't worth it.

3. THE AGE OF INFLUENCE

Decentralization Nation

Marvin Bower had burned an immutable value system into the core of McKinsey. But it was the ways in which he forced McKinsey to adapt that kept it fiercely competitive. When government spending increased, McKinsey was there to offer Washington, D.C., its advice. When corporate Europe was ravaged by war and needed repair, McKinsey came on the next flight and set up a global operation. When competition for finding talented consultants heated up, McKinsey upended the industry's recruiting with a masterstroke partnership with the Harvard Business School. And then, when the talent pool at Harvard started running dry, McKinsey led the way with "nontraditional" hiring—engineers, PhDs, MDs, and graduate students from other departments. This was McKinsey at its best: a rock-solid foundation with an ever-changing house sitting on top.

When Crockett stepped down as managing partner of McKinsey in 1950, there was never a moment's doubt about who would succeed him. Marvin Bower was forty-seven years old. He'd been at McKinsey for seventeen years. He had the respect of his partners, as well as their complete support. The only complaint about him was that he took too much advice from his wife, Helen. They were not that cliché of a detached 1950s couple. They were a team. When asked to name Bower's best friend, his son Dick showed no hesitation before saying, "My mother."[1]

Well, she and the firm. McKinsey was the other great love of Bower's life. He defined the firm, and the firm defined him. In *The Pope of Wall Street,* John H. Coleman wrote of Robert Moses, "Some men aren't satisfied unless they have caviar. Moses would have been happy with a ham sandwich—and power."[2] But Bower didn't want caviar or power. He wanted influence. And McKinsey was the means through which he obtained it.

Bower was both McKinsey's general and its drill sergeant. He guided the firm with big strategic ideas, while also attending to every last detail. There was a right way to do everything. Advertising pioneer David Ogilvy once remarked, "It is said that if you send an engraved wedding invitation to my friend Marvin Bower, the great man of McKinsey, he will return it to you—with revisions."[3] Those who knew him regarded him with a quiet, baffled awe. "When I got there in 1961, Marvin Bower was all over the place," said former McKinsey consultant Doug Ayer. "We must have had lunch once a month for a year. He wasn't a hell of a lot of fun, but he was the most single-minded person I have met in my life."[4]

Like all legendary business leaders, Bower was also quite lucky. The prime of his professional life happened to coincide with the magnificent postwar American boom. From the beginning of World War II through 1973, real per capita GNP grew at 3 percent a year—nearly triple the rate between 1890 and World War II, and 50 percent higher than that from 1973 through 2000. Meanwhile, the U.S. population exploded, growing by half between 1945 and 1973, and the peacetime federal budget soared as Washington wove its way into everyday American life.

The consulting industry was one of corporate America's shiny new toys, growing at a 15 percent clip through the 1950s and 1960s. McKinsey was the clear leader, outhustling the competition for the brightest young workers and endearing itself to CEOs. The postwar boom was marked by two related business phenomena—the rise of gigantism and managerialism[5]—and McKinsey was in the sweet spot to take advantage of both. Between 1947 and 1968, the share of corporate assets owned by the 200 largest industrial companies increased from 47.2 percent to 60.9 percent.[6] When the Celler-Kefauver Act of 1950 prohibited corporations from merging with competitors in the same industry, managers pursued growth by acquiring unrelated businesses, which they typically knew little or nothing about.

Companies that had ten to twenty-five divisions before the war suddenly had forty or more. In 1929, just 15 percent of the largest hundred firms in the country were diversified; by 1960, the proportion was 60 percent and still climbing—it topped out around 76 percent in 1970.[7] In the 1960s, General Electric had 190 separate departments, each with its own operating budget. Overseeing these massive corporate entities required managerial expertise that simply did not exist. This was McKinsey's great opportunity. Its consultants became anthropologists of a modern and evolving social organism called the corporation. They were the first ones to truly understand how this human machine worked.

As its business grew, McKinsey had to modify some of its core principles, such as James McKinsey's original dictum that the firm consult only with a company's chief executive. Work for a massive client like General Electric couldn't all go through the CEO's office. It wasn't possible. So Bower decided that it was tolerable to deal with lower levels of management. "As organizations have grown in size and complexity . . . the CEO we serve now may be the chief executive of a subsidiary or division," Bower wrote.[8] He was unforgiving, though, with regard to his conviction that McKinsey work only on its clients' most pressing problems. In 1963 he fired a partner for doing what he considered too much routine work for infant-formula pioneer Mead Johnson.[9]

In the 1950s, McKinsey was working for just about every iconic American company: Colgate, Chrysler, General Foods, Philip Morris, and Raytheon. The firm did pro bono work for the American Red Cross and the Southern California Symphony. McKinsey also expanded its power base beyond New York and Chicago. By 1960 the San Francisco and Los Angeles offices were bringing in more than a million dollars of revenue combined, 16 percent of overall billings.[10] A September 1955 story in *BusinessWeek* included a two-page map highlighting the headquarters of twenty unidentified McKinsey clients. Individual company names might have been kept confidential, but McKinsey's success was out in the open: It was working with everyone.

Organization Man

In the 1950s, the Company Man was ascendant. William Whyte's 1956 book, *The Organization Man,* gave him a second name, but both figures marched to the steady beat of corporate conformity. Young men happily traded their individuality in exchange for a steady paycheck, an obsequious secretary, and a degree of career stability not seen since before the Great Depression. "They are wry about it, to be sure; they talk of the 'treadmill,' the rat race, of the inability to control one's direction," Whyte wrote. "But they have no great sense of plight; between themselves and organization they believe they see an ultimate harmony."[11] Such willful compliance was a manager's dream. "The training makes our men interchangeable," one IBM executive told Whyte.[12]

While novelists and Hollywood saw menace in the conformity of office workers, the truth was that the nation's suspicions toward large organizations had softened considerably in the aftermath of the war. As Rakesh Khurana pointed out in *From Higher Aims to Hired Hands,* those millions of Americans who had served in the military or worked in wartime production had firsthand experience with the positive benefits of large-scale bureaucracy in action. They saw little reason to reflexively question authority, especially when loyalty and subservience were repaid in the form of stable careers and ever-rising prospects.[13]

A small number of McKinsey consultants did manage to stand out from the rest. In 1951 Arch Patton became the first consultant since the founder himself to pioneer an entire field. General Motors had hired Patton to do a study of executive compensation, and he did so by surveying thirty-seven major companies. The results, published in *Fortune* and the *Harvard Business Review,* showed something remarkable: Worker wages had risen faster than management wages. Management took special note of this development, and demand for Patton's imprimatur on executive pay packages went through the roof. Juan Trippe, then CEO of Pan American World Airways, engaged Patton to work on a study of stock options for his management team. Once started, this demand to increase and "justify" executive compensation became a perpetual motion machine. Patton wrote more than sixty articles on the subject over the years.

Though it enriched the firm, Patton's renown stuck in Bower's craw. Patton himself once overheard Bower tell an associate that the executive comp work was not true problem-solving in the spirit of McKinsey's practice but merely a specialty. Patton nearly quit at the time, but he was convinced to let the comment pass. And no wonder his partners wanted him to stay: For several years, Patton personally accounted for almost 10 percent of the firm's billings. But Bower's distaste for Patton's executive compensation work, as well as for headhunting in general, meant that McKinsey passed on the opportunity to provide executives with advice on the fundamental issue of succession planning. "If you want to know the one *major* weakness of McKinsey, I would say that is it," said a retired partner of the firm. "It has everything else, but not that. Everyone was comfortable with the decision to not be in the headhunting business, but that didn't mean we couldn't provide assistance to what constitutes anywhere from a third to a half of a chief executive's job, which is to think of how to structure people coming through your organization in such a way that it maintains your talent capability. Because of that 'Marvin versus Arch' situation, that weakness got built into McKinsey and it's never been cleared up. It's our big missed opportunity."

Still, Patton's example inspired McKinsey colleagues to branch out into new areas. In 1958 Dick Neuschel—who had joined the firm in 1945 and was later named to Bower's three-man Executive Group—successfully proposed a push to serve insurance companies; the practice has been one of the firm's most successful over the past fifty years.

Bower insisted that no individual could ever be allowed to eclipse the firm, but in a few isolated cases he had no choice but to let a star shine brighter than the rest. Just as Tom Peters would be years later, Patton was awfully good for McKinsey in the 1950s. His legacy to American business in general, however, is controversial. Patton's research was, without question, one impetus for skyrocketing executive pay. Asked in the 1980s how he felt about the effect of his work, his reply was simple: "Guilty."[14]

All that came later. In the 1950s, there was little popular outrage about managerial pay. The American public was optimistic about the future, and nowhere more so than inside McKinsey. Between 1939 and 1956, just a single partner left the firm for a reason other than retirement. In the patriotic fervor of the era, some went so far as to conflate managerialism with democracy, giving McKinsey and its peers a perfect sales pitch. They weren't just helping companies boost profits; they were helping the causes of democracy and freedom. McKinsey's own privately published history credits the firm with "helping capitalism work better at a time when its credibility was still in doubt around the world."[15]

Feeding at the Government Trough

Chicago may have been its heritage and New York its power base, but in the 1950s Washington was McKinsey's milieu. U.S. military spending was a boon to the consulting industry, jumping 24-fold from 1939 to 1945, from $2.5 billion to $62 billion. That was followed by the emergence of big government in the aftermath of the war. McKinsey could smell money as well as any of its competitors, and it opened an actual office in the nation's capital in May 1951.

Less than a year after McKinsey set up shop, newly elected president Dwight Eisenhower hired the firm to advise him on political appointees for the executive branch as well as a reorganization of the White House. One of the major outcomes was the creation of the position of the White House chief of staff. This signaled the start of a near decade of highly profitable, highly influential government work for McKinsey.

McKinsey had, for a time, been earnestly involved in basic headhunting. A 1940 brochure made J. Edgar Hoover–like claims: "We are prepared to assist our clients in locating candidates for executive positions. To that end, we maintain confidential files of the names of men who are doing outstanding work in various fields."[16] But by this time, the company was backing away from the recruiting business—because, in Bower's view, it was another activity unbecoming of a true professional. Caught in a quandary, McKinsey came up with handy new jargon—it redefined its charge and promised to answer the question: If you really wanted to be in charge, what were the key jobs? "Once this question was asked," wrote attorneys Daniel Guttman and Barry Willner in their groundbreaking book *The Shadow Government,* McKinsey offered to help, as a courtesy, find men to fill the jobs.[17]

The executive branch appointment work was headhunting, but it was headhunting informed by a larger strategy. Harold Talbert, a prominent Republican, had told Eisenhower that he would front the money to hire McKinsey to develop a strategy for taking over the government. How many positions did the president need to fill with his own loyalists in order to have the "will of the people" done?

McKinsey's final report to Eisenhower calculated that full control of the two-million-people-strong federal government could be achieved by appointing a mere 610 positions.[18] "This is very valuable," Eisenhower told Bower after reading the report. "We'll use it like a bible."[19] The reward for this crucial work was not small: The firm worked for twenty-five to thirty federal agencies in the 1950s, getting a giant share "of the prestigious contracts awarded by an Administration that it helped create."[20]

One of McKinsey's key roles was consulting on national security issues. In 1953 the firm worked for Nelson Rockefeller in reorganizing the Department of Defense and in 1955 it helped the Atomic Energy Commission identify potential commercial applications of nuclear power. When former AEC commissioner Keith Glennan became the first administrator of NASA in 1958, he hired McKinsey to organize the new agency. That first study led to eight other engagements with NASA for a total of $232,000 in fees—and a staff position in NASA for a former McKinsey consultant.[21]

With deals like this, argued historian Christopher McKenna, McKinsey helped bring about the radical transformation of the United States into a "contractor state." In a study of NASA's contracting policies, McKinsey pushed for "as extensive a role as possible" for private industry, concluding that NASA should "contract for the bulk of research and development services needed."[22] The report quoted McKinsey client Ralph Cordiner of General Electric in support of the idea. And why wouldn't he be? Firms like GE were the first in line for government contracts.

As government agencies turned to outside contractors, they also relied on consultants to help in the contractor-selection process, thereby putting McKinsey in a position to recommend its own clients for government work. Instead of being called in on special occasions, consultants thus became "central to the everyday administration of the contract state," wrote McKenna.[23] North American Aviation, a major McKinsey client, snagged more than a third of the $24 billion spent on NASA's Apollo program.[24]

Naturally, those same clients had a powerful incentive for retaining McKinsey's services. It was a perfect positive feedback loop: McKinsey's work for the government allowed it to bring in other clients who in turn hired McKinsey to help in their work for the government. Decades later, government watchdogs would no doubt have been all over this kind of mutual backscratching, but at the time nobody was complaining.

Just over a decade into his tenure as managing director of McKinsey, Bower had fully arrived: The man once rejected for a job by a Cleveland law firm was now advising presidents. Bower's memoirs include a photo of a luncheon card with John F. Kennedy from October 8, 1963. The menu: Quiche Lorraine, Chicken Breast Marengo, and Pears Belle Helène.

A "Trivial but Well-Publicized" Controversy

In the 1950s and 1960s, McKinsey's government work had gone smoothly. The firm's D.C. envoy, John Corson, had burrowed his way deep into the Washington establishment, popping up on practically every committee of note: the Davis Commission (which studied the organization of the army), the Kestenbaum Commission (federal grants-in-aid), the Gaither Commission (the Russian nuclear threat), and others focused on higher education, public health, and air traffic.[25]

But a bruising encounter with hard-nosed municipal politics in New York caused the firm to reconsider the value of public clients. Carter Bales, an up-and-coming McKinsey consultant, was doing some burrowing of his own, and in 1968 he secured an unpaid position in the New York City government as head of the Division of Program Budget Systems in the city's Budget Bureau. This arrangement was something entirely new. While Corson merely served on commissions, Bales had managed to become a de facto government employee while still working at McKinsey. "McKinsey was . . . in title and in fact, both a public and private organization," wrote Guttman and Willner in *The Shadow Government*.[26]

Bales—and McKinsey—later participated in the creation of a public benefit corporation designed to take over management of the city's municipal hospitals. Bales signed, on behalf of McKinsey, a letter of intent to provide $325,000 worth of "management assistance" to the corporation. Who was one of the people on the other side of the (figurative) table? Carter Bales, in his role as assistant budget director. The city also gave McKinsey a $300,000 contract for help in its Model Cities program, as well as a handful of other contracts that fell under the purview of the Budget Bureau.

When political opponents of Mayor John Lindsay came across

Bales's complicated dual role, they caused a ruckus. Through the summer of 1970, the *New York Times* raked the Lindsay administration and the consulting firm over the coals. Controller Abe Beame initially withheld $1.5 million in McKinsey fees. The first issue, according to Beame, wasn't that Bales was working both sides of the fence; it was that, in several instances, McKinsey was working without a contract—and therefore illegally. In which case, said the controller, the city had no obligation to pay. Bales and his McKinsey colleagues were flabbergasted: The contracts for New York City had nearly *always* lagged behind the work; McKinsey thought it was doing the city a favor by starting work without them. The firm was eventually paid.

The second issue was whether there had been anything unethical going on. An indignant Bales represented himself at the hearings. Both managing director Lee Walton and New York office head Ron Daniel stood behind Bales, though Marvin Bower, conspicuously, did not. Bower thought Bales had besmirched the firm's reputation and he implored Walton to fire Bales, to no avail.

Both the city's Board of Ethics and the Association of Consulting Management Engineers deemed McKinsey's role to have been aboveboard, but the experience focused the firm on the power of perception, and on the idea that doing business with the public sector lacked the safety and privacy of the executive suites in which it was more accustomed to operate.

McKinsey's internal history dismissed the controversy as "trivial but well-publicized," though it certainly did not feel trivial at the time. Walton told a reporter that he'd "suffered and bled with this damn thing," and Bower called it "excruciatingly painful."[27] In the fallout from the imbroglio, the firm found its "urban practice" overstaffed, and New York office manager Ron Daniel was forced to let go forty consultants.

Despite predictions by industry insiders that he was "finished" at

McKinsey, Bales emerged largely unscathed from the controversy. For many years in the 1980s, he was the firm's largest biller. A bull of a man bursting with self-confidence, Bales headed several hundred engagements for the likes of Merrill Lynch, Chase Manhattan, and CBS over a thirty-three-year career with the firm. He was a fierce, unapologetic proponent of McKinsey's methods, including its long, involved relationships with clients. "Difficult problems don't yield to an 'aha!' moment," he said. "Instead, there is the sandpaper, sandpaper, sandpaper theory of progress. Take the performance management system at Merrill Lynch. Their retail brokers were, in effect, subsidizing their wholesale business. We helped them come up with a new way of evaluating and rewarding performance, but it took us eighteen months of hard work."[28]

Bales was also a risk taker. He tried—a little too early for client tastes, it proved—to start an environmental practice at McKinsey, and he ran unsuccessfully for Congress in 1972. Years after the New York City controversy, Bower stood up at a partners conference and decreed Bales to be the most successful consultant in the firm. As one colleague observed, "Marvin acted off a very strong set of principles and had strong opinions. But when his opinion changed, it changed."

McKinsey eventually moved away from government work almost entirely, ceding federal turf to competitor Booz Allen Hamilton and doing only sporadic work for local administrations. McKinsey veterans claim that this was in response to the ever-growing bureaucratization of the federal consulting process. Over time, the procurement function was separated from the users of consulting services, meaning that the building of relationships with its ultimate customer—McKinsey's forte—no longer helped in terms of new assignments. Well, there was that, and the more pecuniary fact that margins were coming down. McKinsey was accustomed to charging high fees, and if government wasn't going to pay them, there were plenty in the private sector who would. Or, in McKinsey-speak, as Bower himself later wrote, "Congress, the press, and the public at large have a negative attitude toward a *sensible* [emphasis added] level of fees."[29] By the end of the 1960s—before the Bales imbroglio—government work accounted for just 5 percent of billings. Nonprofit assignments added up to just 1 percent.[30] For the next forty years or so, McKinsey was content to make its contributions to the world almost entirely through the corporate sector.

London Ho!

As McKinsey established its Washington presence, Marvin Bower began to look beyond national borders. In 1953 he and his wife, Helen, traveled abroad for the first time in their lives—to France and Portugal—and when he returned, he raised the question of establishing a European beachhead in a memo to his partners.[31]

At the time, McKinsey's ambitions were still confined to the United States, where its clients came from all across the corporate spectrum. Between 1959 and 1961, the firm worked for clients in twenty industries, with only one—petroleum—accounting for more than 10 percent of billings. Strategic planning was its largest practice area, accounting for nearly one-fifth of revenue, and the firm was still quite small. "When I joined in 1960, the place was only a hundred consultants strong," said Jon Katzenbach. "I remember the first firm conference I went to at a country club in Sleepy Hollow, New York. We had to room together. The youngest associate and the oldest director shared a room."[32]

By the end of the 1950s, though, McKinsey was ready to expand. It so dominated the domestic market that growth opportunities were dwindling, and some of its clients had already opened offices overseas.

Even though the decentralization movement in the United States was still going strong, Europe was virgin territory for deploying the idea. The war had battered most European multinationals, lending their healthy American counterparts a spectacular advantage: There were 93 subsidiaries of American manufacturing firms in Britain in 1948. By 1971 there were 544.[33]

Broader technological developments also played a part in the firm's global expansion. In the 1950s jet travel became cost-effective for corporate executives, and the first transatlantic phone cable began operating in 1956. Europe suddenly wasn't so far away. Booz Allen Hamilton and Arthur D. Little both opened offices in Zurich in 1957. In December of that year, *BusinessWeek* even criticized McKinsey for thinking it could merely send Americans abroad instead of establishing a presence on the ground. It wouldn't be long until that changed.

In 1955 McKinsey hired Charles Lee, an expert on business in Europe, to work with partner Gil Clee in formulating expansion plans. Clee, who briefly followed Bower as managing director before succumbing to lung cancer, was one of Bower's right-hand men at the firm, and his expertise in finance served as a complement to Bower's obsession with values. Clee and Lee spent the next few years making the case for an expanded overseas experience, but it was slow going. By 1956 McKinsey could count only the overseas operations of Heinz, IBM, and ITT as clients. Its work for IBM World Trade in Paris was credited with helping the computer firm make significant European inroads. But the consultants had made scant progress beyond that.

McKinsey's ultimate push into Europe actually came by way of Venezuela, via a 1956 project that came through a referral from Texaco's Augustus "Gus" Long to Royal Dutch Shell's John Loudon. Loudon asked McKinsey to reorganize the giant oil and gas company's operations in Venezuela as a kind of tryout for further work. The firm passed with flying colors. Upon becoming Shell's chairman in July 1957, Loudon immediately cabled McKinsey about a study of the entire company. Marvin Bower himself went to The Hague for a negotiation in which the American company held a pretty sweet position. Shell's joint Dutch-British ownership had produced a stalemate, as the British side of the firm would not countenance Dutch consultants, nor would the Dutch side countenance British consultants. McKinsey represented a compromise, and it landed a giant new client. A London office became a near necessity.

Still, this being McKinsey, there were memos to write. Clee penned one in March 1958 titled "Proposed London Office." His previous efforts, in 1956, had been rebuffed, in part because the consultants didn't believe Europeans would stand for McKinsey's fees. The Shell contract suggested this was not true. At the April 8, 1958 meeting of McKinsey's directors, when further study of the matter was proposed, Bower replied that it had been studied enough and asked for a show of hands. The vote was unanimous: McKinsey would open a London office. In April 1959, McKinsey announced the opening of its new office at 4 King Street, St. James, London. Just as it had insinuated itself into the American establishment by way of establishment hiring, McKinsey tapped then-New York–based consultant Hugh Parker, who had rowed at Cambridge, as its first London head. Parker was given a budget of $25,000 to get things going, and in the first year he managed to bill $4,625 to the British subsidiary of Hoover.

"He understood the British," Bower later wrote.[34] More to the point: "To establish a staff equivalent in caliber to our U.S. staff, we first needed honors graduates of Cambridge and Oxford who could attract others."[35] Parker was a McKinsey man, through and through, as evidenced by remarks like the one in which he said McKinsey men should have "the basic habit of success."[36] That, and an "Oxbridge" degree—from one of just two schools. Bower had his own chestnut:

"The successful consultant has a personality that causes most people to like him."[37]

Still, Parker was an American. As the bulk of the London office's business shifted from serving the overseas operation of U.S. companies to major UK companies, its staffing had to change. British managers wanted to talk to British consultants. To that end, McKinsey lured Sir Alcon Copisarow, a veteran of the UK civil service, as its first non-American director in 1966. It was an astute move, as the governor of the Bank of England thereafter personally requested Copisarow on assignments.[38]

In January 1959, Shell announced that it had adopted McKinsey's organizational recommendations, some of which remained in effect through the 1990s. This was great press for the firm, but it claimed to be troubled by the publicity. "They go around boasting of hiring the McKinseys," partner Everett Smith told author Hal Higdon. "Our name hits the *Times* regularly, and quite frankly it scares the devil out of us."[39]

Mike Allen, a former McKinsey consultant who went on to found his own successful consulting firm, was another American who helped London get off the ground. "We were like movie stars," he said. "After General Electric had decentralized in the 1950s, we seized on the idea and exported it." Allen recalled challenging the most sacred of British cows: the tea break. "When we worked for the British Post, we quantified it. It was supposed to be fifteen minutes, but it was two hours. They actually only worked about three hours out of eight. The head of the union said it was management's fault. He was right."[40]

Business ramped up quite quickly. By 1962 London's client list included the British subsidiaries of Heinz, Massey Ferguson, and Hoover, as well as local firms like Dunlop Rubber and chemical giant ICI. By 1966 the London office was the second largest at McKinsey, with thirty-seven clients to New York's ninety-six.[41] The product, naturally, was decentralization: In short order, the firm decentralized twenty-five of the top 100 British companies. "Honestly, though, it was like shooting fish in a barrel," said former McKinsey consultant Doug Ayer. "It was okay to be a businessman in the U.S. by that point. But in England, it was still civil service, clergy, or the army. Their businesses needed help."[42]

It's been said that McKinsey consultants traveled across Europe with a copy of Alfred Chandler's *Strategy and Structure* in their briefcases. Chandler's multidivisional model was the sine qua non of organizational structures, and McKinsey acted as its chief proselytizer. According to historian Christopher McKenna, one European manager told his colleagues to save McKinsey's $100,000 fee by merely buying a single copy of the book. *Le Monde* coined the term *prêt-à-penser*—an analog to *prêt-à-porter,* or "off-the-rack." In short, the paper accused McKinsey of selling off-the-rack ideas, tailored only at the cuffs.

If the criticism cut into McKinsey's growth, it was undetectable. McKinsey's European excursion was so successful that the firm entered the popular vernacular. The *Sunday Times* defined the verb *McKinsey* as follows: "1. V. To shake up, reorganize, declare redundant, abolish committee rule. Mainly applied to large industrial companies but also to any organization with management problems. See: British Broadcasting Corporation, the General Post Office and Sussex University. 2. N. An international firm of American management consultants."[43] In the view of many, McKinsey reorganized Europe itself.

McKinsey consultants described their expansion with the same benevolent jargon that had worked so well in the United States. "McKinsey . . . did as much as any institution to rebuild European productivity," said partner John Macomber. "[And] . . . there was never one scintilla of a doubt about what was motivating us. And it wasn't money. It was trying to help them."[44]

Over the next decade, McKinsey "helped" an enviable roster of British clients, including Cadbury Schweppes, Cunard, Rolls-Royce, Imperial Chemical Industries, Tate & Lyle, Unilever, and Vickers. It had even greater success in the public realm, working with the Atomic Energy Commission, the Bank of Ireland, British Rail, the British Broadcasting Corporation, the National Health Service, and, in 1968, the Bank of England. That last one was perceived as an affront by British consultants: "The Post Office was a slap in the face; the BBC was a humiliating blow; but the Bank of England was the crowning disaster," said the chairman of the British Management Consultants Association. Was British management consulting so bad that they had to bring in the colonials?

The public uproar caused by the Bank of England contract only reinforced the perception of McKinsey's competitive superiority. As the London correspondent for *Science* magazine wrote, "And then there is McKinsey, projecting an image which suggests that, if God decides to redo creation, He will call in McKinsey."[45]

By the end of the 1960s, Europe was in full-fledged panic about the economic invasion from the United States. American direct investment in Europe, which had been $1.7 billion in 1950, reached $24.5 billion in 1970.[46] French journalist Jean-Jacques Servan-Schreiber's 1968 book, *The American Challenge,* argued forcefully that American companies' ability to manage their operations over vast geographies was crushing European competition, and that the secret to their success was in their organizational structure: in other words, the decentralized form.

This was *Scale and Scope* all over again, except this time on a global playing field. "Fifteen years from now it is quite possible that the world's third greatest industrial power, just after the United States and Russia, will not be Europe, but American industry in Europe," wrote Servan-Schreiber.[47] But "American industry" was an abstraction. And at the time McKinsey, more than anyone else, was its concrete manifestation.

After London, the firm rolled across Europe like an invading army. It opened an office in Geneva in June 1961, soon picking up Swiss clients like Geigy, Nestlé, Sandoz, and Union Bank. Paris followed in November 1963, and consultants worked for the likes of Air France, Crédit Lyonnais, Pechiney, Renault, and Rhône-Poulenc. In 1964 the firm opened offices in Amsterdam and Dusseldorf and began working for BASF, KLM Airlines, Deutsche Bank, and Volkswagen. By 1969 more than half of the firm's revenue came from outside the United States. In 1950 the M-form was relatively unknown in Germany; by 1970 half of the largest hundred companies in the country had implemented it, most with the help of McKinsey.[48]

From 1967 through 1974, the firm had a notable presence in Tanzania, with more than sixty consultants from nine different offices working with Tanzanian president Julius Nyerere to help him plan the nation's future. While the firm did some work pro bono, journalist Michael Useem reported that the fees were still so high that they became a line item in Tanzania's budget.[49] Indeed, Logan Cheek, who worked at McKinsey from 1968 to 1971, remembers being in the room when Nyerere read the firm's proposal. "He read most of it, and said, 'That's what I want.' Then he saw the fees. There was a long silence, and he said, 'Do you realize that the lowest-paid associate on this team will be making more than my most senior minister?' Roger Morrison thought we'd blown it. But then Nyerere stood up, walked to the window, paused, and said, 'But . . . back in my village, we have an expression: if you offer peanuts, you get monkeys.' We got the study."[50] (That Nyerere was a tyrant who quite literally destroyed his country despite vast infusions of Western and Soviet aid during his reign, from 1961 to 1985, did not seem to dissuade McKinsey from doing the work.)

In 1971 McKinsey was asked to study the administration of the

British crown colony of Hong Kong. That was another old-boy connection: Sir Alcon ran into the British governor of Hong Kong, Murray MacLehose, "in the Club" and walked out with a mandate.[51]

The ease with which McKinsey colonized Europe left the firm wholly unprepared for a fairly sudden leveling of its growth that arrived as the go-go 1960s came to an end and the more turbulent 1970s took their toll on business in general and American business in particular. But for the time being, Europe was McKinsey's for the taking.

McHarvard

In 1953 McKinsey became the first consulting firm to focus on the crème de la crème of students at graduate business schools—choosing youth and possibility over age and experience. At Harvard, these were Baker Scholars, the top 5 percent of each class, and over the next decades McKinsey became so intertwined with the university that author Martin Kihn facetiously coined the term "McHarvard." The first two hires from this group, John Macomber and Roger Morrison, stayed at the firm for a combined fifty-eight years. Morrison eventually ran the firm's London office from 1972 to 1985, while Macomber ran Paris and, after leaving McKinsey in 1973, became chairman of chemical maker Celanese Corporation and president of the Export-Import Bank.

Within the firm, this decision to prize youth over experience was controversial. "I can tell you, I had Roger Morrison on his first assignment and I was sweating blood," said partner Ev Smith. "It was Chrysler and those boys don't play patsy out there."[52] Even Bower himself wasn't totally convinced. "When . . . Marvin interviewed me, he spent the entire time telling me why it was impossible for someone without experience to be an effective consultant," recalled Morrison.[53]

But the idea caught on. Between 1950 and 1959, as the proportion of consultants at the firm with MBAs climbed from 20 percent to over 80 percent, the median age of McKinsey consultants dropped by almost ten years.[54] Younger and hungrier—and a lot cheaper. Betting on potential has become one of McKinsey's defining characteristics. The idea was simple: It was easier to mold a young mind than to change an older one. "Harvard . . . doesn't teach you accounting or finance," McKinsey alum and convicted fraud Jeff Skilling once said. "They teach you how to be convincing."[55]

Most people are convincing when they mean what they say. But Skilling was referring to the remarkable subset of American society known as the insecure overachiever. "Why do people work there?" asked former McKinsey consultant and author James Kwak. "They recruit from the pinnacle of the education system. I spent a lot of time at that pinnacle—I went to Harvard, Berkeley, and Yale Law. The people at these schools are driven by desire for status and fear of failing. You have spent your life trying to get into the best schools and being the best at everything you do. When you graduate, you reach that terrifying point in your life when the next thing to do is not obvious, when there are a lot more choices than before. McKinsey makes it very easy for people whose primary goal is to keep their options open. A lot of people in this situation don't know what they want to do with their lives."[56] It doesn't end there. In a true "profession," one's legitimacy rests on an actual body of knowledge. In consulting, it's mere insecurity mixed with arrogance. The degree to which juniors at McKinsey are bullied is actually quite shocking, if not necessarily unique among professional services firms.

Lou Gerstner, then a young consultant who went on to head RJR Nabisco, IBM, and The Carlyle Group, the king of the buyout firms, wrote of McKinsey's approach of throwing young and hungry but still largely ignorant talent at its clients' problems in his autobiography,

Who Says Elephants Can't Dance? "My first assignment was to conduct an executive compensation study for the Socony Mobil Oil Company. I'll never forget my first day on that project. I knew nothing about executive compensation, and absolutely nothing about the oil industry. Thank goodness I was the low man on the totem pole, but in the McKinsey world one was expected to get up to speed in a hurry. Within days I was out meeting with senior executives decades older than I was."

In other words, McKinsey had perfected personnel development: It hired the young and inexperienced for a pittance, then made its clients pay for their further education. It wasn't as obvious a move as it may seem in retrospect. More than half a century after the first of them had been established, the nation's business schools—including Harvard's—were still struggling for professional recognition, much like the consulting industry. But McKinsey's move started a virtuous cycle that provided substantial reciprocal benefits for both parties. More than perhaps any other firm, McKinsey legitimized the Harvard MBA, giving it cachet that was real and enduring. In return, Harvard has acted as a breeding ground of future McKinsey consultants who understand the firm's values and principles long before they start working there. By the mid-1960s, at least two of every five McKinsey consultants had gone to Harvard. In 1968 the firm offered jobs to twenty-seven HBS graduates, and fourteen accepted.[57] Amazingly, by 1978, when the professional staff was approaching seven hundred, HBS graduates still accounted for more than a quarter of all consultants.[58] (This raises an ironic counterclaim to business schools that claim to groom "leaders" but whose graduates tend to follow each other into safe career paths such as consulting. The cult of "leadership" might better be considered a cult of conformism.)

McKinsey's influence at Harvard ran deep: When Harvard president Derek Bok proposed jettisoning the business school's well-known "case study" methods in 1979, Bower himself wrote a fifty-two-page report arguing that there was no justification for doing so.[59] The idea was scrapped. Ron Daniel later became treasurer of Harvard, overseeing its endowment. The connections continue to this day, with McKinsey hiring a disproportionate number of grads in any given year. About a quarter of business school graduates now *begin* their careers advising experienced executives how to run their businesses.[60]

But even for graduates of Harvard, landing a job at McKinsey is hardly a lifetime appointment. Most young consultants spend just a few years at the firm before being tossed back out into the workforce. Only one in six hires stays at the company for five years or more. This merciless system, widely referred to as "up-or-out," was pioneered by law firm Cravath, Swaine & Moore early in the twentieth century and is sometimes called the "Cravath system" as a result. Bower and his partners began formally employing the policy in 1954, inaugurating a relentless performance review cycle. At least once a year, the firm's consultants are subjected to an exhaustive review, wherein *dozens* of their colleagues are asked to comment on their progress and performance.

The pressure doesn't subside over time, either. In 1963 the firm extended the policy to principals—junior partners—for whom "up-or-out" was rechristened "grow-or-go." It was later applied to directors, who had to "lead or leave." Once they hit age sixty, partners are pointed toward the door, through which they are strongly encouraged to exit at the age of sixty-five. The average age of McKinsey's professionals was thirty-two about fifty years ago; it's still thirty-two today. You don't hold the line on a number like that without constant churn, especially at the top. Longtime partner MacLain Stewart described the McKinsey model not as "dog eat dog" but more as "dog eat old dog." Even so, McKinsey has the temerity to refer to its "tradition" of people leaving the firm to seek greener pastures. In most companies, that's called quitting or getting fired. At McKinsey, it's raised to the level of ritual.

Author Matthew Stewart recalled hearing that at an internal presentation on the future of McKinsey, the presenters joked that in ten years or so, only 1 percent of those in the room would still be with the firm. "It is on account of this pyramid principle, of course, that under normal circumstances the opportunity to become a partner in a respectable firm arises only after eight or so years of youth-destroying labor," he wrote.[61] "[And] in the end, just about everybody who plays the game is a loser."[62] Martin Kihn pointed out an additional paradox in the whole system: At McKinsey (as at other consultancies), one is generally promoted from associate to principal on the basis of one's ability to analyze and present data. But thereafter, one is promoted almost solely on the basis of one's ability to sell the firm's services.[63] "It's the only job I can think of where you start in general management, and then, if you're successful, you end up in sales," said an alumnus of the firm.

Given the turnover, leaving McKinsey is no disgrace. The firm has institutionalized what one author has referred to as a "kind but aggressive outplacement program,"[64] and former employees are referred to as "alumni." By 1959, McKinsey was already maintaining a list of their addresses and sending them annual Christmas letters. (The firm was still solidly WASPish at the time.) Like everything the firm does, this has a strategic purpose, as many will turn out to be future clients. In 1957 a small number of McKinsey people had an informal Christmas get-together at a local bar in New York. They called themselves the Rotten Corps. By 1960 it was mostly ex-McKinsey people who attended. Bower reportedly forbade current staffers to attend but was largely ignored. Ten years later, the firm could count 499 people as alumni, and it had by that point fully embraced the community. McKinsey's thoughtfulness and skill in placing its outbound people is now a distinctive feature of the firm.

A Doctor Who Won't Treat Gunshot Wounds

By the end of the 1960s, McKinsey was the envy of its industry. The notion that only a troubled firm called in the consultants had been turned on its head: It seemed that only successful firms hired McKinsey. "Like the doctor who recently refused to treat a man bleeding of a gunshot wound, management consultants dislike death on the premises," journalist John Huey later wrote in *Fortune* describing the shift. "It can be messy, and people may draw conclusions that can be bad for business."[65]

One outcome of Bower's focus on training and consistency is that the firm's only physical product—the McKinsey report delivered at the end of a consulting engagement—has an identity all its own. "From the 1950s on, you could tell," said historian Christopher McKenna. "They were higher quality. They were better written. They were more thoughtful. And they had a certain kind of style. It would be like picking up a lawyer's letter and actually knowing which law firm it came from."[66]

Mind you, that didn't necessarily mean they contained anything that might shock the client. Most McKinsey engagements begin with the consultant asking the client CEO, "What would you like to get out of this project?" In other words, conclusions can be preordained, or, at the very least, arrived at with no surprises along the way. McKinsey *always* sits down with the client to discuss the work in progress several times during an engagement. Consultants call this process pre-wiring. But it's also a rare thing indeed that the final presentation includes anything at all that the CEO didn't see coming, despite the fact that this flies in the face of the whole truth-telling self-image.

McKinsey may surprise its clients with the rigor of its research, but it rarely surprises them by offering a conclusion the client didn't play a part in arriving at. The firm is not admired for revolutionary ideas; it is admired for its systematic approach to forcing multiple hypotheses to survive or wilt in the hot glare of factual reality. Even so, the firm can—*and does*—sometimes recommend what the client wanted without properly considering the implications. McKinsey deserves a fair share of the blame for the destruction of General Motors in the 1980s, the bankruptcy of Swissair, the charade that was Enron, and many smaller mistakes.

The firm has protected its status as the best by intensive training and review at every level. As early as 1952, the firm had designed a 1,000-point scale for partnership share allocations that included firm development (150 points), leadership (200), recruiting (50), personnel development (100), client introductions (200), tenure (50), prestige clients (125), and building firm reputation (125). There's something a little ridiculous about such a detailed scale, but it demonstrates a belief in the power of the firm's own internal processes.

Training went even further than that. In the 1960s, McKinsey reportedly spent nearly $400,000 a year in psychological evaluations of its employees,[67] something it continued to do sporadically into the 1990s. Most important, in 1956 the firm abandoned the partnership structure and incorporated. The notion had been considered and rejected in 1949 and again in 1951 by Bower and Crockett out of concern for possible changes in the firm's character: The more they moved away from pure partnership, they worried, the more removed partners might feel from the institution. They were ultimately persuaded that the advantages outweighed the risks, and when they finally pulled the trigger, it allowed them to offer tax-sheltered profit sharing for employees, more cost-effective ways of handling retirement and death claims, and more tax-efficient accumulation of capital for growth. (Under U.S. partnership law, partners are taxed on their share of earnings, regardless of whether or not those earnings are distributed that year, making reinvestment an after-tax—and thus more expensive—proposition. Incorporation eliminated that issue.)

There were certainly profits to be shared. Marvin Bower drove a Cadillac and lived comfortably in a series of ever-larger houses in the affluent New York suburb of Bronxville. And along with the rest of the industry, McKinsey embraced the notion of staffing leverage as much as any other. In 1960, 176 nonconsulting staff members supported the 165 consultants at McKinsey. In other words, the 42 partners had 300 other people working for them, a "leverage ratio" of seven to one.[68] Most consultants can bill a maximum of 2,000 hours per year. Utilization between 80 and 100 percent is considered achievable.[69] The challenge of this "pyramid" form is stretching top talent across many projects at once, while fresh-faced Harvard graduates carry on the legwork. Partners then take home the lion's share of the money earned through the work of junior consultants—a departure from earlier, experience-based consulting firms that had no such junior talent to exploit. Still, if they held on to income, they were nevertheless sacrificing ownership, and this is no small testament to Marvin Bower's persuasive powers.

Or to his obsessiveness. While Bower always maintained that the first obligation of the consultant is to be financially independent—otherwise you are unable to act in a professional manner—he nevertheless kept his eye on every penny.

Even as he was getting quite old—his wife, Helen, died in 1985, but he lived another eighteen years, to the age of ninety-nine—Bower still stuck around the firm, reminding people of all the little things that made McKinsey great. One former employee recalled traveling to Dusseldorf shortly after starting his job in the early 1980s and receiving a message that Marvin Bower had called. He promptly called Bower back.

"Where are you?" asked Bower.

"In Dusseldorf, sir," replied the employee.

"Why are you calling me from Dusseldorf?" Bower barked.

"I'm returning your call, sir."

"Well, you're going to have to learn to be more responsible with the firm's money," Bower said. "My call wasn't important and could have waited until you'd returned to New York."

"Yes, sir," said the employee. "But I didn't know whether the matter was urgent or not."

"An unnecessary call is just wasting money," said Bower, ignoring the logic of the response. "I just wanted to set a time to get together and introduce ourselves. Good-bye."

Rumblings of a Seismic Shift

The great open secret of the McKinsey business model is that a large part of its success has come by reselling the insights of others. The primary product McKinsey sold, for several decades, was a customized version of the decentralized, multidivisional organizational structure pioneered by the likes of DuPont. Clients know this. In fact, they often engage consulting firms for the very purpose of finding out what the competition is up to. As Christopher McKenna has stated so plainly: "Consultants will carry information in and information out. The client has to decide which of those flows is worth more."

So it is ironic that the most significant competitive challenge McKinsey has ever faced was a rival firm selling managerial intelligence that came from the very same wellspring, DuPont. In 1963 Bruce Henderson, a veteran of Arthur D. Little, founded the Boston Consulting Group. With a radically simple four-square matrix, he inaugurated the era of "strategy consulting" and sent a shot across McKinsey's bow that sent the firm reeling for several years.

There was nothing new about "strategizing." Companies had been doing it for several decades. What distinguished the approach of managers at DuPont was that they had stopped letting *every* group manager shoot for the moon with aggressive sales projections and instead adjusted their product portfolio—and the capital allocated to each product—on the basis of more realistic and analytically sound projections. This was James McKinsey's theory in practice: Managers had to prove that they could grow their division through sound budgeting and forecasting. If they couldn't, they were out of luck. "Around 1965 or so, [strategy] burst onto the scene as the essential discipline of management," wrote Matthew Stewart. "It became—and has remained—the defining task of CEOs, the copestone course in business education, and the product supplied by the world's most expensive consultants."[70]

Henderson's insight was to package product portfolio management in an easy-to-consume form. His now legendary "growth-share matrix" suggested that executives look at their products as one of four types: a cash cow (to be milked), a rising star that needed that same cash to grow, a dog that needed to be put down, and a question mark that needed further study. By reducing a complicated corporation to a simple, one-page chart, Henderson had out-McKinseyed McKinsey. Major decisions could be made with clarity and confidence. This division is a rising star? Then throw more money at it! This one is a dog? Put the thing out of its misery! And this one's a cash cow? Let's crank prices up and milk the thing for all it's worth before its time has passed!

Strategy was the answer to the end of the decentralization era. Most large companies had already reorganized. What top management needed now was justification for their own nonoperational jobs. Companies might actually make or do something real at the end of the day, but the self-reinforcing management/consulting relationship lived in its own parallel universe.

This new focus on strategy unleashed a torrent of concepts, and reinvigorated the business-school curriculum. Whether it was Total

Quality Management or Management by Objectives, a cycle of management ideas had begun. Peter Drucker, who once claimed to have "invented" management, was its first truly famous purveyor. His 1946 book on General Motors, *Concept of the Corporation,* put him on the map as a management theorist, and a half century of demand for his teaching and consulting services followed. Others came after, most famously Harvard's Michael Porter, but most of the new theories—including Porter's famous Five Forces—were new recipes from the age-old ingredients: product, customer, supplier, and competitor. And they all had the very same goal: how one could contemplate one's competitive position in a brand-new light.

There's no shame in recycling, as long as you finesse it properly. McKinsey earned great acclaim in the 1990s for arguing that companies in the United States were engaged in a war for talent. No matter that the Carnegie Corporation in 1956 had decreed the existence of the Great Talent Hunt. If three decades have passed, any management idea is fair game for reconstitution, which is just what Henderson did with insights DuPont had figured out in the 1930s. McKinsey didn't know it yet—and disdainfully dismissed Henderson's firm for nearly a decade after its founding—but the ground was moving beneath its feet.

The Emergence of Arrogance

By the end of the 1960s, McKinsey was working for so many companies that clients started to worry about conflicts of interest. Some refused to keep hiring its consultants if they worked with direct competitors. What was the professional response? Bain & Company, another new consultancy founded in 1973, took the view that it was proper to serve just a single major client in any industry. McKinsey came to the opposite conclusion: that to truly understand an industry, the firm needed to work for any and all comers.

This issue had come up a few times over the years. In 1960 the CEO of Texaco—then McKinsey's largest client—had demanded that the firm drop Socony Mobil, Union Oil, and Sun Oil. The consultants balked, and Texaco backed down.[71] The petroleum company had enjoyed such success in cost cutting with the help of McKinsey that, when faced with the repercussions of its demands, it relented. Therein is one of the closely guarded secrets of McKinsey: As much as it might tout its expertise in top-level strategic thinking, it is often most valuable to its gigantic corporate clients in finding new ways to slash costs. There may be no better army of cost cutters on the planet.

In the late 1960s, McKinsey faced a similar showdown with Citicorp, which did not want to share a consulting firm with its archrival Chase Manhattan. This time things didn't go quite so smoothly. "We were very well on the road to building Citicorp into quite an attractive long-term client when, lo and behold, we received an inquiry from David Rockefeller, who was then the chairman and CEO of Chase," recalled Jon Katzenbach. "We decided that we should be able to serve both banks because we have a policy of serving competitors. In fact this single event is one of the most interesting tests of that policy. The firm decided to go ahead and serve Chase. [Citicorp CEO Walter] Wriston made good his threat. We were fifteen years without ever doing a piece of work over there."[72]

That setback aside, McKinsey's work with Citicorp is a showcase of its ability to reach into all aspects of its clients' businesses. First, McKinsey helped organize the bank around discrete markets—retail, wholesale, and private—rather than functions: lending, deposits, and processing. Then it was on to strategy, planning in particular for the coming wave of deregulation that allowed the New York–based company to grow into a financial services conglomerate. Such contemplation entailed endless possibilities and therefore endless work.

A February 1965 story in *Fortune* by Walter Guzzardi Jr.—"Consultants: The Men Who Came to Dinner"—outlined a development that had actually begun in the 1950s. The title was a riff on the hit 1939 play *The Man Who Came to Dinner,* about an acerbic houseguest who breaks his hip and is put up in order to convalesce but who presumably never leaves. In like manner, once they get their hooks into a client, McKinsey consultants never let go. "The best of the management consultants scorn[s] the hard sell as unnecessary and ineffective," wrote Guzzardi. "He scoffs at the standard soft sell as unimaginative and unworthy. True to the traditions of his craft, the big-time management consultant has invented something new: the self-perpetuating sell."[73]

Citibank and Mobil were two of the firm's first megaclients—the latter in particular provided a river of consulting assignments from the 1950s through the 1970s—but many more followed. A late 1960s boom in mergers and acquisitions had developed into a full-grown mania by decade's end. Whereas in 1965 there were 2,000 such transactions in the United States, in 1969 there were more than 6,000. (That number dropped to 2,861 in 1974, in line with a collapsing economy, but for the time being the M&A market was on fire.)[74] Chief executives buying businesses that they had no business buying were suddenly in great need of outside help—thus, there was even more demand for consulting. The pell-mell buying and selling of companies for diversification purposes among American conglomerates soon spawned its own evil offspring—Wall Street's business of buying and selling businesses themselves.

There were missteps. The firm lost Philip Morris as a client for a time after McKinsey consulted with New York City about a tax on cigarettes based on their tar and nicotine levels. The McKinsey motto, "The client before anything" can clearly run into complications when two clients are seeking precisely opposite outcomes. But that was a rare instance. McKinsey has almost invariably won in stare-downs with clients who insist on exclusivity, something that McKinsey has steadfastly refused to offer.

And why not? Because for an extended moment, it surely seemed as if the sky was the limit, that double-digit annual growth could continue unabated. Consulting—and McKinsey in particular—was now a part of the American establishment. In 1965 *BusinessWeek* pointed out that there was one consultant for every hundred "managers" in the country. (By 1995 it was one for every thirteen.)[75] "To hear some consultants tell of it," *Fortune* magazine added, "their appearance on the scene ranks with the Second Coming."[76]

McKinsey had become a luxury brand, and luxury brands do not apologize or explain. Considered in that light, the firm's high fees were justified for their own sake. Said a colonel in the U.S. Air Force, a McKinsey client at the time: "Consultants lend a lot more credibility to what you're doing. A fellow who works for us at a billing rate that amounts to $166,000 a year is making ten times my salary. This lends him a certain amount of stature. You can use a consultant as a communications aid."[77] In other words, when you hire McKinsey, your employees should know that you're not kidding around anymore. Still, it's a costly communications aid: McKinsey charged clients three times what it paid its consultants, to cover salary, overhead, and profit. In that light, there's another way to look at it: Hiring McKinsey was a sign of affluence.

Marvin Bower had predicted that the surest route to elite status was to act as if you already were elite. He was right about that. But by the end of the 1960s, the consultants' posturing had evolved into self-appraisal. Suddenly, they couldn't find *anyone* who was good enough to join their club: In 1965 the firm ran a blind help-wanted ad in the *New York Times* and, despite a thousand replies, hired not a single person. Four ads in *Time* magazine a year later—ads that cost $20,000—were equally unproductive.[78] Everyone at McKinsey—from Bower on down—had begun to believe in the firm's exceptionalism. But it had a sting in the tail: Because of it, they got sloppy.

To be fair, not everyone thought that the firm was invincible. In 1966 Gil Clee, a member of its four-man executive group—the others were Ev Smith, Dick Neuschel, and Bower himself—wrote a memo to his partners voicing concern that McKinsey's growth had more to do with growing client demand than with McKinsey's exceptional services. Dick Neuschel added his own concerns in a memo the next year titled "Whither McKinsey & Company." Several consultants expressed concern that the firm's generalist model was losing its appeal with a more specialized clientele, but those fears were generally drowned out by the applause for continuing growth numbers.

One problem was that the firm had never taken good care of its stars, in the misguided belief that the company was all that mattered, that individuals could be replaced. This cost it talent: People like Rod Carnegie—so revered by associates that they called him "Rod the God"—left the firm in 1970 to become finance director (and later CEO) of Cozinc Rio Tinto. Carnegie was the typical McKinseyite. He didn't just go to Oxford; he rowed varsity crew. (He also redesigned the blade used by rowers for the previous hundred years.) He didn't just go to Harvard Business School; he became its top-performing Baker Scholar. And he didn't just join McKinsey; he became the youngest director in its history. But he eventually tired of the company's self-satisfaction. "It was a question about what they wanted to do," Carnegie later said. "There was no gripping vision which led everybody to feel that this was a place that could really take a next major step forward."[79] This was widely interpreted as a swipe at then-managing director Lee Walton, but it also pointed to the larger fact that McKinsey was resting on its laurels.

As much as McKinsey consultants attributed their performance in the 1950s and 1960s to their own skill and intellectual prowess, they were aided by the giant wave of American corporate success that followed World War II. For two decades, most leading industrials maintained their domestic market share without substantial price competition.[80] Business was, in a word, *easy*. Despite their claims to glory, managing the problems of giant oligopolies (or, better yet, monopolies) was not that big a challenge. Without the pressure that came from competition, operational problems were relatively easy to solve.

Internationally, McKinsey had utterly failed to plan for a slowdown. After a period of largely unrestrained growth, McKinsey had conquered Europe, at least in terms of organizational consulting. By 1970, more than half of Britain's largest industrials had engaged the firm. It should have been clear that such rapid growth could not be sustained, but the firm continued hiring and expanding. Bower later observed that "in 1965 we were overextended on the Continent incurring considerable quality risks in the countries where we had offices."[81] He wrote those words more than a decade later, though, and it's not entirely clear whether he'd had that understanding at the time.

Where's the Value-Add?

Marvin Bower had impeccable timing. He hitched his wagon to James O. McKinsey's star just when consulting was starting to take off in the United States, and he stepped down as managing director in 1967, just before demand for consulting services fell off a cliff. His stewardship had been a profitable one: In 1967 firm revenues hit $21 million, more than 10 times the amount when he had taken over. The number of consultants had grown from 84 to 390. The firm served 19 of the top 25 industrial companies in the United States, and 58 of the top 100.[82] In the early 1950s, McKinsey had been an idea in search of business success. Marvin Bower thought he knew the best way to run a professional firm, and he set about implementing that philosophy. By the time he stepped down, his vision had been ratified. His plan had been the right one.

But for whom? Things had certainly worked out for McKinsey. And there was no question that most of its clients—in particular, their CEOs—felt McKinsey had worked out for them. The only remaining question was whether McKinsey was good for society. Despite all its claims to big-picture thinking, the firm had, since James O. McKinsey's days at Marshall Field, made the bulk of its money helping its clients slash costs. In this sense, McKinsey was a true forerunner of the 1980s revolutions in reorganization, downsizing, and rationalization—which are really just layoffs in different guises. One British journalist coined the term "to be McKinseyed" to describe this often painful corporate experience. McKinsey once argued that it "only assesses situations, not people."[83] But that's just a bullet point. The theory might be about company structure, but the reality is about people's jobs.

It's an impossible number to quantify, given that McKinsey doesn't actually make final decisions for its clients, but it may not be too far off the mark to suggest that McKinsey has been the impetus for more layoffs than any other entity in corporate history. While many of those layoffs were surely called for—at ailing firms, or ailing divisions of ailing firms—the notion surely raises the ultimate question of whether McKinsey is a net increaser of value or merely the most capable mercenary force in the corporate world. Here's the problem for mercenary forces, though: When the fun stops, they turn on each other. And that's precisely what was about to happen to McKinsey.

Marvin Bower created an entity that reflected the triumphant story of American business in the mid-twentieth century, a global empire the likes of which the world had never seen before. Like all empires, though, it faced its challenges, the greatest of which came in the 1970s, when, for an instant, both McKinsey and America itself lost the compass.

4. THE DECADE OF DOUBT

Lost Moorings

In the heady days of the postwar boom, nobody had particularly minded that managers were sprouting like weeds. But the social contract between business and society—work hard, sublimate your personality, and we will give you something approaching lifelong employment—broke down in the economic crisis of the 1970s. When the turmoil also exposed a clueless managerial class that had failed to prepare its companies for rough sledding, public—and intellectual—opinion turned sharply against it. As Alfred Chandler put it, "Top managers began to lose the competence essential to maintaining a unified enterprise in which the whole is more than the sum of its parts."[1]

Since the dawn of the American conglomerate, so-called managerial capitalism had been the dominant business philosophy in the United States. In 1920 the ratio of so-called administrative (i.e., managerial) employees to production employees had been 15.6 percent. By 1970 it had nearly doubled, to 30.3 percent. Economists call this a measure of "managerial intensity"—and it demonstrates just how far Organization Man had come since he had stepped out from the shadows of the robber barons.[2]

But he'd actually made a fine mess of things: By 1973, fifteen of the top two hundred American manufacturing companies were conglomerates, and analysts began to doubt that any value had been created.[3] In fact, it looked suspiciously as though most conglomerates were worth decidedly less than the combined value of the companies they owned. And so the great dismantling began. Whereas in 1965 there were eleven mergers or acquisitions for every divestiture, by 1977 the ratio was just two and a half to one.[4] Wall Street investment banks had nary a mergers and acquisitions department in the mid-1960s. By the late 1970s, M&A departments were the banks' biggest earners.

It's hard to imagine that in October 1967, after holding power at McKinsey for more than two decades, Marvin Bower didn't have these enormous changes in mind when he did what few men of his stature ever do: He left voluntarily. He was sixty-four years old. Those who knew him were not the least bit surprised. A graceful, timely exit was in keeping with a life lived according to principle. It was nearly a foregone conclusion that a member of the three-person executive committee he'd set up in 1963—Gil Clee, Dick Neuschel, and Ev Smith—would succeed him. The only question was which.

McKinsey hadn't dealt with such a momentous transfer of power since the death of James O. McKinsey himself. It was about to lose a cherished leader, and the future was therefore unclear. All three members of the executive committee were respected partners of the firm, but none of them was *Bower*. The transition set the firm on a course of uncertainty from which it took almost a decade to recover.

In preparation for the change, Bower appointed an election committee that produced an elaborate set of rules. There would be a secret ballot, for starters, with the results tallied by McKinsey's auditors, Arthur Andersen. A 60 percent supermajority would be required for victory, and managing directors could serve multiple three-year terms until the age of sixty.

Like Franklin Delano Roosevelt with the presidential term limit, Bower helped establish a system that practically ensured his tenure as managing director would forever rate as the longest at McKinsey—a crafty move for a man obsessed with his own legacy. But it was nevertheless an *elective* process. There are precious few private enterprises of comparable size or influence in the world that actually allow the senior people to elect their leaders.

Still, the partners couldn't keep themselves from adding a classic piece of McKinsey casuistry: There was to be no campaigning. Of course, with so much at stake, that was impossible. If campaigning weren't permitted to be overt, it would be covert. Factions emerged, as did aggressive behind-the-scenes lobbying. In the first election, international partners lined up behind Clee, who had spearheaded expansion outside the United States. Domestic partners, particularly those in New York, lined up behind Neuschel, known as the Silver Fox for his stylish gray hair. Smith, lacking a meaningful constituency, withdrew from the race and threw his weight *against* Neuschel. When the first round of votes was tallied, Neuschel was out, leaving Clee to face the forty-one-year-old Lee Walton, the Chicago office manager whose support among younger partners forced a number of votes. On June 21, 1967, Clee was victorious.

"I know that any former holder of a leadership position can best assist the new leader by standing aside," Bower wrote in a note to the firm the following day. He stayed true to his word over the next thirty-six years.

The orderly transition proved short-lived. Clee, who was the son of a Presbyterian minister and had served in both houses of the New Jersey legislature, took office in October. A tall and attractive man, he famously wore just one type of suit: dark blue with white pinstripes. He was also one of the most widely liked consultants in the firm, and this made it all the more jarring when in February 1968, he was operated on for lung cancer. He stepped down as managing director the next month. A nervous partners group begged Bower to retake the reins. Never mind the bylaws, they pleaded. Those could be changed. He refused, though, and Lee Walton was elected on March 30 without significant opposition. Clee died in July. He was the second McKinsey leader to pass away in two years: Guy Crockett had died in August 1966.

According to Ian Davis, who served as managing director from 2003 to 2009, Clee had one particularly significant achievement in his brief reign: He reaffirmed a basic tenet of how McKinsey governed itself. Talented people *don't like* to be managed, Clee argued, and so if the firm wanted to attract and retain talented people, it had to trust them to do the right thing without undue oversight. It is a challenge the firm has had to confront as it has grown larger: Can McKinsey allow partners the autonomy they seek while still maintaining enough control to keep the thing from spinning apart? One way it has done so is by strict enforcement of its cult of servitude, but even servants can act contrary to instruction.

On the day of Walton's election, Clee wrote a memo to his partners titled "Notes on the Election of a New Managing Director." It was a moving tribute by a dying man to the ideals to which he had devoted his career. "I know of no other profession and no other firm within this profession where there is such a rich balance of challenge, satisfaction, and material rewards," he wrote. It was a perfect distillation of the McKinsey ethos, the firm's sense of itself as a collection of the *smartest,* most *stimulated* group of people on the planet. But in the hard years that lay ahead, that ethos would be put to the test.

Between 1967 and 1972, McKinsey enjoyed a final burst of growth. The firm opened six new offices—in Toronto, Milan, Mexico City, Sydney, Tokyo, and Copenhagen—and increased its professional headcount to more than 650. Revenues doubled again, to $45 million. In each new country, too, the firm was able to attract an elite clientele: Alitalia in Italy, Pemex in Mexico. But McKinsey was about to discover the downside of riding a sidecar attached to the American economy: When the tank is full of gas, it's a nice ride. But the tank was about to run dry.

A Perfect Storm

America's belief in itself was badly shaken in the early 1970s. There was the Vietnam War as well as the oil embargo, runaway inflation, a brutal recession, the abandonment of the gold standard and subsequent devaluation of the dollar, and the revival of European and Asian industry. The American economy—and, by extension, its consigliere, the consulting industry—went into a tailspin. After two decades of nonstop growth, the consulting industry's revenues stalled at $2 billion in 1970, and the figure wouldn't tick upward for the next six years.[5] For a firm accustomed to limitless horizons, this was nothing short of devastating.

McKinsey suffered a financial squeeze in its 1971 fiscal year, as flattening client demand and the expense of opening new offices drained the firm's cash accounts. The experience revealed the extent to which McKinsey had not prepared for tough times—it had no rigorous cost controls. It also led the firm to resolve that it would borrow only to fund operations. Capital expenditures would have to be self-funded.

The 1970s were not merely an inflection point for the American economy; they were also an inflection point for the American self-image. Company Man finally looked in the mirror and saw what others had long seen: Conformity had its costs, and the flush postwar years had left him fat and lazy. The era of managerialism was coming to a close, to be replaced by a more aggressive, less genteel era of so-called shareholder capitalism. Along with it came an emphasis on leaner companies—and thus less demand for McKinsey's bread-and-butter business, organizational consulting. In 1969 the United States was home to forty of the world's top fifty industrial firms. By 1974 that number had dwindled to less than thirty. Management was indicted—justifiably so—for its failure to prepare for such seismic shifts in the global economy. The auto industry was hit hardest. In 1950 85 percent of *all* cars worldwide were made in the United States. By 1980 Japan had overtaken the United States as the world's largest producer of cars.[6] America was in the throes of its own corporate Pearl Harbor.

Billings disappeared virtually overnight, and McKinsey found itself dealing with its own executive bloat. "Almost overnight, McKinsey's enormous reservoir of internal self-confidence and even self-satisfaction began to turn into self-doubt and self-criticism," explained a Harvard Business School case study.[7] A 1971 Commission on Firm Aims and Goals concluded that McKinsey had chased growth at the expense of quality.

"We realized that we didn't have nearly as strong a partner group as we should have, that we had elected a lot of partners who should not be partners, that the [firm] was capable of doing bad work, and that we weren't necessarily on a winning streak forever," future managing director Ron Daniel said later. "It was an era of coming to terms with the fact that the giddy growth of the 1960s was over for us."[8] As for Bower, semi-retirement didn't bring contentment. The firm's troubles were his troubles, and the years 1967 to 1972 have been called his "dark years," as the institution he had so painstakingly built struggled for balance.

Second Generation

Lee Walton, a five-foot-seven Texan partial to gold steer cuff links,[9] had joined the firm in 1955 after stints in the Air Force and oil industry. He had worked in the Chicago office, in Venezuela on the Shell project, then in London, Amsterdam, and Chicago again. While he'd been a favorite of Bower, particularly due to his contributions to European expansion, he was no Bower acolyte as managing director. In fact, he pointedly chose not to consult the older man on major decisions, a move he later conceded might have rubbed Bower the wrong way. He even made a ruling or two contrary to Bower's cherished "professionalisms," such as when he decided to let Bower's contemporary John Neukom serve on a few corporate boards while still working at McKinsey. To Bower, such arrangements presented glaring conflicts of interest.

Walton was the first of the second generation of McKinsey leaders. Only forty-two when he was elected, he took the brunt of the frustration that the firm's older partners surely felt at turning over their creation to a band of ungrateful youngsters. Worse yet, his era as managing director—from 1968 through 1973—was a painful time for the firm, as was that of his successor, Al McDonald. The nine-year period following Bower's stepping down in 1967 through the election of Ron Daniel in 1976 is quite clearly one the firm would like to forget. McKinsey had to contend with not only lackluster growth, but also the appearance of savvy new competitors.

Walton opened his tenure as head of the firm in a way that has since become tradition. He formed a number of new committees, like the Management Group Administration Committee, to evaluate candidates for advancement to director, as well as compensation for both principals and directors; and the Principal Candidate Evaluation Committee. These were, in effect, his cabinet.

He also devised new ways for the firm to study itself, putting together the Commission on Firm Aims and Goals. (McKinsey's navel-gazing knows no bounds). A year later, the commission reported that the targeted growth of the firm's professional staff should be 7 to 8 percent annually, and that its associate-to-partner ratio should be no more than 5 or 6 by 1975. These were reasonable targets, and ones the firm unremittingly stuck to for two decades.

Like the law firms it emulated from the start, McKinsey was fundamentally conservative. But its model of white Protestant males in dark suits counseling other white Protestant males in dark suits was out of sync with the times. The firm responded belatedly to the civil rights movement, not hiring its first black consultants—Bob Holland and Jim Lowry—until 1968. Holland became the firm's first black principal in 1974, before leaving to become CEO of Ben & Jerry's in 1981. At the end of the 1990s the firm had just five black principals, and it didn't name a black director until 2005.

Likewise, women made slow progress up the ranks, due to both internal and external factors. "I remember working for a prominent CEO at the time," said current McKinsey director Nancy Killefer. "I was pregnant with my first child, and I had to explain to him that I wasn't disabled, I was just pregnant."[10] Four years after hiring its first female associate, the firm put a woman in charge of a study for the first time: in 1968 Mary Falvey headed an engagement for the Insurance Company of North America, a predecessor to CIGNA.

Not long after taking office, Walton told a *New York Times* reporter questioning the firm's lack of diversity that he, Walton, was evidence of diversity: a Roman Catholic heading a firm that, to that juncture, had been a Protestant stronghold. The company could even count several Jews among its ranks.

The Phone Stops Ringing

McKinsey's foreign strategy was modeled on its British experience. It seeded the new enterprise with proven American managers and then tried, over time, to develop a consulting staff of local nationality. By 1969, of the seventy-six consultants in London, fifty-six were British. (Thirteen were American, and eight from elsewhere.) The American presence helped establish and maintain the important one-firm ethos, and the gradual shift to local talent ensured that the firm could relate culturally to its clients, while also providing a buffer against any flare-ups of anti-Americanism.

The problem was that the firm was no longer able to find new clients in huge, critical markets like London. McKinsey was a victim of economic woes but also of its own success: It had successfully reorganized Europe. "Somewhere around 1970, the phone stopped ringing,"[11] said London office manager Hugh Parker.

Christopher McKenna has pointed out that developments in England paralleled those in the United States: Once the decentralization business was done, the firm needed government work to pick up the slack. But that came with major drawbacks. Executives at private companies have occasionally tried to publicly pin their problems on their consultants, but not often, in large part because it might raise the issue of their own competence. Politicians face no such constraints. Savvy cabinet ministers in England love shifting blame to consultants, especially when they have to lay off government workers.

What's more, the firm was facing up to the fact that some high-profile clients were less than enamored with the work McKinsey had done for them. The firm had been brought into Volkswagen in Germany in 1968 by CEO Kurt Lotz to help with organization and marketing issues, including helping Lotz devise a successor for the "Bug." But when Ernst Leiding succeeded Lotz in 1971, he fired McKinsey and disregarded all its work to that point.[12] Other German manufacturing firms were also abandoning the M-form structure and reverting to earlier organizational forms because McKinsey's one-size-fits-all model of decentralization had proven more problematic due to a number of local factors, including the role of the banks in corporate affairs, concentrated shareholders, and the country's dual system of corporate boards—one of which represented shareholders and the other management.[13,14] The sheen from the 1950s and 1960s had faded. When Parker stepped down as London office manager in 1973, *no one* wanted the job. Jan van den Berg finally filled the vacant position two years later.

By 1972 it was clear that Walton had abjectly failed to restart the McKinsey engine: In fiscal 1972, revenues fell for the first time in a decade. Both the volume of work and the profitability of that work were sagging. What's more, it was getting more difficult to corral the firm's far-flung consultants and focus them on common goals. Whereas the Bower era had been marked by centralized power, the Walton era was defined by the opposite. Power migrated to new places. In the mid-1960s, the managers of the Amsterdam, Dusseldorf, London, and Paris offices had become known as the "barons"—a powerful group that wielded growing influence, from hiring to staffing to a tendency to vote as a bloc. Walton's tenure was described as "weak king, strong baron."[15]

Remarkably, though, the firm was still able to summon the strength to turn down work when it was obvious that it couldn't meet Bower's mandate of having a true impact on a client. One client in the late 1960s was the Railway Express Agency, a national monopoly set up by the U.S. government in 1917 that functioned much like UPS today, except via rail. One of the REA's predecessor companies was the railway express division of Wells Fargo. When McKinsey consultants visited some storage facilities in New York City to see what the REA had been paying to store over the decades, they discovered about thirty roll-top desks and a couple of stagecoaches. Rod Carnegie, the director in charge of the engagement, resigned immediately. "I remember what his exact words were," recalled former consultant Logan Cheek. "He said, ' I lack faith in the client's ability to execute.'"[16] (Carnegie replied that the finding of the relics in the warehouse wasn't *the* reason for resigning the engagement, but that it certainly was an indication of management's likely inability to "respond to the modern world.")[17]

Having Their Lunch Eaten

If McKinsey was stalling in the early 1970s, Bruce Henderson's Boston Consulting Group was on a roll. In addition to his four-box matrix, Henderson had recently added a second weapon to his arsenal: the experience curve. Its purpose was to help clients see how costs go down systematically along with experience and market share. For each doubling of experience, the curve suggested, total costs declined by 20 to 30 percent due economies of scale and innovation. This was not rocket science—Henry Ford had long before proven that volume begets cost savings—but a generation of American managers latched on to BCG's insights for dear life.

Some clients were surely attracted by the eye candy: the charts, graphs, lists, and matrices. And while the idea of strategizing wasn't even new—there were talented managers who had been "strategizing" for decades—it turned out that most managers couldn't name their top customer across business units, couldn't say how profitable that customer was, and couldn't identify which division was eating more capital than it was creating. Organization Man had been asleep at the wheel.

McKinsey had never imagined that its sophisticated clients could be sold "products" such as the growth-share matrix and the experience curve. Under Bower's lead, the firm had deliberately avoided flavor-of-the-month ideas, thinking that its clientele wanted smart people, not smartly packaged ideas. It was dead wrong about that. Its clients apparently wanted both.

Black & Decker was a typical BCG client of the time, wrote Walter Kiechel in *The Lords of Strategy*. By using the tools of the experience curve—both analyzing and predicting costs—the consumer product maker took its circular saw business from 50,000 units to 600,000 units, a result of pushing its retail pricing down from $35.00 or so to $19.95. Although the iconic brand at first had trouble with its distributors when it suggested slashing prices, it quickly won converts when it used the curve to show how rapidly increasing volumes negated any margin loss when a market leader used its power to take market share.[18]

The appeal of BCG was in the tangibility of its advice. It was not a process or an intellectual exercise. "While McKinsey was selling its own innate brilliance, BCG was selling products and selling lots of them,"[19] said business author Stuart Crainer. Henderson took a direct shot at McKinsey when he told a reporter that "good strategy must be based primarily on logic, not . . . on experience derived from intuition."[20]

McKinsey had been through lean times before. But now the firm had to ask itself: Was this our own fault? The Boston Consulting Group had seen the end of the organizational consulting boom coming and had adjusted accordingly by inventing the business of strategy consulting with its growth-share matrix. McKinsey had nothing to counter with, and by the late 1960s, the firm's client share of the top fifty industrial companies was declining. In 1969 BCG outrecruited McKinsey at Harvard Business School. "[BCG] hurt us by outrecruiting us, and for a while we weren't even in the contest," one insider told *BusinessWeek*.[21]

After the oil crisis, many corporations concluded that long-term planning was meaningless and that BCG had the antidote—a cold, hard look at the present state of affairs. Pretty much every consulting firm abandoned McKinsey's expansive approach and followed BCG's lead. Boston Consulting Group spawned Bain & Company and Braxton Associates, as well as Strategic Planning Associates, Kaiser Associates, and Marakon Associates. Corporate executives had always relied on the experience of the McKinsey crowd. Now they had a second option: the ideas of the BCG retinue. McKinsey had its *Quarterly*; BCG began sending out *Perspectives,* a less substantive but more compelling broadside that didn't feel like homework. BCG and Bain were the Apple to McKinsey's Microsoft.

McKinsey even found itself in the wrong town. In the early 1970s, New York City was falling apart and approaching the nadir of its national popularity. Boston, by contrast, was Silicon Valley's antecedent, a cleaner, safer, and more humane place to start one's career as a young consultant. Competition for recruiting Harvard's best and brightest became a multifaceted argument, not the least factor in which was quality of life. New York was fit for the likes of Lew Ranieri, the Salomon Brothers hustler who sold real estate bonds like a used car salesman. If you were refined, Boston was your town.

Bill Bain bolted BCG in 1973. He made two decisions that distinguished his new consulting firm, Bain & Company, from McKinsey and BCG. First, he would work for only one company in an industry, but only if that company agreed to a long-term relationship. Second, he and his colleagues argued that the quality of its consulting boosted the share price of its clients. While this was a refreshing departure from McKinsey's long-stated claim that it was impossible to measure the consultants' impact, it took credit for things over which consultants had no influence. On the other hand, Bain was putting real skin in the game.

When the firm established Bain Capital in 1984—headed by Mitt Romney—at least a portion of its investment dollars were targeted for investment in clients of Bain & Company. For Bain Capital, share price *was* a true measure of success, and so the claim that stock appreciation was a good measure of success was arguably as good a yardstick as one might find. Bain & Company was deliberately eschewing the consulting industry's traditional routine of passing along competitors' secrets—the economy of knowledge gained by talking to all players—so its consultants were forced to come up with truly company-specific advice and its fortunes could actually rise and fall along with those of its clients.

The idea of taking similar action was discussed, and then rejected, in the corridors of McKinsey. In the face of real innovation in its competitive set, the firm chose to stick to its knitting. Not for the first time, some critics argued that McKinsey had become what it counseled against—hidebound—and was stuck in what *Economist* editor Adrian Wooldridge later described as a "complacent torpor."[22] As late as 1976, then-managing director Al McDonald referred to BCG as a "disconcerting strategic actor of no concern." A charitable explanation is that he was bluffing.

Still, it was hard to say whether BCG's emergence marked a genuine revolution in consulting or was merely a triumph of salesmanship. Consultants at Bain & Company referred to "the million-dollar slide"—a single chart or graph that told a company so much about itself that it was worth a million dollars in fees.[23] For all the rhetoric about the "strategy revolution," companies continued to make the same mistakes they've always made despite having paid through the nose to chart their bold course into the future. "The most reliable way to make money from strategy," observed Matthew Stewart, "is to sell it to other people."[24]

He's right. "Strategy," as it is sold by consulting firms, is essentially a pipe dream. Why? Because you can sit in a boardroom and plot all you'd like, but once the game has started, it's pretty much improvisation from that point forth. The best companies stay efficient and effective, and they do well because their people are trained to do their jobs. The hardest thing in any big organization is to keep execution discipline in the forefront. There is a huge usefulness to *that* kind of consulting—process improvement—versus the elusive promise of big breakthrough thinking. The idea that executives need to be smart and heroic is a new invention. The essence of efficient management is hiring and training unheroic, ordinary people to play by certain rules. You need to take care of that before trying to create leaders or heroes.

That said, there's nothing wrong with looking for big insights—strategy with a capital S—that can take you to where the market opportunities will be. But that wasn't what McKinsey and its peers were selling. Consultants sell an analytical approach to strategy, argued McGill professor Henry Mintzberg, but that's never going to give you the big insight into what product or service will make you profitable again. No amount of reductive analysis of customer needs, market sizing, or competitive positioning can do that. For that you need to innovate, and there's something about the whole analytical mind-set that effectively drives the ability to innovate out of the building.

"McKinsey people are very sharp analysts; there's no doubt about that," said Mintzberg. "And that's what you should look for when you hire them—analytical advice. They may couch it as managerial or strategic advice, but it's merely analysis. You won't hear it from them, but strategy is a learning process; you can't just buy it from someone. Any chief executive who hires a consultant to give them strategy should be fired."[25] And, truth be told, McKinsey had been as guilty of this sleight of hand as anyone—it promised big breakthrough thinking, but what it really delivered was lots of analysis. It made sure its clients didn't do anything really stupid, but was that really what companies were paying it the big bucks for?

Over time, McKinsey regained some lost ground. Even if Henderson and his ilk were making inroads with some clients, McKinsey was still the consultant of choice, especially for the largest of firms. In 1968, GE CEO Fred Borch asked McKinsey for help in evaluating his corporation's strategic planning. GE had deemed BCG's four-box matrix intriguing but inadequate for the real world. A three-month study produced the GE/McKinsey nine-block matrix. If it seemed a petty response—you have four? *we* have nine!—it still satisfied the client.[26]

GE's problem was typical of the conglomerates of the era. Up until that time, the assumption had been that all business units were created equal and that all general managers should grow their own businesses. The result, though, was that GE was growing profitlessly. Revenues were up, but profits were flat. The same thing was happening at Westinghouse. The great insight of the strategy practitioners was that not all businesses are created equal, and it is the job of the CEO to divvy up capital according to which ones could put it to best use. This wasn't a new idea, but it had been lost in the enthusiasm regarding growth and success of the postwar boom.

Some answers to the complexity served a purpose, but in the end they were like Band-Aids on a broken bone. A lot of CEOs of the era, for example, had gotten to the top by exercising internal control. GE's Borch, for one, read the profit-and-loss statements of all his departments every year and told them to stop spending on paper clips. Budgeting and control were at least one part of leadership, but such immersion in detail has its obvious limitations. If you're wearing a green eyeshade, you're not looking at the battlefield. Suddenly you look up, and—whoops!—Napoleon is coming for you!

With McKinsey's help, GE created strategic business units, or SBUs, that were organized not for span of control but for businesses around which a cohesive competitive strategy could be developed. BCG talked about market share and growth rates; McKinsey threw industry attractiveness and competitive strength into the mix. GE needed to shift its focus from internal control to external factors, the consultants argued. While it had sold a lot of televisions, for example, the corporation suddenly had no answer to Sony. The problem was that GE was too inward looking, and it wasn't thinking about its business units in the right way—outwardly, analyzing all manner of factors beyond just production costs. The sprawling conglomerate—GE had 360 departments before the study—ended with just 50 SBUs. This organizational idea then swept the world, and it helped McKinsey stem the tide of competitors.

Former McKinsey consultant Mike Allen argued that McKinsey's work at General Electric laid the groundwork for Jack Welch's acclaimed career. "Without McKinsey, he would have not had an organization that worked," said Allen. "He would have had no strategic planning or organizational structure to work with. We helped put him on the map. It was the high point of our interaction with GE, from a creative standpoint."[27]

Though BCG and Bain took a toll, they didn't deter McKinsey from its global march. In 1971 the firm opened offices in both Tokyo and Sydney. Early clients in Tokyo included Japan Airlines and Sanwa Bank. In 1972 Copenhagen; 1973 Stamford; 1974 Caracas and Dallas; 1975 São Paulo, Munich, and Houston. (Although Caracas was shuttered that same year due to a lack of business.) McKinsey also worked on a few signature engagements, like the one in 1973 in which the firm, while engaged on an electronic coding project for Heinz, did work that led to the creation of the universal product code—or bar code—for food. McKinsey research correctly predicted that the code would revolutionize the grocery business and improve Americans' quality of life at the same time. That is exactly what they did, making stores vastly more efficient and dramatically reducing checkout times.

By the mid-1970s, the existential threat posed by the likes of BCG had largely passed. Some of this was McKinsey's doing, and some of it was because the fad had burned out. Henderson had grown so enamored of his ability to conjure up salable theories that he veered off into folly. In 1976 he wrote an essay titled "The Rules of Three and Four," in which he claimed that a stable competitive market never has more than three significant competitors, the largest of which has no more than four times the market share of the smallest.[28] The rule was merely a hypothesis, he said, and "not subject to rigorous proof." Henderson was fat and happy from his decade of success, and this was a casual and careless approach to providing insight to clients—to which McKinsey had successfully defined itself in opposition. "In my view, the best thing that ever happened to the Firm was the onset of BCG," said Fred Gluck, who succeeded Ron Daniel as managing director of McKinsey in 1988. "I think that the Firm's market success in the 1960s had developed into a sense of smugness and self-satisfaction that was counterproductive."[29]

Not that McKinsey had stopped taking pages out of Henderson's playbook. In a belated response to *Perspectives,* McKinsey later began sending missives of two thousand words or less out to prospective clients. Called "spill a cup of coffee on that," the briefs had a threefold goal. First, the McKinsey partner asked the prospects what they thought of the work. This appealed to the client's vanity. Second, it compelled the client to then read McKinsey's latest thinking. And third, it gave the firm a chance to follow up. One rival suggested the firm has captured more business through these informal communiqués than through big, important papers on the future of hedge funds or capitalism on which the media so eagerly feed. And this gets at what has been one of McKinsey's enduring competitive advantages: the firm's ability to build enduring relationships with its clients' CEOs and then use those relationships to spin off study after study. This is something that no other consulting firm has been able to do nearly as well.

Alternate Futures

If there was one thing Bower had unquestionably given the firm, it was certitude. But just a few years after he stepped down, the consultants were second-guessing almost everything about themselves and what they were doing. A representative moment came in 1974 when consultant Jim Bennett made a presentation to the Chicago office titled "Mismanaging the Change Process: The Best and Brightest at Their Most Brilliant and Their Worst." In it he spotlighted controversial consulting work that the firm had done for Air Canada, work for which the consultants had been portrayed as "hatchet men" for the airline's management when it came to light that 135 managers had been let go as part of a reorganization. Bower's back-channel man Warren Cannon soon reined Bennett in, forbidding him to make the presentation again, but it had struck a chord. McKinsey was wrestling with doubts about its purpose in the world.

In one way or another, the firm had been wondering about its future since the moment Bower had ceded the top post. In 1968 then-managing director Lee Walton set up a task force to rethink how the firm went about its business. Should it, for example, begin making venture investments in companies it advised or form an alliance with—dare it contemplate the thought?—a Wall Street firm?

In October 1969, at their annual meeting in Madrid—the first-ever partners' meeting in Europe—the directors considered a specific proposal to form a joint venture with boutique investment bank Donaldson, Lufkin & Jenrette. The idea was compelling in theory: DLJ would acquire underachieving companies, reinvigorate them with McKinsey management know-how, and then flip them back into the market. The two firms would share the spoils.

Bower spoke out against the hookup at the meeting, one of just two times he did so in thirty-plus years after his semi-retirement. Being owner/operators was a violation of professional principles, he said, and would compromise McKinsey's character. Wall Street was a polar opposite, he argued: "promotional" as opposed to "professional." The idea was voted down. "Marvin broke out of his cage," Warren

Cannon said later. "He apologized for breaking his vow of silence, but he felt that the whole character of the [firm] was at stake . . . Then he went back into his cage."[30] One other memorable detail about the meeting was the fact that Bower flew coach to Madrid while many of his partners flew first class. It is instances such as this that can carve a man's reputation for frugality in stone.

Though the partners resisted getting hitched to a Wall Street firm, they still hungered to do a deal of some sort. After all, everybody else was doing it. In 1970 Booz Allen Hamilton sold shares to the public. That same year, another consulting firm, Cresap, McCormick and Paget, sold itself to Citibank. Citi's first choice for an acquisition had been McKinsey, but the partners rebuffed the inquiry. The firm did consider selling out to both the Systems Development Corporation (an air force spinoff) and the publicly traded systems analysis outfit Planning Research Corporation. But neither idea went very far.

The staunch refusal of Bower and his partners to sell is quite likely the key to McKinsey's enduring lead over its competition. Bower understood that selling shares to the public at a multiple of earnings (as opposed to selling back to his partners at book value) was a surefire way to become very, very rich. But it also created classes of haves and have-nots that most likely would eventually lead to the dissolution of the firm. That he chose not to do so is perhaps the most important road not taken in the history of the firm. John Forbis, at McKinsey from 1971 through 1983, put it simply enough: "Marvin not taking McKinsey public is like George Washington refusing the title of king—it did not match the founding principles."[31]

Turnover and turmoil at those firms that did sell—Cresap was a money loser for Citibank, and Booz consultants took their firm private again in 1976 after its shares plunged—validated Bower's vision. "Is Marvin Bower right?" *Consulting News* asked—and then answered in the affirmative.[32]

That didn't mean McKinsey wasn't facing serious challenges to its standing, and not just from interlopers like Bruce Henderson. The sputtering economy meant that its biggest customers were cash strapped. And the rise of Wall Street and the era of the modern CEO also threatened the self-image of a group of people who had previously luxuriated in their self-confidence. Consultants had long worn their IQ on their sleeves; bankers their W2. But things were starting to get out of hand.

The competition for talent from Wall Street firms—which started paying their people multiples of what McKinsey consultants made—was especially fierce, and the New York office watched with increasing alarm as associate turnover rose to unprecedented levels. Bower had long extolled the nonfinancial rewards of a professional career. But many consultants weren't as drawn to them as he was. The partnership was concerned enough to yield to younger colleagues' desire for more alternatives in the company's profit-sharing retirement trust. In 1968 McKinsey added a second option to its investment choices in the trust. With a more aggressive tilt, the new fund lost value in the early 1970s, but it had bounced back by the end of the decade and was up 50 percent from its inception by 1977.

It wasn't just Wall Street that was pushing up the cost of talent. Corporate executives, who up to that point had shown a "sense of stewardship and moderation"[33] about their pay, started grabbing a larger portion of company profits for themselves. McKinsey consultants, accustomed to considering themselves equal, if not superior, to their client executives, were suddenly the poorest players at the boardroom table.

As much as McKinsey will argue that its people are not primarily motivated by money—and, in large part, they don't seem to be—they still fought bitterly over their share of the annual spoils. Firm policy had been to set compensation according to two basic criteria: the quality and quantity of one's actual work during the year, and the squishier concept of one's "enduring contribution" to the firm. "The most acerbic debates among senior directors were about that split," recalled Peter von Braun.[34] "People were always trying to claim that their enduring was more enduring than your enduring." Von Braun's contemporary Ed Massey put it more bluntly: "If you didn't bring in clients, you argued your enduring contribution."[35]

In the end, McKinsey started paying its people more than it had in the past. But to do that, it needed to grow, thus beginning a multiyear expansion process that strained the firm as much as its dry years had done.

The Last of the Great Generalists

Of all the painful ways that McKinsey had to adapt to a new era, perhaps none was more unsettling to the McKinsey ego than the waning of its time-honed generalist model of consulting. As late as 1967, Gil Clee had bragged to *BusinessWeek* that "many of [the firm's] partners are generalists who will take on any problem and rely on logic and intelligence to arrive at answers."[36] Behind closed doors, many partners were not so sure. Arch Patton had already told a "skeptical"[37] Marvin Bower that he thought a firm with six hundred generalists was untenable. He argued for a greater specialization by consultants. Bower countered that specialization would eventually entail flying people into and out of various local markets, undermining the firm's practice of insinuating its consultants into the local business community.[38]

This issue with its push and pull was a constant for McKinsey, and one it wouldn't ultimately resolve until the tail end of the century, when it stumbled on a characteristic solution. The firm capitulated to client demands for more specialized consultants while still maintaining a generalist veneer. In time, McKinsey offered its clients specialists in a range of industries and functions (e.g., supply-chain management, corporate finance) but at the same time managed to hold on to a vaunted image as boardroom consultants. The result: As with many things McKinsey, surface appearance didn't tell the whole story. But the transition didn't just take years; it took decades.

In 1970 Lee Walton established a Practice Development Committee to look into carving out specific practice niches. The only problem: There weren't too many consultants who wanted to put on such straitjackets. "Everyone wants to have specialists around and to have access to them, but no one wants to be one," said one partner at the time.[39] Author Hal Higdon compared the specialist role at a consulting firm to that of a field goal kicker on a football team: You might need one, but McKinsey men were trained to be quarterbacks.[40]

The firm hadn't avoided specialization altogether. Arch Patton was a world-renowned expert on compensation studies. Dick Neuschel and Peter Walker were heavyweights in insurance, Lee Walton was highly regarded by railroad executives, and Andrall Pearson was already a giant in the world of marketing. Lowell Bryan was recruited from State Street in 1975 to help establish the firm's banking practice.

But over the years, it had been the generalists who had proven the most successful at attracting and retaining clients and therefore wielded the most power. There were six key nodes in the firm's power structure: engagement directors, who ran individual client projects; the partners (directors and principals); the associates; the office managers; the managing director; and the firm's governing bodies, in particular the shareholders committee (basically its legal board of directors), the executive committee, and the various personnel committees. Engagement managers were the first-line managers on a study. They were the core of the firm, and if you flamed out in that role you would never make director, because one essential skill needed in a director was the ability to jump in and rescue a study if the engagement manager was struggling. That's a relationship skill, not one that demands high specialization. Sure, an associate or principal could choose to specialize, but the two main career roads led either to a generalist relationship director or to an administrative office manager director. There was no specialist lane on either.

Walton's Commission on Firm Aims and Goals tried another tactic, endorsing the idea of the "T-shaped" consultant—one with breadth of perspective *and* depth of understanding. Amazingly, a study commissioned by the firm—in which other consultants consulted for the McKinsey consultants—found that the firm had been neglecting the professional and technical development of its people by taking on "routine assignments from marginal clients."[41] Principals and directors, in other words, were at fault for not being more selective with their studies. (This phenomenon wasn't entirely dealt with until the 1990s, with the creation of an internal market for projects. Partners would put their studies up on the intranet and associates would choose which they wanted to work on. Boring, marginal studies wouldn't get staffed, and the projects would be turned down.)

The conclusion was, on its face, startling: McKinsey's lack of expertise was somehow . . . the fault of its own clients?

Though it took years, the firm had no choice but to relinquish its generalist approach and become more specialized. "Consultants once prided themselves on being generalists," said partner Frank Mattern. "You went to your client and said, 'I know nothing about your business,' and that was a strength. If you said that to a client today they would think you were in the wrong movie."[42]

A parallel development at the time—equally resisted by the old guard—was a shift to more visual client presentations. Up to that point, the firm's style had sprung directly from Bower's lawyerly roots, and his insistence on dense, highly structured, wordy presentations was still the model.

But across the industry, new techniques were evolving. Consider ex-McKinsey consultant Barbara Minto's *The Pyramid Principle: Logic in Writing, Thinking, and Problem Solving,* a text that is really a primer on modern McKinsey report writing. Minto's principle wasn't about pretty pictures or overlapping ovals. It was about laying out conclusions and supporting data and analyses of a study in a structured way that presumably wouldn't overburden the already strained intellectual resources of the average CEO, whose available time for the consultants' presentation and attention span during that presentation were often both denominated in minutes.

The pyramid principle is a kind of consulting poetry. Longtime McKinsey director of visual communications Gene Zelazny, a legend at the firm, further made the case in his 1985 book, *Say It with Charts*. Just as the generalist-versus-specialist impulse was a conflict, so too were the inclinations toward pictures and words. In both cases the old school lost out to the new one, but, as with all things McKinsey, it took years of thrashing through debates for the firm to find its new way.

Not all changes were improvements, either. While *The Pyramid Principle* was a terrific way to organize one's thoughts on a PowerPoint presentation, it was also a very poor structural guide for writing in plain English. The unfortunate side effect of pyramidizing was that some young consultants became so enamored of the logical, rational format that their actual writing began to verge on the unreadable. "We would frequently get article submissions to the *McKinsey Quarterly* that were completely unreadable—full of pure *consultese,*" said former partner (and third editor in chief of the *Quarterly*) Partha Bose. "We found ourselves constantly de-pyramidizing some of these young consultants."[43]

The Rise of Investor Capitalism

While McKinsey battled new competitors and struggled to rethink its antiquated methods, it had to deal simultaneously with a much bigger and more fundamental change: the end of one era of modern capitalism and the start of another.

So-called neoliberal economists like Michael C. Jensen and William J. Abernathy were arguing that the lack of an active market for corporate control—corporate executives, once entrenched, can be hard to dislodge—had resulted in little managerial accountability. They espoused a new form of market logic that prized corporate takeovers as the optimal way to value companies. Making managers fear for their jobs was the best way to keep them honest and focused. This was the start of the era of investor capitalism.

The work of Jensen and others amounted to a direct assault on the Protestant precepts that Marvin Bower had so painstakingly laid down. Bower's professional manager was a man who had an *obligation* to his community, "in the service of a higher end than self-interest."[44] And whereas Bower and his contemporaries believed that their management consulting had contributed to society in many ways, including as a bulwark against Communism during the Cold War, a new agency theory arose suggesting that if a corporation is merely a sum of contractual arrangements, then the managers have no claim to the idea of social good. They are pretty much just looking out for themselves. There's nothing wrong with that, but it certainly contradicted Bower's ideal of the professional consultant.

"Rarely, if ever, in American history had there been such a wholesale reinterpretation of economic history as that which occurred during the . . . decades of the 1980s and 1990s," wrote Rakesh Khurana in *From Higher Aims to Hired Hands*. "As the narrative was revised, managerial capitalism was portrayed no longer as the key to America's economic success but, rather, as a liability. . . . Corporate takeovers came to be seen as a means of restoring power to the group now believed to be the only one with a legitimate claim to the value created by corporations—shareholders."[45]

There really is no such thing as "shareholders" as a coherent entity. "Shareholders" is code for "Wall Street," and starting in the late 1970s, that's where power began to be concentrated. Corporate boardrooms were not where the action was anymore. McKinsey recognized that shift, helped it along, and made a lot of money along the way. But because of Bower's own principles, it avoided being swallowed up itself, an astonishing feat.

While McKinsey never did hook up with an investment bank, partners spent years wondering how to become a bigger player in financial restructuring. Why? Money, of course. An internal McKinsey report from 1989 addressed the fact head-on: In the late 1980s, buyout shops like Kohlberg Kravis Roberts were pulling down revenues per professional of about $5 million, versus McKinsey's mere $250,000 or so. The pressure to pay its people as much as Wall Street could strained McKinsey's fabric over the next fifteen years.

From the 1920s through to the mid-1970s, the giant American corporation had been the ne plus ultra of organizations. Then capitalism took an axe to itself, and the never-ending era of cost cutting and rationalization was under way. Consultants often get called in to assist with such planning. But they can also be a casualty of the process.

The Axe Man

Of all the managing directors of McKinsey, none has a more complicated relationship with his former partners than Al McDonald, who served from 1973 to 1976. He helped steady the firm during its most turbulent times, though his tenure is one the firm doesn't celebrate too much.

An ex-Marine, McDonald had joined the firm in 1960 in New York, then went to Europe, where he ran the Paris office and oversaw stupendous growth: The number of consultants climbed from twenty in 1968 to sixty-four just five years later. And yet he was voted in as managing director to do just the opposite: to slash the budgets of a bloated organization.

When Walton stepped down in 1973—he stayed with the firm, opening the Dallas office—the enthusiasm for the top job was muted. Ron Daniel, a favorite of Bower's who was running the New York office, chose not to run, as did Jon Katzenbach. No one wanted the thankless job of cutting costs and saying no to his colleagues. So into the breach stepped McDonald. He wasn't an instant favorite. He ran against Jack Cardwell of the Chicago office, and neither he nor Cardwell obtained the 60 percent majority required for election in the firm's bylaws. The partnership decided to change the requirement to a simple majority, and McDonald won on the next ballot. That vote for managing director in 1973 took place at the Racquet Club in New York City. It was the last time the partnership met face-to-face to elect a managing partner.

Walton had been a laissez-faire leader, with a style that had lulled the firm into a sense that things were going to be okay. But the firm was in worse shape on the day he stepped down than it had been when he took over. Operating profits in 1972 were close to zero. It took nearly a whole year to pay back bank loans the firm took out in June 1973 to pay partner bonuses. The firm had been struggling with its cash position since 1971, with the New York office putting constant pressure on other offices to expedite the transfer of cash back to headquarters. If things got any worse, the whole enterprise might collapse. In a shocking turnaround, London was now operating in the red.

Consultant turnover was also abnormally high. It had been 14 percent annually for the decade through 1972, then jumped to 25 percent in 1972 and 1973. It remained at 20 percent through 1978. But there's another way of looking at it. McKinsey downsized by tightening its promotion criteria and then invoking the "up-or-out" rules: Whenever business turns down, instead of laying off people, the firm simply lowers the percentage that gets promoted at each level and the problem takes care of itself in a year or two. Voilà! The firm, which had 627 consultants on the payroll in 1971, had just 532 in 1975. Even more disturbing: Some partners were concerned that the value of the firm's shares might be worth less than what the partnership was asking new principals to pay for them. Considering that most principals took out loans to buy into the partnership, McKinsey was running the risk that newly appointed partners might refuse to buy in completely.

McDonald tried to stop the bleeding as quickly as he could. He negotiated a new credit line at U.S. Trust. He changed the share buyback from departing partners to take place over five years, at 20 percent a year, instead of as one immediate lump sum, making it less attractive for partners to leave for greener pastures while also relieving capital pressures on the firm. And he insisted that the firm raise its fees. The San Francisco office refused at first, and McDonald told it that it would enjoy disproportionately lower income than the rest of the firm. Nine months later, it relented.

McDonald also instituted a number of changes designed to make sure directors still performed in the interests of the firm, including the extension of the up-or-out policy to the director level. Previously, directors effectively had tenure. Henceforth, they had to justify their existence along with everyone else.

"I also put financial controls and higher performance expectations on offices and office managers who had tended to operate as independent baronies," recalled McDonald. "And I include myself in that group, from my time as manager of the office in Paris and earlier in Zurich."[46] McDonald was ruthless: He changed office managers in half of the firm's locations in his first eighteen months and terminated a partner a month for nearly the entire thirty-six months he was in office.

Bower resented McDonald's laser focus on finances. While frugal himself, he'd always argued that if the firm focused on serving clients, the finances would take care of themselves. But the economic climate had changed everything. The removal of the United States from the gold standard had resulted in inflation and then recession. United States gross domestic product fell from October 1973 through early 1975, a sixteen-month decline that was the longest since World War II. New investment in the nation dropped by a startling 39.8 percent. "Al made us pay attention to financial planning and budgeting," said Jack Vance, head of the Los Angeles office. "At first we needed those controls. But as soon as we didn't, the partners didn't really want them."[47]

When McDonald initiated a project to develop a new "firm description" so the outside world would better know McKinsey, the knives truly came out. Arch Patton, one of the old guard, wrote a scathing memo to McDonald on March 3, 1976, attacking what he saw as a "sales piece." But Patton's memo was more revealing for what it said about McKinsey's inflated self-regard than for what it said about McDonald's effort. He cautioned against talking down to outsiders, displaying McKinsey arrogance in the process: "This version gives me [the feeling] that we are simply superior people. I think we are, but hate to see us say so." More important, he killed the sacred cow: "We would like people to consider us a profession (we are not, of course)." It was all a construct, he was saying, and unless McKinsey was careful, people would see right through it.

McDonald's dramatic changes were driven by a realization that McKinsey wasn't invulnerable. But many partners preferred to believe in the myth that it was—and to see McDonald himself as the cause of their problems. They derided his focus on costs. They saw imperiousness in his use of gold-toned paper for memos from the corner office. "Al kind of committed hara-kiri by thinking he was in charge," said one of his colleagues. "That's a big mistake. You can be very influential and make a lot of things happen as managing director of McKinsey, but you are definitely not in charge. Marvin was in charge, but no one has been since." A few understood what McDonald was trying to do—"It's very hard to manage an orderly retreat, but Al did," said partner Charles Shaw[48]—but they were a small and not particularly vocal minority.

In short, Al McDonald was the kind of guy you didn't elect in good times. Even he knew that. And when the next election came around, he didn't really stand a chance. "I think Marvin was pleased that I wasn't reelected," said McDonald. "The same goes for a few others who thought my enforced disciplines and higher performance expectations might put them in a less favorable light. But I had not been elected based on popularity, but because people knew I would do what urgently needed to be done for the firm. And I did it, to the satisfaction and relief of some and to the concern of others."[49] Bower was so excited to see McDonald leave that once Ron Daniel had been elected as his successor, Bower encouraged McDonald to step down immediately, as opposed to governing (as was his right) in transition. McDonald refused.

"There were a few times when things got a little out of control," said ex-McKinsey consultant Peter von Braun. "In one of those instances, Al McDonald was brought in to clean things up. But they didn't reelect him because they didn't want that kind of directive management anymore."[50]

In an interview more than twenty years after losing reelection, McDonald was reflective. "At the time, it was a big disappointment since we had achieved a major turnaround of firm results and future prospects in those three years," he said. "Even so, it was not a big surprise. The partners had accorded me a great honor by choosing me to lead them through one of the firm's most uncertain and traumatic periods, internally and externally. Although there was still much to do, I was proud to leave office with the [firm] greatly strengthened and rapidly gaining momentum, with a renewed, more confident, and brighter outlook ahead."[51] McDonald, who had been the firm's largest shareholder, went on to work in the Carter administration before becoming a corporate executive and private investor.

In Bower's eyes, McDonald also committed an unforgivable sin when he terminated residual payments to Zip Reilly, who had been receiving them since coming up with a much-needed capital injection to the firm in the 1930s. But Bower was angry for a lot of reasons. He couldn't stand to see his glorious creation under siege. And he chose to pin all that on McDonald: "He was not able to provide the push and drive to take the [firm] forward and he didn't have the capacity to think in terms of strategy for the [firm,]" the older man later said. And then he stuck the shiv in even farther: "Al McDonald had one fatal flaw," said Bower. "He was for Al McDonald." (The firm history concludes: "That judgment was not quite fair.")[52]

Bower's view of McDonald seems myopic in retrospect, another piece of evidence that he was losing sight of the plot in his final years. In reality, Bower was merely fighting the fight that all great leaders eventually must, which is the decline of one's own relevance. What's more, for all the strong values he had instilled in the firm, he had never been very good at anticipating changes in the business world. When he stepped down as managing director, the firm was woefully ill prepared for how hard its business was about to become. But by the end of McDonald's single term as managing director, McKinsey was on a far stronger footing than it had been just five years before. Just as the American economy would soon do, the firm had adapted to a changing world and capitalized on new strengths.

5. A RETURN TO FORM

The Man from Central Casting

If Hollywood were to cast the part of a McKinsey consultant, Ron Daniel would win the role hands down. Intelligent, gracious, and of regal height and bearing, he was once described by a colleague as "so smooth he could skate on your face and not leave a mark." Daniel succeeded Al McDonald as the firm's managing director in 1976 and led the firm over the next twelve years.

When Daniel was elected, McKinsey was still managed intuitively. He would change that on the basis of a conviction that in order to thrive in the next cycle, McKinsey had to institutionalize. He established committees to elect and evaluate junior partners and installed more formal ways to evaluate senior partners. The personnel processes he put in place allowed McKinsey to govern itself effectively as it grew. Equally important, Ron Daniel yanked the firm out of its generalist torpor and invested systematically in the creation of domain knowledge. He also proved the best judge of talent the firm had yet known, nurturing a number of McKinsey superstars during his tenure.

A mathematics graduate of Wesleyan, Daniel went to Harvard Business School and then served in the navy before landing at McKinsey in 1957. As of 2012, he still held an office at the firm, which means he's worked there for more than half a century. He recalled one of his first clients—a public utility in Arkansas—that took four or five flights to get to: New York to Washington to Knoxville or Memphis and then Little Rock. "[After arriving,] I had Sunday night dinner at the Toodle House," he told McKinsey's in-house magazine in 1996. "You could get a steak wrapped in bacon, french fries, chocolate cream pie, and chocolate milk—all for $1.19."[1]

Elected principal in 1963, Daniel took over Harvard recruiting for the firm in 1965. In 1970 Lee Walton asked him to manage the New York office, and in 1973, when the job of managing director opened, Daniel presciently chose not to run, waiting until 1976, when the firm had regained its footing. This time around, Daniel ran against Al McDonald and Jack Cardwell. Fearful that Daniel and Cardwell would neutralize each other and McDonald might be elected again, a group of partners got together and convinced Cardwell to bow out. Cardwell dutifully agreed and soon after left the firm to become president of Sara Lee and later of New York investment house Bessemer Securities.

The firm was already on the mend when Daniel took office. Austerity had stopped the internal bleeding, and client hours, which had bottomed in 1974, were rising along with the American economy. Only one office was in the red in 1976—Tokyo—and its losses had been halved. The firm's net operating profit was twenty times its low in 1973, and it was sitting on the largest capital reserve in its history. Shares were worth more than four times what they'd been worth when Marvin Bower stepped down in 1967.

McKinsey men were supposed to be great communicators—sufficiently wise and trusted to tell their clients bad news without losing the business—and on that front, Daniel eclipsed all those who had come before him, including Bower. "Marvin was cantankerous and sharp edged," recalled one McKinsey consultant. "He was like medicine. But it didn't feel that way with Ron. He brought force of opinion and strong will but delivered it in a way that was polished as well."

Through his tenure, as the media's fascination with McKinsey grew, Daniel kept an extremely low public profile. "We can't see how it serves the firm's interests," he told *BusinessWeek* in 1986 while declining an interview request. "Besides, we're kind of a dull, anonymous bunch, and we cannot talk about our clients."[2] Of all the long-serving managing directors in McKinsey's history, Daniel stayed the farthest beneath the public's radar.

Yet, other than Bower, he also stayed on as managing director longer than any in the firm's history. During Al McDonald's tenure, the shareholders committee had approved increasing the voting requirement for an incumbent director to remain in office: 60 percent in the director's first election, 70 percent in the next, and 80 percent in a third, making it nearly impossible for a director to stay on for more than two terms. During Daniel's first term in office, the change was rescinded, reducing the requirement to just 60 percent regardless of tenure, thereby allowing Daniel to glide through four elections. "But that's okay," said one former director. "He deserved it. He sacrificed his whole life for the place, just like Marvin."

Compared with McDonald's forced rehabilitation, Daniel was a soothing balm. "Al McDonald made Ron Daniel both possible and necessary," reads the firm's internal history.[3] Why? Because McKinsey men don't like constraints. More important, they don't like autocratic rule, even if the times demand it, and they needed a leader after McDonald who would loosen the reins again.

"The funny part about Ron Daniel is that he wasn't much of a consultant," said one of his longtime partners. "He only had one big client, and that was Mobil. But he was a gifted judge of talent." Daniel nurtured future McKinsey managing director Fred Gluck from the get-go, while also presiding over the emergence of McKinsey standouts like Tom Peters and Kenichi Ohmae.

Daniel wasn't much of a revolutionary thinker himself. But he believed, above all, in the partnership. He knew how to bring people inside and how to lead. He took risks by pushing as yet unproven consultants into important positions. Within five years of his election, 40 percent of the members of every committee—except for the members of the shareholders committee, who were elected—owed their appointments to Daniel.[4] But he didn't overly rely on committees. He was too smart for that. He wasn't going to come up with the next great theory about economic value, but he, as much as anyone, was responsible for helping McKinsey transition from a primarily domestic concern to a global partnership. The man sailed through twelve years of leadership without a challenge.

Some managing directors of McKinsey enjoyed a rising economic tide as the backdrop to their tenure—Marvin Bower, for example, and Rajat Gupta in the late 1990s. Ron Daniel had the 1980s boom at the end of his term, but when he took over in 1976, neither the U.S. nor the global economy could be called healthy. This was the era of Jimmy Carter and stagflation. How did Daniel keep McKinsey headed up and to the right of the growth chart? One major way was by embracing the idea of the "transformational relationship" and encouraging consultants to push it to their clients. McKinsey no longer pitched itself as a project-to-project firm; from this point forth, it sold itself to clients as an ongoing prodder of change, the kind a smart CEO would keep around indefinitely.

The sell worked: Once ensconced in the boardrooms of the biggest corporate players in the world, McKinsey rarely left, ensuring a steady and growing flow of billings for years if not decades. In 2002, for example, *BusinessWeek* noted that at that moment, the firm had served four hundred clients for fifteen years or more.[5] Not only that, but the firm continued to raise billing rates even in the face of stiff competition.

Some problems are solved once and solved forever. Others are piano-tuner problems. McKinsey decided that the real money was in the latter. One great trick was to issue a progress review at the end of any study—raising the implication that the completed work should necessarily lead to further work. An internal joke at the company, according to journalist Dana Milbank: "A transformational relationship is where we transform their money into our money."[6] You will never hear this from McKinsey, but with its business concentrated in continuous clients, a huge part of its effort is spent figuring out how to turn a middling client into a $10 million-per-annum cash cow.

Critics of the firm conveniently ignore that it wasn't just luck that turned one-off clients into relationship clients. Even when there was no hope of any billings, either immediately or in the near future, McKinsey partners would make it their business to meet the CEO and his top team on a regular basis. They would inform the C-suite on an issue they knew its members were grappling with or an emerging issue that the industry might be addressing. "I never thought twice about boarding a plane and flying from New York or London to São Paulo or New Delhi to accompany my partners in meetings for clients where there was no hope of any commercial benefit right away," said former partner Partha Bose.[7]

One former consultant recalled that the *only* time he heard talk of a client's actual profitability was when a young principal had just learned that a senior director he'd managed to cross had just used the firm's internal billing processes to put him in his place. The director ran a big proposal effort for the client and then billed the effort to the principal, who then saw his internal profit and loss measurements collapse. The principal left McKinsey soon after, acrimoniously.

Overall, the numbers were increasingly coming in as they had before the rough transition out of the Marvin Bower era. In 1973 McKinsey had the highest billings of any consultancy. In 1978 it was in fifth place, behind Arthur D. Little, Booz Allen Hamilton, Arthur Andersen, and Cooper's & Lybrand. [8] The firm had never prided itself on being the industry's largest player—it just felt it was the most important one—but losing ground opened the eyes of partners to the ways in which the firm had become a hostage to its traditions. Whereas McKinsey had always focused on its image and its relationships, BCG, Bain, and other upstarts had shifted the battle to the realm of ideas, where McKinsey had little to offer. "BCG and Bain had convinced the world that they had better ideas than McKinsey," said academic Matthias Kipping.[9] Under Daniel's leadership, McKinsey created the machinery to produce ideas of its own. By the time he was done, the firm had recaptured the client mindshare that had gotten away from it.

Superteam

Under Bower, McKinsey had a small, idiosyncratic leadership structure. He managed the firm with a kitchen cabinet of three or four people at most. Lee Walton expanded that, creating a shareholders committee of some forty-five members. Daniel brought more than a hundred partners into firm management decisions, a power-sharing arrangement that enabled the firm to become a global force. What Daniel proved was that McKinsey could evolve. In the Bower era, the firm rode the wave of growing demand for basic organizational consulting, first in the United States and then in Europe. The next four managing directors had to contend with a stagnation of demand and the internal complications that ensued. To find new opportunities for McKinsey, Daniel shifted the focus of the firm to "knowledge."

This is a critical concept, and one that took a while for McKinsey old-timers to absorb and get used to. They were accustomed to working with industrial firms that never needed to explain to their customers what they "knew"—they had a product, and the customer could choose to buy it or not. Some professional services firms—lawyers, for instance—have no need to explain themselves either. People know when they need a lawyer. But consultants have to, in essence, constantly make an argument for their own existence, which by the mid-1970s McKinsey had grown confused about. What exactly was its expertise, and how could it convince the world to keep buying more of this?

After his election, Daniel made a point of asking the firm's partners what they thought the firm should be focusing on. Fred Gluck responded with a memo detailing how McKinsey was falling behind, not only in strategy but in operations and organizational consulting too. Sure, BCG had outflanked McKinsey with a couple of savvy charts, but there was an underlying problem more insidious than that: Clients now wanted consultants who knew something, and McKinsey's database of knowledge was razor thin.

The partners agreed that the most pressing need was to expand its offering of strategic planning tools. Daniel asked Gluck if he would head up a new strategy practice. Gluck was concerned about being pigeonholed—the generalist ethos still held great sway at the firm—and he offered instead to act as head of a strategic steering committee. As Walter Kiechel pointed out in *The Lords of Strategy,* this made him, de facto, the head of the firm's strategy practice, but at McKinsey, where semantic subtlety was an art form, the compromise worked for everyone.[10]

Peter Foy, who managed the London office from 1984 to 1991, said that McKinsey's fortunes changed after a June 1977 meeting of the firm's strategy experts at the Westchester Country Club. Twenty-three of McKinsey's top strategy buffs sat around bouncing ideas off each other. And even in a gathering of that much intellect, Tokyo consultant Kenichi Ohmae stood out. At the end of the meeting, Foy offered the group a scorecard: "Lions 10, Christians 5, Ohmae 37." Years later, he sent Gluck a silver tray with that inscription. Although he was one of the firm's first champions of a strategy practice, Ohmae became famous for his later repudiation of the idea of formal corporate strategy—arguing a variant of Prussian general Helmuth von Moltke's dictum that all strategic plans become nullified on first contact with the enemy. By definition, you improvise in battle, and he who improvises best wins.

The meeting was an early step in the firm's belated response to the major competitive threat posed by BCG and Bain. Gluck soon put together an immodestly named group, the Superteam: a half-dozen consultants from different offices who were to midwife a strategy practice over the next decade. It was about time: One 1979 survey showed that 45 percent of the *Fortune* 500 were using some sort of BCG-style matrix analysis in their strategic planning.[11]

One thing Gluck didn't want to do was merely mimic BCG. "People were saying, 'What we need, Fred, is not a lot of complicated stuff. We need a conceptual supernova, a direct response to BCG's matrix. And I rejected that notion. That was exactly what we didn't need. We want to help our clients solve the problems they have, not the problems we know how to solve. We don't want to be a solution in search of a problem, and that's what the four-box matrix was. That's what the experience curve was. Sometimes they worked. And sometimes they didn't."[12]

Gluck continued: "I said we should forget about trying to do what BCG did. That we should tip our hat to them for what they accomplished, and then get on and do what we do best, which is to understand our clients' strategic problems and bring our extensive knowledge and experience to solving them." To that end, Gluck introduced practice bulletins, one-page summaries of what had been learned on a particular engagement or series of engagements with clients, so as to keep all consultants abreast of current work being done by the firm. Gluck intended to build an internal McKinsey knowledge network one piece of paper at a time.

And McKinsey approached strategy in a far more nuanced way than drawing a couple of graphs on a page. Gluck's 1978 paper, *The Evolution of Strategic Management*—the inaugural McKinsey Staff Paper—was something of a battle cry, marking the firm's intention of taking back lost market share. The paper's approach to strategy was the furthest thing imaginable from the General Survey Outline. The GSO was based on the premise that by following a checklist, managers could better understand their companies. But it was too inward looking. The strategic revolution was about looking outward, and adding exhaustive competitive analysis to the simple data gathering that was the core of the GSO.

Gluck's paper laid out four phases of a company's evolution in strategic decision making. The first, financial planning, was essentially old-school budgeting. The second, forecast-based planning, considered a far larger number of factors affecting the company. The third, externally oriented planning, called for in-depth analysis of a company's "business environment, the competitive situation, and competitive strategies." The fourth phase was full-fledged strategic management.

In a lengthy and colorful breakdown of the four phases, Walter Kiechel, author of *The Lords of Strategy,* credited McKinsey with bringing the discussion of strategy back around to organizational structure. The answer to a desire to be strategic, Gluck and his colleagues were arguing, was to organize one's company around that desire. And nobody understood organization better than McKinsey. By the end of 1979, some 50 percent of the firm's billings came from fine-grained strategy work, making it a bigger player in the realm than either BCG or Bain. "Bain and BCG turned consulting into a rock star profession," said former McKinsey partner Clay Deutsch. "But we benefited more than they did. Once we got our act together, we cornered it."[13] Indeed: Whereas in 1980 BCG was over one-third the size of McKinsey, by 1985 it was less than one-fifth.[14]

Snowball Makers

The revolution in how the firm collected and synthesized just what its consultants knew went far beyond its push into strategy. McKinsey also put two overlays on its geographic setup, establishing fifteen functional groups (e.g., corporate leadership, finance, organizational behavior) as well as increasing the number of industry specialties (e.g., banking, insurance, consumer products) from three to eight. The smart consultant maintained a generalist image while cultivating a niche in one or more functional or industry practices. Gluck oversaw this effort too, a clear indication of his status with Daniel.

In beseeching his colleagues to develop something more than a generalist expertise, Gluck uttered a line that became enshrined in McKinsey lore. In arguing that the firm needed both "snowball makers" (specialists) and "snowball throwers" (generalist rainmakers), he said, "Every McKinsey consultant needs to be a generalist, but it's not necessarily a handicap to know what you're talking about." He later added, "Would you want your brain surgery done by a general practitioner?"[15]

It was under Daniel that the firm first produced its practice-information system (a database of client engagements), its practice-development network (for knowledge gleaned by the firm's different practice groups), and a knowledge-resource directory (basically, an in-house phone book of experts and document titles). The last of the three—which didn't become computerized for years—became one of the McKinsey man's prized possessions, a little red spiral-bound book running to several hundred pages, never to be let out of his grasp.

What's more, a real premium began to be placed on being part of this knowledge oeuvre—not just in what McKinsey knew but in who at McKinsey knew these subject areas. An unstated understanding emerged that if you were a logistics expert in, say, the retail sector and you were called by a partner you had never met who mainly did work with pharmaceutical companies, you would nevertheless return the call. That reputation for contributing was *your asset* in the firm. It was endlessly discussed and recognized, and in the process, such sharing really did enter the firm's culture. "Other places have extensive systems for knowledge management, but what Daniel and Gluck built was a culture for sharing that was completely in the service of the firm," said former partner Partha Bose.[16] Such a profound shift does raise the question of what constitutes knowledge of an industry or function and whether consultants can actually capture it, but clients were keen to let them try to do so in any event.

Despite Gluck's resistance, the firm *did* produce a direct response to BCG's matrix—the nine-box McKinsey matrix—but it also set about formulating a series of frameworks through which the consultants could analyze companies in new and important ways. Hours upon hours of data collection and analysis went into each framework, and the degree of intellectual engagement required of a McKinsey associate was substantial. By the end of the 1980s, the firm required that new recruits learn more than a dozen core analytical frameworks, ranging from "the raider's perspective" to return-on-equity trees, business systems, industry cost curves, value-delivery systems, economic value to the shareholder (or customer), and the strategic game board.

While the inputs and thought processes differ greatly, most frameworks try to achieve the same goal, which is breaking down one's business into component parts and thinking about them from a fresh perspective. The business system comes in two flavors, for example—the traditional product-orientated system and the value-delivery system. In the former, consultants break down a client's business to its basics: *create the product* (product design, process design), *make the product* (procurement, manufacturing, and service), and *sell the product* (research, advertising, promotion, pricing, and sales and distribution. The latter is about the "value" involved—*choose the value* (understand desires, select the target, define the benefits), *provide the value* (product process design, procurement, manufacturing, distribution, service, and price), and *communicate the value* (sales message, advertising, promotion and PR). It all sounds simple—even banal—but every executive can lose sight of such fundamental issues when bogged down in the day-to-day, and McKinsey and others were offering to help them get centered again.

The frameworks also looked into the future. For its part, the strategic game board offered CEOs a way to think about their companies much as the BCG matrix did—with four types of potential strategic "moves." Whatever it is you make or sell, McKinsey's consultants learned to advise their clients, you should continuously be deciding whether to choose to do better and more of the same; re-segment the market to create a niche; create and pursue a unique advantage; or exploit a unique advantage industrywide.

Such were the more prosaic frameworks. The real ball-busters, though, were heavy on the numbers, from cost of capital to returns on all manner of investments. Just looking at a return-on-capital-employed tree can make the head spin with its accounting jargon overload, from "days sales in inventories and payables" to asset utilization, depreciation, and costs per unit made and sold. This was strategy via microeconomic analysis—getting to the on-the-ground numbers at the heart of the issue—McKinsey's expertise. Work for Citicorp in 1984, for example—code-named Project Alpha—was aimed at a so-called Activity Value Analysis, a database-heavy analysis of how the bank's corporate office functioned and where cost savings could be found.

This increased focus paid off: Whereas banking clients represented just 3 percent of the firm's revenues in 1975, by 1983 they accounted for 25 to 30 percent in both New York and London. This was not by accident. When brought to bear on a specific subject, the collective McKinsey intellect is powerful. In 1988 two consultants, Jim Rosenthal and Juan Ocampo, wrote *Securitization of Credit*, a road map that helped Citibank and Chase Manhattan survive the South American debt crisis. The book, the first on a subject that soon washed over the financial world like a tsunami, showed the banks, unable to earn their way out of their bad debt situation, that by securitizing the loans on their books—packaging them up and selling them into the secondary debt markets—they could effectively walk away from the loans, albeit while still taking a hit to their balance sheets.

The subtext to all the knowledge development was that consultants had to participate in cataloging and disseminating that knowledge into the firm's burgeoning repositories of such. While Bower had paid lip service to contributions to the firm beyond billings, his consultants still largely ate what they killed. Top compensation went to top billers. But as Daniel began emphasizing knowledge development, the soft side of the compensation discussion became meaningful. With Gluck by his side, Daniel slowly persuaded his colleagues that knowledge development deserved to be a core, ongoing pursuit.

McKinsey's efforts in this area would take the firm into uncharted territory: popular culture. The holy grail of the consultant is an idea that attracts clients but is still vague or complex enough that they need your help in carrying it out. This is why consultants are great progenitors of buzzwords, ideas like scientific management or lean production or reengineering. If it's got its own name, you probably want to hire the expert on it, don't you? In the 1970s and 1980s, the argument extended all the way to the land of the rising sun. Having lost significant market share in industries from automobiles to consumer electronics, managers gladly paid through the nose for the inside scoop on Japanese management techniques, such as just-in-time production, total quality management, and continuous improvement. It was the existential threat posed by Japan that led to one of the most idiosyncratic achievements in McKinsey's history: Its consultants produced a book that even Joe Six-Pack wanted to read.

The Secrets of Excellence

While Ron Daniel relied on Gluck for strategy, he asked Cleveland-based director Jim Bennett to oversee work on bulking up McKinsey's knowledge base in organizational effectiveness. Bennett, in turn, recruited an energetic San Francisco associate named Tom Peters to help lay the groundwork on the project, including a survey of all the extant literature as well as a poll of McKinsey clients. Later, Bob Waterman replaced Bennett as head of the effort. At the time, though, this was not a big priority for McKinsey. Expectations for the organizational work were somewhere between low and very low.

In fact, it transformed McKinsey. But that took years.

Though his tenure was relatively short and he left under contentious circumstances, Peters is the most famous consultant McKinsey has ever produced. His influence on the firm was enormous and helped raise its profile beyond Bower's wildest dreams. More like Bower's nightmares, actually. Peters helped *rebrand* McKinsey as a group of thinkers while at the same time revealing some less-than-great qualities of McKinsey, such as its utter incapacity to deal with a star in its midst.

Peters, a Cornell graduate who majored in civil engineering, spent four years in the navy, then eventually got his MBA and PhD in organizational behavior from Stanford. After a stint in the Office of Management and Budget, he landed a job in McKinsey's San Francisco office in 1974. "McKinsey was as cool as it gets at the time," recalled Peters. "If you didn't have some grand desire in life, it was the place to be."[17] (That idea—the delaying of one of life's major choices—still holds true for many McKinsey recruits today.)

Waterman, a graduate of the Colorado School of Mines with a Stanford MBA, had been at McKinsey since 1963. After focusing on banking and forest products in the San Francisco office, he'd been sent overseas to help open the Osaka office in 1970 and later took over management of the Melbourne office, which he ran for three years. He then did what few have done at McKinsey: He took a sabbatical with his wife and two kids that included some teaching in Switzerland. But teaching is expensive business: After nine months, Waterman found himself running a little short on cash, and he returned to San Francisco and to McKinsey.[18]

In 1977 Bennett put Peters in charge of the project that aimed to find out what made companies effective beyond the areas of strategy and structure in which McKinsey excelled. Over the course of a few years, Peters and Bennett (and then Waterman) researched the question—Peters hopscotched all over the globe, visiting twelve business schools and a number of companies in both the United States and Europe[19]—and eventually compiled their findings in a twenty-page folio they called "Excellence." It was presented to Shell in July 1979, along with talks from Fred Gluck on strategy and Ken Ohmae on "life."

Even though Peters and Waterman had gotten Hewlett-Packard

president John Young and others to answer the question "What do you do to promote excellence at your company?"—a topic they thought would resonate with any executive interested in emulating the success of an iconic American firm—the presentation fell flat.[20] The problem: Shell was a confident company. It knew what it knew and didn't need the anecdotes of Hewlett-Packard executives to show it how to run its business.

"We got an awful response," recalled Peters. "Gluck was long-winded and Ohmae was talking about the Japanese taking over the world. We had prepared the shit out of the stuff and finished up with twenty minutes. Shell didn't want to hear it."[21] Luckily, German partner Herb Henzler was in the audience. *He* liked it. And he sold the idea of the project to the German conglomerate Siemens. Suddenly the work was paying for itself. From the fall of 1979 through the spring of 1980, Peters and Waterman continued conducting research to fill out their theses. But a subsequent presentation to PepsiCo's top hundred managers in Lyford Cay, Bahamas, in May 1980 also fell flat. Peters said the content was there, but he'd felt his delivery was uninspired.

Still, the work was slowly gaining converts, albeit primarily from outside McKinsey. Bill Matassoni, the firm's communications chief, set up a meeting with Lew Young, the editor of *BusinessWeek*, and the next thing they knew, the research was trumpeted on the magazine's cover on July 21, 1980. Harper & Row then came calling with an offer to publish a book. The consultants jumped at the opportunity, and before long they had a working title: "The Secrets of Excellence."

Even though a book contract was in hand, however, the project still failed to garner much internal support. "The Secrets of Excellence" was, in part, offensive to the McKinsey mind. Peters and Waterman were suggesting that the secrets to success were not necessarily quantifiable, that they might be impervious to rigorous analysis. They talked of focusing on the customer and on the employee, not just on org charts and spreadsheets.

The project took on a little more momentum when Waterman recruited two professors to aid in the effort, Anthony Athos and Richard Pascale. It was Athos and Pascale who suggested that Peters and Waterman organize their mushy and not always memorable concepts with a series of easy-to-grasp alliterations that came to be known as the 7-S framework. Whereas before, Peters and Waterman had been talking about a range of topics—from people to involvement, trust, listening, and wandering—with this new insight, the ideas now slid off the tongue: skills, staff, style, systems, structure, shared values, and strategy. (And propagating a tradition that has become accepted in most consulting circles but definitely within McKinsey: Every idea needs an *odd number* of bullet points to be explained.)

In one sense, this seemed right out of kindergarten. Did serious managers require such spoon-feeding? In another sense, though, it was homage to BCG: the virtue of simplicity. In the end, *Excellence* showcased forty-three American companies going about their business in "excellent" ways. Peters and Waterman cataloged the qualities of excellent firms: They had a bias for action; closeness to the customer; autonomy and entrepreneurship; productivity through people; a hands-on, value-driven emphasis; stick-to-the-knitting persistence; simple form, lean staff; and simultaneous loose-tight properties—new-age management jargon for simultaneously keeping overall control while still letting your top performers roam.

The book hit one notable roadblock. After hearing of the proposed title, Bower decreed that it had to be changed, because it sounded as if they were giving away the secrets of McKinsey's clients. The compromise: *In Search of Excellence*. "We were royally pissed off," said Peters. "But it turned out to be the best thing. *In Search of* is better than 'Secrets of' anyway."[22]

In Search of Excellence was published in October 1982. The message on its back cover neatly distilled its appeal: "There is good news from America. There is an ART OF AMERICAN MANAGEMENT—and it works!" The idea was that despite being pinned down on both sides by Japanese and German competitors, American management still had what it took to win.

In many important ways the book really was an attack on McKinsey thinking, on the idea that the secrets of success could be found in an analytical framework or in a new corporate structure. It was an attack on the rationalist idea that businesses were machines that could be fine-tuned. The work of Peters and Waterman served to remind managers about first principles in business: If they didn't listen to their customers or employees, then the rest was irrelevant. If the strategy revolution was forcing companies to look outward more than they ever had before, what *Excellence* did was force that gaze right back inside again. And it wasn't talking only about financial management. It was also talking about how you treated the people who worked for you. It was, in short, the first great manifesto of the idea of corporate culture.

Looking back on it, Peters thinks the book was misperceived as a Pollyannaish take on American business. "Consultants live with problems," he later said. "That's what they get paid for. So we were always working with broken things. *In Search of Excellence* was the first book written about things that work. It was purposeful. Admittedly, the logic of the book was that American management was fucked up. It was a brutal, upfront attack on American management and McKinsey thinking. Okay, it was 75 percent about islands of hope, but that was what they were: exceptional. I consider *In Search of Excellence* a bad news book."[23] Bad news or good, it was roping in a whole new contingent of fans: If traditional management literature was about how to get ahead, Peters and Waterman were now telling readers how not to get left behind.[24]

The first piece Peters had nationally published on the subject—well before the book came out—was an op-ed in the *Wall Street Journal,* in which he stressed the importance of execution and dismissed the whole idea of strategy. "Far too many managers have lost sight of the basics—service to customers, low-cost manufacturing, productivity improvement, innovation, and risk-taking," he wrote. "In many cases, they have been seduced by the availability of MBAs, armed with the 'latest' in strategic planning techniques. MBAs who specialize in strategy are bright, but they often cannot implement their ideas, and their companies wind up losing the capacity to act." This was not an oblique attack on McKinsey thinking; it was a frontal assault. Mike Bulkin, then running the New York office, demanded that Daniel fire the heretic. "Why there should have been so much friction, I cannot tell you," recalled Peters. "But I clearly irritated a lot of people."[25]

The management elite, including Peter Drucker and the academics at Harvard Business School, attacked the book. It was called "careless, anecdotal stuff" and "strikingly banal." It was also full of what Matthew Stewart, author of *The Management Myth,* referred to as nonfalsifiable truisms. The authors cited a "bias for action" (who would vote for inaction?) and advised one to "stay close to the customer" (who would advise otherwise?). "Since Peters, it has become clear that the market for inanities masquerading as profound insights knows no limits," wrote Stewart. "Aspiring gurus seem to understand that the road to riches is paved with garbled clichés and transparently unsubstantiated pseudotheories. No sentiment is too obvious or banal to count as management wisdom, provided it makes use of one or two bits of jargon and is followed by an exclamation point!"[26]

Stewart was not the only critic who condemned the book's "scientific findings" as practically tautological, at least to anyone who has ever worked with a group of people. Most *were* banal. You might want to pay attention to people when they have something to say, for example. Teamwork is a good thing, for another. Helping people find meaning in their work will have positive results, a third. Maybe the most autocratic of CEOs had lost sight of how to manage people during the postwar boom, but the book could hardly surprise anyone who had ever stopped to think about such things. Still, people loved it, and you could hardly board a business class section of a plane without seeing someone reading it voraciously. The economy was in the dumps at the time—with 10 percent unemployment—and readers were hungry for any way forward.

In December 1981, Peters left McKinsey, eight months before the book even landed on shelves. Indeed, both he and Waterman had realized that they no longer fit in the McKinsey scheme of things. At that point, in fact, it was obvious to everyone. "Tom got to be more and more independent of the firm, to the point of wearing shorts to work and little hats with propellers on them," recalled Waterman. "It was like a child saying, 'I will get away with this stuff as long as you don't discipline me.' Eventually, I said that if he kept behaving like that, he was going to get us both fired."[27] Waterman helped Peters negotiate an exit package that included a $10,000 monthly retainer to finish the book (which he was obligated to pay back) and a 50 percent share of royalties with McKinsey. It turned out to be a very good deal.

No one had any idea how big *In Search of Excellence* was going to be. This wasn't like signing up Jack Welch to write *Straight from the Gut* and ordering a first printing of a million copies. Outside McKinsey, Peters and Waterman were nobodies. The first printing was five thousand copies. Three years later the book had sold five million, the first management book to ever top the bestseller list. Peters's next book, *A Passion for Excellence,* was the second.

Interestingly, Waterman got nothing for *Excellence* beyond his McKinsey compensation, which the firm had even cut while they were finishing the book, a result of the fact that Waterman's own client billings had fallen off. When the book started to sell like gangbusters, he began to agitate about how it was Peters and McKinsey splitting royalties. McKinsey tried to mollify him by boosting his pay—in one year he made more than Ron Daniel—but partners groused about Waterman's special treatment. When Bantam Books offered Waterman a multimillion-dollar deal for two more books in 1984, Daniel urged him not to sign the contracts until the firm could sort out how profits might be shared. After a meeting with Jim Bennett, Daniel, and Waterman failed to come to any conclusion, Daniel told Waterman, "If you sign those contracts, you're going to have to leave." Waterman saw his only course: "I told him I knew that, and I went ahead and signed them anyway. And that was that."[28]

Both men were in such demand on the speaker circuit that they rarely made it home. Waterman said he slept in his own bed just fourteen days in the first year after the book came out. Both went on to hugely successful careers as speakers and authors, with Peters becoming the world's most successful management guru.

There's a question about which effort—Gluck's strategy work or Peters's and Waterman's organizational work—had the bigger effect on McKinsey and its newfound love for knowing what it knew. You can split the difference. McKinsey obviously valued Gluck's more—witness his eventual election as managing director—and it's likely that his work led to more actual billings for McKinsey than Peters and Waterman did. On the other hand, *In Search of Excellence* was the opening bell of the age of corporate culture, and McKinsey took massive advantage of that. "Whatever is finally written on the 7-S tombstone about its real value, it certainly seemed to be an invaluable revenue generator in the 1980s," said one ex-McKinseyite. "The fact that 'serious' consultants thought the ideas were too soft and squishy to be legitimate manly fare didn't stop them from capitalizing on their almost magical ability to generate work."

While sales of the book have held up well over time, many of the "excellent" companies have not. *BusinessWeek,* which helped launch the book into the stratosphere in the first place, came back two years later to perform a drive-by shooting on *Excellence*: In a cover story titled "Oops!" (inside headline: Who's Excellent Now?"), the magazine suggested that two-thirds of the forty-three companies profiled were no longer "excellent." From Atari to IBM, many were in serious trouble. It says something about McKinsey's status at the time that this was new *BusinessWeek* editor Steve Shepard's first cover story. McKinsey was officially a target worth aiming at.

Peters still has a testy relationship with the firm. "McKinsey has a stratospheric belief in itself," he has said. "If intellectual arrogance had not yet been invented," he continued, " it would have been invented for that crew. But let me tell you this: I am sixty-seven years old, and I have had the luck of God smile on me, but I am still scared shitless of McKinsey people."[29] The firm even found a way to needle him in its privately published internal history. "There's a caption under a picture of me that made me laugh hysterically," he said. "I am described as undisciplined but brilliant. I have no problem with 'brilliant,' but 'undisciplined' made me turn purple in the face. You don't write sixteen books, give three thousand speeches, and work eighteen hours a day for thirty years and be undisciplined. It's typical fucking McKinsey. Why do you need to say things like that?"[30] (A McKinsey partner responded: "He just said it. Three thousand speeches and sixteen books is exactly what we meant. He's undisciplined. He should have focused on two clients and one book.")[31]

Waterman has fonder memories. "Marvin Bower scared the hell out of me at first," he recalled. "I was not much in his eyes until I made director. After that we got to be close friends. He was absolutely in love with *In Search of Excellence*. He was in his nineties when he called me up and said, 'Do you mind if I quote you?' I said, 'God, Marvin, you can quote me on anything you want to.'"[32] Still, Waterman could be as dismissive as Peters. "For what it does, McKinsey is probably the best in the world. But in the grand scheme of things, maybe what it does just isn't as important as it thinks. . . . McKinsey thinks it sells grand strategies and big ideas when really its role is to keep management from doing a lot of dumb things. They do great analysis, but it won't get your company to the top."[33] Of course, there is a large contingent that thinks *In Search of Excellence* was mere pap. McKinsey may spread pap in the corporate suite, but management gurus can be accused of committing a similar crime in book form.

The Occasional Guru

The popularity of *In Search of Excellence* alerted McKinsey to the possibility that not all publicity was bad publicity. The firm had long practiced its nonmarketing approach to marketing—the writing of papers for the *Harvard Business Review,* the providing of background for the occasional reporter, the publication of the occasional informational brochure—while adhering to a strict prohibition on outright self-promotion. But maybe it was time, the consultants told themselves, to be a little more proactive about burnishing their public reputation as management thinkers. They had already brought on Bill Matassoni, a Harvard Business School grad turned marketing expert, to serve as communications chief in 1979. True to form, McKinsey described the job as "reputation building"—the firm didn't like the term "marketing"—but Matassoni was a marketer through and through.

Peters and Waterman weren't the first employees known to the outside world. Arch Patton, for one, had developed a following as a business philosopher of sorts. "But he'd written the same article twenty-seven times for the *Harvard Business Review,*" said Matassoni, who helped push for new public profiles. He helped shepherd into the *Wall Street Journal* an op-ed from John Sawhill about breaking up big oil. "It wasn't about managing big oil," recalled Matassoni, "but within weeks, John was in the boardroom of every big oil company, at their invitation. Because they respected him."[34] And once you're in the boardroom, the engagement dollars start to flow.

Singling out individuals didn't come naturally to a firm that had always sold itself as a collective. When you hired McKinsey, you weren't supposed to ask for a certain consultant; you were supposed to think that whatever team was assigned to you, the work would be superlative. But the rise of BCG had challenged that orthodoxy. Books were now a big part of the game. Between 1960 and 1980, McKinsey published just two books. Since then, it has published close to a hundred, with titles ranging from the vague (*Knowledge Unplugged,* in 2002) to the precise (*Say It with Charts,* 1985; *Achieving Excellence in Retail Banking*, 2003) to the perennially salable (*The Power of Productivity,* 2004). There have been two big changes since the days of *In Search of Excellence*. One: McKinsey now retains control over any book written by a consultant. And two: Unlike most consulting firms, McKinsey, after several disastrous experiences of senior partners taking months off to write books that neither sold nor moved the needle in management thinking, does not give partners time off from their day jobs to write books.

Likewise, the firm embarked on a more open relationship with the press. While McKinsey still tended to avoid having its consultants quoted, it began to accede to the occasional profile—every two or three years—in the likes of *Fortune* or *BusinessWeek*. Later, the firm also began engaging the international media to give McKinsey's ideas more prominent play overseas—in the *Financial Times,* the *Economist,* and overseas versions of the *Wall Street Journal*. There were so many conversations going on between McKinsey and top media platforms in the mid-1990s that one editor in chief of a major publication demanded to know of his own editors what McKinsey's influence was on their pieces. Sometimes journalists would approach the firm to write about its workings, not its ideas; and every now and then—say, around the time of a managing director's retirement—the firm would cooperate. And if such coverage wasn't *always* positive, the power and influence of McKinsey was never seriously dented.

Consultants embraced the idea of getting their writing out in public so much that the firm had to eventually tighten the portal to the outside world. Under the aegis of Alan Kantrow and Partha Bose, the *McKinsey Quarterly* became the platform to which the best writing got steered, so much that one editor in chief of the *Harvard Business Review* bemoaned that McKinsey had cut *HBR* out of the loop and was offering only its second-tier work to external publications. One consultant who'd had a piece turned down by *HBR* was advised by its editors to submit the piece to the *McKinsey Quarterly*. "Are you kidding?" he asked them incredulously. "They turned me down months ago."

But while the firm could control *some* of its big egos and force them to submit to the greater good, some consultants nevertheless still managed to achieve a level of renown—both internal and external—that set them apart from their otherwise inconspicuous peers.

King Herb

In 1987 Edzard Reuter, then CEO of Daimler-Benz, made a remarkable claim: "Nothing happens in Germany without McKinsey being consulted first." More precisely, nothing happened in Germany without Herbert Henzler being consulted first. From his base in Dusseldorf, Henzler had turned McKinsey's German operations into the envy of his colleagues, eventually achieving the greatest penetration of major businesses of any country in which McKinsey had a presence.

At one point in time, the office served twenty-seven of the top thirty companies in the nation. The German magazine *Wirstschaftswoche* ran a cover story about Henzler called, simply, "King Herb."

It wasn't always this way. When former McKinsey consultant Logan Cheek, who worked for the firm from 1968 to 1971, arrived for a two-year stint in Dusseldorf in 1969, he felt as if no one in Germany had ever heard of management consulting. "The Germans couldn't understand why someone in authority would pay someone else to tell him what to do," recalled Cheek. "Many of our German friends concluded that McKinsey had something to do with Alfred E. Kinsey, and that we were nothing other than a front for sex consultants."[35]

By the time Henzler was done, few in Germany were so confused, and the German office was the V8 engine under McKinsey's hood. "I remember very clearly another twentieth anniversary," Ron Daniel once said, "this time in the German office, where Henry Kissinger was a speaker. He was amazed. He got to that party in Munich and found sixty major industrialists at our semi-private seminar, many of whom he had heard of but never met, all of them top drawer. . . . Mobilizing the firm's network and power is something we do every day on behalf of our clients."[36]

While the firm strives to make its decisions through consensus, there have been a number of uniquely powerful consultants over the years, from Bower to Daniel to the relatively unknown Warren Cannon, who was consigliere to both men. Henzler too was a breed apart. His colleagues referred to him as the last of the barons. Fred Gluck, of German ancestry himself, even used to call Henzler and his German colleagues Friedrich Schiefer and Helmut Hagemann "the U-boat commanders."

In the fourteen years Henzler headed the German office, it grew from a hundred consultants to eight hundred, getting him tagged with another nickname: "Growth Herbie."[37] By 2011 there were 150 partners in Germany and another 80 German partners in other McKinsey offices internationally. "Herb had this thing where he would say, 'We will know we have arrived when the cabdriver picking you up at the airport knows exactly where to take you when you simply say *McKinsey*,'" recalled a former partner of the firm. "We would joke, 'Let's hope that cabbie isn't one of the five million people in Germany who have been laid off as a result of McKinsey's work.'"

While he's admired for what some describe as a ruthless German efficiency, Henzler had the good fortune of running the show when Germany underwent a fundamental transformation in the 1980s and 1990s. During that period, the German establishment shifted toward a much stronger market orientation than in the past, dismantling the stolid and collusive Germany Inc. and opening up industries to genuine competition and innovation. McKinsey played a huge role in that, and also became a valued consultant to the trillion-euro reconstruction of East Germany.

Henzler helped McKinsey's European contingent gain an equal voice in the firm's governance against the "New York mafia." "The gravity of the firm was moving anyway, but Herb was the one that came to symbolize the shift," said former managing director Ian Davis.[38]

To some, Henzler also symbolized a growth-at-all-costs attitude that Rajat Gupta later embraced as managing director of the firm. "He was dictatorial and driven and arrogant," said a former colleague. But Henzler was also a forceful proponent for changing the way the consultants paid themselves. Even as Ron Daniel succeeded in bringing to the fore considerations of consultants' noneconomic contributions to the firm, in the 1980s McKinsey nevertheless shifted much of the economic portion of the conversation away from one's effects on the long-term value of the institution and toward a "What have you done for me lately?" approach.

A young and aggressive German contingent resented what they saw as older American consultants coasting on past glories, and they succeeded in radically changing how the firm managed its finances. Henceforth, McKinsey would liquidate itself at the end of every year—paying out all profits to the consultants—a move that encouraged short-termism over true stewardship of the long-term value of the institution. McKinsey may say it encourages its clients to think long-term, but its own people value today over tomorrow. "Germany has been the piston that keeps the engine going for many years," said one European alumnus. "McKinsey has been more German than American for some time. That's why they asked for more of the cash in the 1980s."

Indeed, Henzler accumulated enough power that at one point he openly defied Ron Daniel. Daniel had closed the firm's São Paolo office in 1977, just two years after it had opened. When Henzler told him that a German client, which had a significant trucking operation in Brazil, wanted McKinsey to reopen an outpost there in the mid-1980s, Daniel told him to focus on Germany and to leave Brazil to the Americans. Henzler did no such thing, dispatching Stefan Matzinger to set up a covert operation. He then presented the office to the shareholders committee as a fait accompli. Some partners were upset, but Henzler got his way in the end.[39] Twenty-three years later, the firm had 230 people in Brazil. The German office also played a part in opening practices in Russia, Taiwan, and Turkey, all of which were the result of Henzler's edict to young partners: "You want to prove yourself? Do something completely entrepreneurial, like opening a new office."

Henzler's abiding goal was to be considered the *equal* of his clients, not just a hired hand, and in this he succeeded. His connections within Germany ran so deep that there was talk he might become chancellor. When Henzler retired in 2001, he later told author Walter Kiechel, he had consulted for Siemens with no interruption for twenty-seven years, and with both Daimler and Bertelsmann for nearly two decades.[40] "Our partners have become very respected senior business figures," said subsequent German office head Frank Mattern. "We've established ourselves as true peers of the leaders of German industry."[41]

Henzler's singular ambition was tolerated because of his staggering economic contributions to the firm, although in time he eventually managed to alienate a partnership that thought he was getting a little too big for his McKinsey britches. But he had a strong competitor on that front in Japan.

Emperor Ohmae

If Herb Henzler was the last of McKinsey's barons, Kenichi Ohmae was its one and only emperor. But whereas Henzler was a sales machine, Ohmae was more of a rabble-rouser. He was the firm's most prominent and oft-quoted consultant in the late 1980s, head of its Tokyo office, and author of several international bestsellers, including *The Mind of the Strategist* and *Triad Power*.[42] McKinsey had always hired smart people, but Ohmae was truly brilliant. His PhD in nuclear engineering from MIT told only part of the story. He was known in Japan as *Keiei no Kamisama*—the "God of Management."

Bill Matassoni was an ardent supporter of Ohmae. "I remember one time I told Ron Daniel that I wanted to place a full-page ad for $22,000 for Ohmae's *Triad Power* in the *Wall Street Journal,*" Matassoni recalled. "He said he couldn't spend the firm's money on one book. And he was right. But *Triad Power* did just fine. Ohmae wrote thirty-seven editorials for the *Wall Street Journal*. He didn't need any help."[43] That's not entirely true: The unsung man in the background of this event was Alan Kantrow, who moved to Tokyo for several years to be

Ohmae's "thought partner." Ohmae's 1990 book, *The Borderless World,* correctly foresaw the era of corporations overtaking governments as the most powerful entities on the planet. The firm's 1993 annual report included the joke: "We published 11 books last year. Only 3 were by Ken Ohmae."

The first native Japanese to run the Tokyo office, Ohmae became office manager in 1979, and the office made its first positive financial contribution to the firm in 1981.[44] More important, Ohmae helped establish an elite reputation for the firm in Japan. Nicknamed "Mr. Strategy," he led high-profile engagements for the likes of Sumitomo Bank and helped change Japanese attitudes toward management consulting. This was another example of Ron Daniel's deftness. At one point all of the firm's office managers were American. After he installed Ohmae in Tokyo, Daniel did likewise all over the world: Gerard Thuillez in France, Peter Foy in London, Henzler in Germany, Paco Moreno in Spain, Christian Caspar in Denmark, and Rolando Polli in Italy. (Mind you, Thuillez was not a Frenchman but a *Belgian*—and this was a source of great consternation for the firm's French partners.)

In a company overflowing with big egos, Ohmae managed to stand far above the rest. This was a man prepared to draw up a manifesto for the government of the entire world, after all. "I didn't know Ohmae," said one former McKinsey consultant who overlapped with him. "But everyone told the story that when you met him, you would realize that you were talking to the smartest person that ever lived. And that's because he would tell you that it was so. It was cause for great ridicule." It also drove many senior partners to distraction that Ohmae had a bodyguard, who sat all day long with a thick pistol on his desk for all to see.

That said, counter other McKinsey consultants, he was also hugely generous and charming if you engaged with him on the right issue.

"In my sixth month at McKinsey, I got home to White Plains in New York, where I lived with my wife and nine-month-old daughter," recalled Partha Bose. "At ten p.m., I got a call from Tokyo: 'Ohmae-san wants to speak with you.' I motioned to my wife with my finger going across my neck that I must be getting fired. But it was nothing of the sort. I had sent Ohmae a report our Cleveland office had done on the future of Japanese auto suppliers in the United States and he spoke to me for half an hour about it, asking for my perspective on a number of its conclusions. I kept thinking: 'Does he realize he's speaking to someone with only six months at the firm?' But that was Ohmae for you. If you had a good idea, you were in. But he didn't tolerate fools lightly."[45]

Many McKinsey directors speak fondly of spending time with Ohmae and his family at one of the many houses he owned around the world. Ohmae was also a concert-level clarinetist, a bon vivant, and a connoisseur of the finest things in the world. Including himself: In 2009 he saw the need to write a paper titled "The Inside of Ohmae's Brain."[46] After he wrote in *Triad Power* that multinational corporations ought to have the "Anchorage perspective"—it was equidistant from New York, London, and Tokyo—the mayor of Anchorage presented him with a key to the city for putting it so forcefully on the map.

Ohmae's high profile was a double-edged sword for McKinsey. Business flowed from Japanese clients enamored with him, but his reputation also put a stress on McKinsey's firm-before-individual ethos. He came to personify the firm's Tokyo operations to such a degree that when he left the firm in 1994, McKinsey found that many Japanese clients didn't want to work with just *any* McKinsey consultant. They wanted Ohmae, and if they couldn't have him they didn't want to work with McKinsey at all. So great was Ohmae's popularity that a poll conducted in the 1990s by one Japanese newspaper ranked him as the nation's most trusted man.

Ohmae also favored a command-and-control method of management that even his supporters have described as "tyrannical." There's that, and the fact that the Tokyo office didn't actually generate much profit under his leadership. After leaving McKinsey, Ohmae experienced a comedown familiar to many a McKinsey man who finds that the rarefied air of consulting doesn't always play well in the real world. In 1995 he ran for governor of Tokyo and lost to an entertainer (and occasional drag comedian) named Yukio Aoshima. (Another comedian, Isamu Yokoyama, won in Osaka the same year.)

Still, along with Fred Gluck, Ohmae came to symbolize the true intellectualization of McKinsey, and he helped give the firm an answer to BCG's Bruce Henderson and Michael Porter, who had gone on to consult on his ideas through the firm he and several of his close associates formed: Monitor. And it was Ron Daniel who gave them the freedom to do so.

Three of McKinsey's biggest stars—Tom Peters, Herb Henzler, and Ken Ohmae—poked their heads above the rest for a time. All three gave McKinsey something invaluable. But after they'd all left, McKinsey went back to a system that quietly rewarded a brigade of high-performing no-names.

McKinsey Ist Überall!

By the mid-1980s, McKinsey was as big and complex a company as many of its clients. In 1972 revenues had totaled $45 million. By 1987 they had topped $500 million. (They doubled again over the next four years, topping $1 billion by 1991.) The German magazine *Manager* wrote in 1984 that *McKinsey ist überall!* (McKinsey is everywhere!) And it truly seemed to be: The firm had employed 537 professionals in 1970. In 1987 it had more than double that, with 1,300. Between 1976 and 1988, it opened fifteen offices around the globe, including Boston, Madrid, Lisbon, and Stuttgart.

McKinsey partners had always done well; now top directors were pulling down as much as $500,000 a year. That's the kind of thing that happens when your income growth far outstrips growth in head count. The firm had accumulated so much money that in 1985 it established the McKinsey Investment Office, which operated as a kind of internal family office/fund of funds from that point forth. At a later conference of firm partners in Boca Raton, Marvin Bower asked his partners: "Do you know when you're making too much money? When you need someone else to manage it for you." While those in attendance nodded in agreement with the old man, they still wanted to know what their bonuses would be that year.

Everyone wanted to talk to McKinsey, in part because its massive scope certainly did give it perspective on the best practices of one's competitors, whether they were in New York, London, or Tokyo. Merrill Lynch and Citicorp both hired the firm to help plan for a newly deregulated world. Japanese financial institutions Nippon Life Insurance and Sumitomo Bank hired McKinsey to help them determine in which Wall Street firms to take a stake. The firm helped guide Nippon to Shearson Lehman and Sumitomo to Goldman Sachs.[47]

Not surprisingly, the consultants exhibited a renewed confidence that occasionally veered right into arrogance. "There are only three great institutions left in the world: The Marines, The Catholic Church, and McKinsey," one partner told *BusinessWeek* in 1986.[48] London office manager Peter Foy suggested, "There is no institution on the planet that has more integrity than McKinsey and company." In a *Forbes* article, a McKinsey partner summed up the self-image neatly: "We don't learn from clients. Their standards aren't high enough. We learn from other McKinsey partners."[49]

"There is nothing so exhilarating as listening to one of our consultants . . . hold forth on a subject that he has thought deeply about and that he can apply to a client's particular situation with confidence and impact," Fred Gluck wrote in a 1982 memo to his colleagues. Former San Francisco office head Ted Hall was notorious for his sky-high opinion of his own worth. "I saw Ted Hall in a room with two guys who'd won Nobel Prizes, and yet he still thought he was the smartest guy in the room," recalled a colleague. Hall was notorious for passive-aggressive office-speak: he pretended to engage others but was not really interested in doing so. He would suggest that colleagues "rise up a few levels of abstraction with me" or "invite" them to reconsider their position. "At the end of his career at McKinsey, he'd mellowed a bit," said a former colleague. "He actually acknowledged that there were others in the room."

That said, the man *was* smart. He was credited with helping the Federal Reserve shift the way it counted money from counting bills to a weight-based approach. (Las Vegas casinos owe him a debt of gratitude.) Hall and former partner George Feiger also helped launch the consolidation of the U.S. banking industry by pushing Wells Fargo to acquire Crocker Bank in 1986. "We'd been hired by the Comptroller of the Currency to find out what would happen with deregulated interest rates," recalled Feiger. "The answer was consolidation. So we took that work and explained its implications to private companies. Anyone can buy a competitor, but we showed Wells Fargo how to make money at it."[50]

"The real competition out there isn't for clients, it's for people," explained Daniel. "And we look to hire people who are: first, very smart; second, insecure and thus driven by their insecurity; and third, competitive. Put together 3,000 of these egocentric, task-oriented people, and it produces an atmosphere of something less than humility. Yes, it's elitist. But don't you think there has to be room somewhere in this politically correct world for something like this?"[51] Then again, another partner said, "People ask who our greatest competitors are . . . it's our clients. Their first choice is not McKinsey or someone else, it's hiring anybody at all." It seems inevitable that one will soon say that McKinsey's greatest competition is itself.

When Walter Kiechel wrote a cover story for *Fortune* in 1982 titled "Corporate Strategists Under Fire," the article was accompanied by a cartoon of a boxing ring filled with different-sized boxers, McKinsey being the biggest among them. "Everybody loved it," said Matassoni. "Ron Daniel even bought the original art. But I thought it made the wrong point. I told Ron, 'We need to get out of the ring entirely.'"[52] This wasn't a new idea: McKinsey had always pushed people to believe that it didn't "compete" with BCG, Bain, or any other firm. Bower had elucidated it first: As far as he was concerned, McKinsey didn't have *any* competitors.

"Partners in consulting firms have a natural tendency to view your issues through the prism of their own experience and capabilities," wrote the authors of *Extract Value from Consultants*.[53] McKinsey took this to an extreme: From the late 1980s onward, its advice to many clients was merely to be more like McKinsey. The firm has launched countless initiatives studying itself in order to pass that wisdom on to clients. But that's exactly what some clients wanted. "Everyone asks McKinsey how they do it," said Jim Coulter, a co-founder of private equity firm TPG Capital. "They're a global matrix organization based on knowledge. The key to running that is to know where your knowledge is and to keep your people steady in their seats so you don't have high turnover. We have studied and admired them, as we have thought about our own multiproduct, multicountry growth."[54] Law firm Latham & Watkins hired McKinsey in 1999 to help it with its plans to go global. "One of the attractions of working with McKinsey was that we shared a similar culture, which made it easier for McKinsey to understand us," said chairman Robert Dell. "Unlike other consultants, McKinsey didn't just present canned recommendations that had been used elsewhere, but rather really listened to us, understood us, and provided recommendations that were tailored to us."[55]

In May 1987 *Business Review Weekly* ran a cover story titled "The Power of McKinsey: Why Top Companies Seek Its Cure." The piece was timed to Gluck's elevation to managing director. Five months later, *Forbes* responded with "The McKinsey Mystique: Is It Worth the Price?" McKinsey wouldn't deign to answer that question. The firm's official position is that measuring its value is difficult, evoking a kind of Heisenbergian notion that the intervention of consultants themselves destroys any basis for such a calculation. There's some merit to the argument: According to Professor Matthias Kipping, the product of consulting is hard to evaluate in advance, because it is both intangible and also consumed at the same time it is produced. In the end, impressions can be all that matter.

McKinsey also drove the competition to distraction with its ability to bounce back from any setback. In 1985, when Steve Jobs was first exiled from Apple in favor of John Sculley, the computer company saw a large drop in its market share in schools. Former McKinsey consultant Fred Sturdivant saw an opportunity and landed the company he then led, the MAC Group, a choice consulting assignment. "We came in and did a bang-up job," he recalled. "We got applause. I was convinced that we were in the catbird seat to have a relationship with Apple. We were home free. But within weeks, word came out that a big new strategy engagement had been taken on by guess who? McKinsey." How? "They never go away," answered Sturdivant. "They were wining and dining executives and walking the halls while we had our heads down working on their channel strategy."

The firm continues to frustrate competitors in similar fashion more than a quarter-century later: "I lost a project to a UK-based client because the new chairman of the company was ex-McKinsey," said a former McKinsey partner now working for a competitor. "Their head of strategy wanted to work with us. The chairman told him he could hire whomever he wanted to, as long as it was McKinsey."

The firm eventually institutionalized its high opinion of itself. Whereas Marvin Bower had defined McKinsey's mission singularly—to provide outstanding client service—in 1984 Daniel added a second piece: the building of a great firm. By that he meant hiring, training, and retaining the best people it could. At the time McKinsey was pretty sure it was succeeding in this regard. Daniel also tilted annual evaluations away from a singular focus on one's direct economic contribution to one's overall contribution to the firm—including developing people and building knowledge. To this day, partners serving on the firm's various evaluation committees spend five to six weeks a year on the task, forgoing client work while doing so.

Plus Ça Change

But under Daniel the idea of building a great firm never meant stretching the definition of a McKinsey consultant too far in new directions. Despite slight advances in diversity, the firm was still a white male bastion in the 1980s. By the early 1990s, when the firm approached Bill Clinton's pal and Washington operator Vernon Jordan for help in expanding into South Africa, he asked how many black partners McKinsey had. The answer: none. He reportedly replied, "I'll try to help you, but for God's sake, man, if you want to do business in Africa, get yourself some black partners."[56] The firm didn't elect its first black director—Byron Auguste—until 2005.

McKinsey did only slightly better with women. One of the firm's most famous female alumni, Barbara Minto—author of 1987's *The*

Pyramid Principle: Logic in Writing, Thinking, and Problem Solving—joined the newly opened Cleveland office in 1963 and stayed with the firm for a decade before leaving to start her own consulting firm. The firm elected its first female principal in 1979—Linda Levinson—and a total of nineteen to the partnership in the 1980s. Still, by the end of the 1990s, women constituted just 5 percent of the partnership.

The firm later embraced India as a talent source. Tino Puri, one the first Indians to join McKinsey, in 1970, had long set his eyes on opening an Indian outpost for the firm. McKinsey finally opened a Bombay office in 1993, though it had served clients in India for a full fifteen years before that.

"The problem with McKinsey is that it's a suffocating environment," former McKinseyite Don Carlson told *BusinessWeek* in 1986. "They want a certain person, a certain look, a certain way of doing things."[57]

The kind of consultant McKinsey produced did change over time, and by the 1990s the firm was favoring a scientifically bent technocrat. Ron Daniel might not have as much success at McKinsey today as he did in the 1980s. As one of his former colleagues noted, he—along with many of his contemporaries—might not have the IQ required to survive in the global institution he helped build. When he was hired, the fact that you had been to Harvard Business School was enough. Today that doesn't even guarantee an interview. The consultant of today is more likely to look like Daniel's successor, the proudly geeky Fred Gluck—a man who ran an antimissile program at Bell Labs before he came to McKinsey—as opposed to one who merely knows the right people from the right places. Indeed, outside the U.S. government's national laboratories, McKinsey is the biggest recruiter of scientific and engineering PhDs at places like MIT, and it is also a top recruiter at law schools and medical schools.

Partner Jon Katzenbach thought the firm shortchanged itself by being overly focused on analytical smarts instead of creative qualities in its recruiting. "At McKinsey, hard guys are better," he told *Fortune*. "Issues like organization and leadership are thought of as soft. Unfortunately, that's where client demand is increasing. We have major corporations asking us to help them change their culture; we need to make major changes in our own culture. . . . We're really good at tapping into intellectual smarts, as measured in quantitative and conceptual ways. But in our search for bright guys, we throw out a lot of creative ones. We've got to be less cookie-cutter in our hiring."[58] When he left McKinsey after a storied career, Katzenbach founded a rival firm with the intention of doing precisely that. It didn't work out quite as planned, and he ultimately sold his firm to Booz & Company in 2009 after an eleven-year run that had shown promise at first but sputtered along with the global economy. The soft stuff, in other words, is for the good times.

Since the early 1980s, Bower was a lonely voice in thinking the firm had grown too far, and too fast, and was therefore being forced to serve clients it shouldn't have served, or work on issues that weren't really of importance to top management. At an internal conference around this time when one consultant explained how technology would speed McKinsey's growth, Bower growled from the back of the room, "The firm should not be growing at all. It's far too big already. It should never have gotten above 700 people." But it was far too late to turn back.

When Daniel took over, there was not a lot of separation from Booz Allen and other competitors. When he stepped down, McKinsey was unique and dominant in its industry. And he accomplished all this without shutting the door on tradition.

6. THE CRUCIAL QUESTION: ARE THEY WORTH IT OR NOT?

Even as McKinsey consultants will go to their grave saying it's impossible to measure their impact precisely—thus providing cover for their sky-high fees—at some point in a history of the firm the question must be asked: Has that money been well spent?

The short answer is yes. No enterprise lasts nearly a century without delivering value of some sort. The real question, then, is: Who has benefited from its advice? The executives who continue to hire McKinsey time and time again certainly seem to find the corporate expenditure worthwhile. Do companies themselves benefit? On balance, one can only conclude they do as well, since the forces of competition would surely drive an inferior product out of the market over the years, and certainly over decades.

As Stuart Crainer, author of *The Tom Peters Phenomenon,* put it, "Management theorizing has become expert at finding new angles on old topics. (*In Search of Excellence* was, after all, a 1982 reworking of the oldest managerial chestnut of them all: How can you be successful?) There is nothing wrong with this. Indeed, management is fundamentally concerned with seeking out modern approaches to age-old dilemmas. The final word . . . is unlikely ever to be uttered."[1] In other words, there is no Rosetta stone of management, no unified theory. It's pretty much about making it up as you go along.

But has the spread of McKinseyism been good for business in general? Or for society? When McKinsey spreads the gospel of downsizing in order to enhance corporate profitability, it surely helps individual clients, but is the overall effect a good one?

If you're AT&T in the 1980s, McKinsey provided terrible advice. If you're Condé Nast in 2009, it helped you convince your employees that the time had finally come to cut costs. If you're General Motors under attack from Toyota, McKinsey missed the point entirely. But if you're North Carolina National Bank, it put you on the path to greatness.

Clearly, where you stand on the value of McKinsey depends very much upon where you sit.

Yes, They Are

When McKinsey is at its most effective, it thoroughly identifies and analyzes a problem for its client, enumerates all available options, presents them in easily digestible fashion, and then helps the client choose a course of action.

And even at McKinsey's lofty price, most clients have concluded that hiring the firm is more than worth the fees paid. Mellon Bank chairman Frank Cahouet paid McKinsey $16 million over a six-year period but estimated that the return on that expense was at least twenty times as much.[2] "I joined Mellon in 1987," recalled Cahouet. "It was a tense time, and there was a real question of whether we were going to survive. Regulators were openly hoping that we would be acquired. But I didn't join Mellon to sell it. I joined it to build it."

One important project Cahouet assigned the McKinsey team, led by partner Clay Deutsch, was separating Mellon into two parts—the so-called Good Bank/Bad Bank exercise. They spun the Bad Bank off to shareholders, leaving the Good Bank on a much more solid financial footing. "McKinsey did a lot of the analysis for us," said Cahouet. "And their reputation and credibility helped us in the market as we raised the capital for that." Cahouet subsequently hired McKinsey consultant Ron O'Hanley to join him running Mellon as vice chairman.[3] In 2010 O'Hanley was made copresident of Fidelity Investments.

Work done for the Dutch government in the late 1980s shows the firm in optimal interaction with the client. Dutch officials had contacted McKinsey about a plan to impose a moratorium on subsidies to the steel industry, which would severely hamper the company's largest producer, Hoogovens. They asked McKinsey to come up with a figure for how much money it would take to shore up the company's finances so that it could stand on its own two feet. McKinsey studied the situation for six months and came up with a shocking number: $1 billion.

The country's minister of economic affairs then asked McKinsey for advice on getting the parliament to approve such a gigantic corporate capital injection. The resulting presentation explained the state of the global steel industry, rising Japanese competition, and the powerful effect of Hoogovens on the Dutch trade balance and economic infrastructure. Working with both the government and Hoogovens at this point, the consultants spent another six months figuring out how the money would be invested, down to the last dollar. The result was a twenty-two-page bill, which the minister presented to parliament. It passed on the first round.[4] The company survived and in 1999 merged with British Steel to form Corus Group, one of the world's largest steel producers.

Another remarkable public sector project involved work the London office did around the same time for the Scottish Development Agency. Glasgow was mired in unemployment and crime. Partner

Norman Sanson and a team of Scottish consultants helped devise a survival strategy for the city. The consultants offered a number of ideas, from encouraging tourism to shifting away from manufacturing toward a service economy, and focusing on the importance of the city center as an anchor of development. The consultants also proposed an idea that fits quite well in the history of McKinsey advice: a public/private partnership that would allow private sector interests to partner with politicians to push for a revival of the city's core. "We literally saved Glasgow," said former London office head Peter Foy, in a typical display of McKinsey self-regard.[5] But the remark may also have the virtue of actually being true: Less than a decade after McKinsey's 1984 arrival on the scene, and in no small part due to urban regeneration efforts, Glasgow was named the 1990 European City of Culture. McKinsey helped Carlos Salinas privatize Mexico and Margaret Thatcher on similar efforts in England, and it would go on to aid in privatizing government assets in newly liberalizing countries in Latin America, Central America, Eastern Europe, and Asia.

In 1981 Hugh McColl, then the new president at then-tiny bank North Carolina National Bank (NCNB), asked McKinsey for help in designing an organizational structure that he wouldn't have to change until NCNB became the biggest bank in the country. If he was going to go on an acquisition spree, in other words, he didn't want to be modifying the company's organizational structure at every turn. This was ambition on a huge scale, considering that NCNB's $6 billion in assets were paltry in comparison with industry leaders like Citicorp and Chase Manhattan. But it was also McKinsey's bread-and-butter, organizational advice. The firm's suggestion: to shift the company's customer focus from geography to types such as retail customers or commercial banking clients. That way the company didn't need to introduce whole new units when it entered new territories; it just added these territories to the existing customer groups. Seventeen years later, when what was then known as NationsBank acquired Bank of America, it created the largest bank in the country. That had been McColl's goal, so McKinsey's advice had been worth whatever McColl paid for it.

All of the above point to the fact that McKinsey can do very sophisticated work.

And then there's this: While it may seem simplistic, the job of a CEO is to keep his own job. Even your most reliable lieutenants have a tendency to stab you in the back. So the smart CEOs hire expensive (albeit structurally disloyal)[6] lieutenants in the form of consultants. Even if consultants have long been accused of fomenting uncertainty rather than eradicating it, the life span of current CEOs impels them to ignore that deleterious side effect, while simultaneously extending their own tenure. Roger Smith leaned on McKinsey to keep his grip on the top job at General Motors, Robert Allen did the same at AT&T, and Phil Purcell (a McKinsey alumnus) did the same at Morgan Stanley. McKinsey may proclaim its capability to tell truth to power, but in reality it rarely bites the hand that feeds it.

No, They're Not

An important question: Should the arrival of McKinsey at one's door always be seen as a positive for any particular client? Or, by extension, for business itself? Stanford professor Harold Leavitt, a proponent of the human aspects of business over the numerical ones, answered in the negative in the 1980s: "The new, professional MBA-type manager began to look more and more like the mercenary soldier—ready and willing to fight any way and to do so coolly and systematically, but without ever asking the tough pathfinding questions: Is this war worth fighting? Is it the right war? Is the cause just? Do I believe in it?"[7]

In *House of Lies,* his 2005 attack on the industry, later turned into a series on the cable network Showtime, ex-consultant Martin Kihn wrote of the "Slide" that McKinsey showed at the end of recruiting sessions in 2000. "The Slide is deceptively simple," he wrote. "[It] is simply a curve showing 20 percent annual growth. That's 20 percent compound annual growth over the past decade in both revenues and in the size of McKinsey's staff. . . . To put it bluntly, the Slide implies that *McKinsey is on a path toward total world domination.* . . . If you don't get a job with them this time around, you can always wait. You'll be very old in May 2060—but it won't really matter. They'll have to hire you. Every single man, woman, and child in the U.S. is a McKinsey consultant by May 2060. Every person on earth is a McKinsey consultant by 2075."[8]

Tales of failed consulting engagements—or failed attempts to carry out a McKinsey strategy—don't usually make the front page of the business section. McKinsey won't talk about its clients, and corporate executives don't like to talk about failed projects of any sort, whether or not a consultant was involved. Every now and then, however, a project has a high enough profile—or its failure is public enough—that McKinsey's role comes into full public view. And it is in these instances that McKinsey's grand bargain with its customers—take no credit, take no blame—can prove unworkable. "It is the same with the medical profession," Hal Higdon wrote. "A doctor can perform a thousand successful operations, but everyone remembers the one where his scalpel slipped."[9]

One such engagement was a 1980 project for AT&T. AT&T had invented an early version of wireless technology but was worried about the return on its investment in radio towers, among other things. McKinsey, as always, carefully studied the issue and came up with an estimate that was, to say the least, laughably off the mark: In the year 2000, McKinsey deduced, the total wireless market would have less than one million subscribers.

It's worth remembering that at the time, handsets were so clunky and expensive and bandwidth was so limited that the only customers were very wealthy people and corporate executives. It's also worth remembering that predicting the future is hard. However, this was clearly a blunder, and a very costly one. AT&T dropped the project, dooming the company to playing catch-up in wireless and necessitating its eventual sale to SBC Communications in 2005. That's the consultant's equivalent of a malpractice case, in which the patient dies an awful, avoidable death.

Sometimes McKinsey has been accused of selling not just faulty research but defunct strategy, such as when it worked for the Continental Illinois Bank, then one of the nation's hottest banks, in the 1970s. Continental saw itself on a par with Chase Manhattan and Citibank, two well-known McKinsey clients, and wanted a new organizational structure. The consultants told Continental the same thing they had told numerous other banks: It needed to move away from its hierarchical management structure toward something called "matrix management." The idea, in simple form: In a matrix system, different people may work in one department and may technically report to one manager, but they may also be assigned to a different project and a different manager at any point in time. The result is a theoretical increase in flexibility in return for a diffusion of responsibility and accountability. At first the reorganization seemed brilliant. Between 1976 and 1981, Continental had the fastest asset growth of any major bank, a remarkable 110 percent. Lending grew at an ever-faster rate, 180 percent. The bank's return on equity during that time—14.4 percent—was second only to Morgan Guaranty.

But James McCollom, a former employee of the bank and author of *The Continental Affair,* claimed the advice doomed Continental. The bank's loan-to-asset ratio also increased to 69 percent in 1981, the highest in the industry, arguably making the bank the riskiest of its peers. McCollom pointed to the findings of Peters and Waterman, who later wrote in *In Search of Excellence* that executives "shared our disquiet about conventional approaches [of organizational design]. All were uncomfortable with the limitations of the usual structural solutions, especially the latest aberration, the complex matrix form." In other words, McKinsey was pushing on Continental a structure that its own employees had concluded didn't work. "McKinsey had sold us matrix management, the very snake oil that excellent companies avoided," wrote McCollom. "They had sold us lawyers, secrecy . . . [and] buzzwords. . . . McKinsey had sold the Continental Bank its obsolete equipment."[10] A few years later, Continental earned the dubious distinction of being the biggest bank failure in U.S. history to that point.

In the consulting the London office did for the National Health Service, McKinsey failed to move the stultified British bureaucracy an inch. (The consultants were still in there in 2012, with critics still questioning the benefits of their work, as apt an example of the controversial nature of the McKinsey transformational relationship as any.) McKinsey was in the BBC for years with similar effect, at one point pushing the idea of an internal market in which BBC staffers bought and sold services to one another. This was another consulting theme that looked good in theory but was to be poor in practice, one that forced producers to engage in endless negotiations *internally* just to do things as simple as reserving a studio or finding airtime for a project. In other words, the consultants pushed excessively complex management systems on an oblivious client. One project reportedly had the consultants working with BBC staffers by cutting out paper frogs and pretending to sell them to one another.[11] A scathing June 1995 newspaper investigation had already put the lie to the notion that McKinsey had helped cut costs in return for its extravagant fees: "The BBC now costs more to run while employing less people than ever before," the investigation concluded. "The 'savings' have turned out to be an extra staff cost of 140 million pounds compared to four years ago."[12]

And McKinsey never really left the building. A decade later, when John Birt, then director-general of the BBC, stepped down from his job, McKinsey brought him on as a part-time consultant. In 2005 Birt severed all ties with the firm after critics suggested that working for 10 Downing Street in London *and* McKinsey posed a conflict of interest—as if hiring him shortly after extracting millions of pounds out of the BBC hadn't been. Birt's replacement at the BBC's helm—Greg Dyke—immediately slashed spending on outside consultants by 75 percent.

Few clients are going to hire McKinsey and then say the consultants *weren't* worth it. In a sense, the firm is a spiritual relative of "La Belle" Otero, a courtesan living in Paris in the early part of the twentieth century who was once considered the most sought-after woman in the world. Carolina Otero was very selective about her clientele and charged outrageous fees that reportedly topped $1 million in 2012 dollars. Her customers included Prince Albert I of Monaco and the king of Serbia, and it was widely argued that everybody who had the means had to have her at least once. And once you'd done that, what could you say? Once you'd paid a million francs for a roll in the hay, you weren't about to admit it wasn't worth the price paid.

It's actually quite difficult to make the case that McKinsey has had any lasting—or fundamental—effect on the way businesses are managed since a few signal accomplishments such as reorganizing American conglomerates in the 1940s. Silicon Valley has surely had a far larger impact on the way businesses are run in the last thirty years than McKinsey might claim to have had. "What have they fixed?" asked former McKinsey consultant Michael Lanning. "What have they changed? Did they take any voice in the way banking has evolved in the past thirty years? They did study after study at GM, and that place needed the most radical kind of change you can imagine. The place was dead, and it was just going to take a long time for the body to die unless they changed how they operated. McKinsey was in there with huge teams, charging huge fees, for several decades. And look where GM came out."[13] In the end, all the GM work did was provide a revenue stream to enrich a group of McKinsey partners, especially those working with the automaker.

The last time McKinsey was influential at Apple Computer was when John Sculley was there, and that's because he'd had a brand-marketing heritage from Pepsi. And Sculley was a disaster. Did McKinsey do anything to help the great companies of today become what they are? Amazon, Microsoft, Google? In short, no.

Still, McKinsey's high self-regard survives even in the face of evidence to the contrary. McKinsey consultant Tom Steiner recalled a strategy study done for the New York office by another partner, Chuck Farr. "He had two slides. The first was the top clients of the New York office, by billings—companies like AT&T, American Express, and Manufacturers Hanover. All the partners got up to talk about what special thing McKinsey had done to become so vital to those clients. Before we knew it, there were only fifteen minutes left of what was supposed to be a two-hour meeting. Someone said, 'What's on the second slide?' It was Booz Allen's top clients. And they were pretty much the same companies."[14] McKinsey may have been earning more than Booz at the time, but it was from a client base that was clearly willing to pay for advice from *everyone*. There's nothing special about that kind of product.

A General Disaster

McKinsey's work for General Motors in the early 1980s showed quite clearly that consultants can sometimes do far more harm than good to a company, even if it's one of the most important clients they might ever have. At the time, General Motors—the *Titanic* of American business—was being pummeled by Japanese carmakers like Toyota. Chairman Roger Smith decided in 1984 to embark on the most massive reorganization of a company in American history. He hired McKinsey to devise it with him. The carmaker soon accounted for more fees than the rest of McKinsey's entire U.S. manufacturing practice. According to one report, at one point GM was paying McKinsey as much as $2 million a month.[15]

McKinsey interviewed the top sixty-five executives in the company and eight hundred employees, asking them what organizational problems they saw. With their poll results in hand, the consultants proposed a new structure. Instead of organizing the company by brand—Chevy, Cadillac, Buick, et cetera—the consultants said it should be organized by type of car—large, small, truck. This was a basic McKinsey maneuver—don't organize around *this,* organize around *that*—and it had worked in the past. The consultants had successfully helped AT&T organize around its markets as opposed to its technologies, for example. But it was not the right prescription for GM.

"At the time, neither McKinsey nor General Motors understood the true nature of Japanese competitiveness," said Maryann Keller, author of *Rude Awakening: The Rise, Fall and Struggle for Recovery of General Motors*.[16] "Only later did people begin to realize that it wasn't the fact that the Japanese had a compliant low-paid workforce that got up every day and sang the Toyota hymn. It was that they built cars with fewer parts, fewer defects, continuous improvement processes, and took man-hours out of making cars without compromising productivity. I'm 100 percent sure McKinsey had no clue about these revelations."

Instead, McKinsey just moved people around, and this had the effect of destroying institutional knowledge and the informal networks of people who knew how to get things done inside the massive company. "They were flying perpendicular to where they should have been," said Keller. "It was the thousands of little things Toyota did well that mattered, not the organizational design of General Motors."

The reorganization was such an unmitigated disaster—it ran up huge costs with no measurable improvements in output or efficiencies—that Keller claimed it planted the seeds for GM's bankruptcy in 2009. "But is it such a surprise?" she asked. "These are not people who have ever run anything. These are people who have spent their lives talking to high-level executives. And what do high-level executives know about making things? Not much, usually. Do you think Roger Smith knew anything about making a car?"

Whose fault was it? Not McKinsey's, said McKinsey. Despite refusing to discuss the work in specific, one senior director told *Fortune* writer John Huey that the fault lay squarely with the General Motors management. "We told them like it was. We weren't passive at all. We told them to take their medicine," he said. "It's like being a doctor. You do the best you can, but if the patient won't quit smoking, he still dies. This is a problem the world over. Corporate executives are not risk takers. They don't see trouble clearly until they're going down the drain."[17]

General Motors offers one of the great lessons of strategy consulting. As Matthew Stewart so elegantly pointed out, "The idea of strategy, like the owl of Minerva, typically arises just as the sun is setting on an organization. An old saw has it that strategy is when you're running out of ammo but you keep firing on all guns so that the enemy won't know. As a rule, corporations turn to strategy when they can't justify their existence in any other way, and they start *planning* when they don't really know where they are going."[18]

It Depends

The most valued possession of a McKinsey consultant is a long-term client relationship. That's not so different from any business, but at McKinsey, with no particular products to speak of, the relationship is all. In any given year, some 85 percent of McKinsey's revenues come from existing clients. "We insinuate ourselves," Ron Daniel told *Forbes*.[19] It is a talent that bedevils the firm's rivals and amazes even its alumni. "May we all get there, when clients just keep coming back to you," said Alan Kantrow, former editor of the *McKinsey Quarterly*. "They have follow-on work not just because they're good at what they do, but because they are trained in how to manage these kinds of client relationships. They understand that the core reality is the relationship and the conversation, and that any particular engagement is merely epiphenomenal."[20]

Smart clients say that the best way to use McKinsey is *not* to let them insinuate themselves—to prohibit walking the halls of the client's offices looking for new business. Jamie Dimon of JPMorgan Chase, for example, will hire McKinsey, but for one-off projects in which the entire body of knowledge generated is transferred to JPMorgan Chase at the end of the project. The firm's operating committee has to approve any consulting engagement, and the JPMorgan Chase executives don't take just any consultants; they pick and choose the specific people they want on the project.

"We're not selling time and answers, like law or accounting firms," Ron Daniel told Forbes in 1987.[21] "We're selling a benefit called change. Change is where the value is." Daniel told *Forbes* that clients must "trust McKinsey" to set a fair fee. But clients don't always comply. When Jamie Dimon was CEO of Bank One, he hired McKinsey to look at the bank's credit rules in 2002, something no one had done for years. He told the consultants they would get 50 percent of their fee up front and 50 percent based on performance. McKinsey earned its full fee. A year later, on a project overseen by Dimon's deputy Heidi Miller, Bank One decided McKinsey hadn't earned its performance fee and refused to pay the second installment. The consultants were flabbergasted, but McKinsey partner Clay Deutsch conceded the argument, and the firm took home just half its "fair" fee. Despite Daniel's lofty rhetoric, every now and then McKinsey is confronted with the simple fact that for some customers, consulting is little more than a packaged goods business. At the end of the day, the dogs have to eat the dog food.

And that brings the focus back to the difference between the elusive promise of big-picture, blue-sky thinking and the true value that a consultant can almost always provide. Real consulting, writer Kevin Mellyn has argued, isn't about change or leadership or vision. It's about helping people manage what one might call Industrial Prussianism—organizing activities through highly rational bureaucratic routines that promote effectiveness, efficiency, and honesty. The Prussians beat the French in 1871, but not because they had inspired leadership. They won because their system was based on rules, orders, and norms that allowed their army to run efficiently and *without the need* for heroes. Likewise, Industrial Prussianism skips the heroes and focuses on efficiency and frugality, with training and accountability. The only point of strategic planning is to think through all contingencies in advance so as to make fewer tactical execution errors; he who makes the fewest and has the best-organized and best-trained troops wins. The companies that survive, like the best armies, can recover from unexpected blows of fate and competitor breakthroughs.

Bower and his contemporaries understood this. They understood that when businesses become big, they need efficiency experts to help hone their internal processes. McKinsey was part of that wave of consulting engineers. Even today, the best consultants are ex-engineers, not perfectly designed social operators with a Harvard MBA. Engineering teaches you to define your solution space, determine the relevant levers you can pull or push, and then find your solution. Strategize all you want, but if your processes aren't well oiled, you're a goner.

Hiring McKinsey Just to Make a Point

By the end of the 1980s, McKinsey's brand had moved into a whole new realm. Observers had long been comparing it to IBM in the context of "you never got fired for hiring" either one of them, but now companies had begun to hire McKinsey *just to make a point*. The mere announcement of the hiring of the firm now had its own legitimizing effect: the press release as cattle prod of the corporate sphere. Every consulting firm does this. McKinsey just does it better than the rest of them. More than forty years ago, London's *Sunday Times* put it thus: "Calling in McKinsey has proved to be a highly effective way of nailing the red rag of revolution to the masthead."[22]

When you hired IBM, you were hiring it to do something specific and real—revamp your entire technology infrastructure, say, or outsource your payroll and personnel processing. With McKinsey, the hiring of the consultants could be a mere tactic. If, as CEO, you felt you needed to cut 10 percent of costs but didn't feel you were getting buy-in from your employees, the hiring of McKinsey generally got the point across quite clearly. Companies still hire McKinsey to send this type of message.

In 2009 publisher Condé Nast famously hired the firm to ram the message through to a staff used to spending extravagantly that 30 percent needed to be removed from the company's cost structure. Likewise, Warner Amex Cable Communications hired McKinsey in 1984 because of infighting that was getting in the way of executing a turnaround. "We had to go outside for a view that wasn't biased," said then-CEO Drew Lewis. "And McKinsey did a fine job."[23]

In 1993 Delta Air Lines was bleeding money as the result of some newly acquired European operations. Shareholders were in revolt. What did management do? It hired McKinsey, and told the world about it. "Such an announcement sends out several messages," John Huey wrote in *Fortune* at the time. "'We know we have a problem. We're doing something about it. We hired the most expensive help we could find. Give us some time, okay?'"[24] This brought McKinsey a whole lot closer to the bond rating-agency model than it liked—the McKinsey engagement as corollary to the AAA rating. But AAA-rated bonds can (and do) fail. So do some recommendations made by McKinsey.

McKinsey claims that it tries to avoid this kind of situation, going so far as to build into its contract language that prevents clients from mentioning that the firm has been hired: "McKinsey's work for the Client is confidential and intended for the Client's internal use only. McKinsey does not make public client names, client materials or reports prepared for clients without their prior written permission. Similarly, the Client agrees that it will not use McKinsey's name, refer to McKinsey's work, or make the Deliverables or the existence or terms of this agreement available outside its organization without McKinsey's prior written permission."

"We do that for this explicit reason," explained senior partner Larry Kanarek. "So that we cannot be purchased for a Good Housekeeping seal of approval. I was on a recent call when we flat out said no. We lost the work, because the client [wanted] to cite us in an IPO prospectus. We don't want to be hired so somebody can say, 'McKinsey says this is a good strategy.' We are advisers, and it is management's job to take all the advice they receive and make their own decisions. Not to say that McKinsey told me to do this."[25]

There's that disconnect from ultimate responsibility again. McKinsey doesn't ask for credit, but it won't take the blame. Kanarek saw nothing wrong with this arrangement. "We have a different form of responsibility," he said. "But we are also disconnected from the rewards. If our advice is consistently bad, the client will stop using us. But there have been many more times where the advice has been good and clients and shareholders get wealthy and we do not. Our rewards are damped because that's what being a professional is all about. Theirs are higher and lower because they are the real players. Whenever someone in McKinsey tells me they think they know how to run a company, I tell them to go do it. Because that's *not* what we're doing here."

While McKinsey may have a problem with *public* use of its name, it doesn't have any whatsoever with corporate executives using the firm to provide justification for a major decision. When First Interstate Bancorp made a bid for Bank of America in 1986, McKinsey was brought in to show how the combined organization would enjoy $700 million in savings, the big sort of number that First Interstate needed to convince board members and shareholders that it could take over a bank nearly twice its size.[26] "Sometimes there are situations in which you want to impose an answer," said a former McKinsey consultant now working at a rival. "In those cases, McKinsey is usually the better hire. There is a degree of arrogance about the place that works."

Nor does McKinsey take issue with being brought in to provide ammunition for an executive who is having trouble convincing his colleagues of a particular course of action. After General Electric purchased NBC in 1987, GE-installed president of NBC Bob Wright suggested a "budget exercise" aimed at achieving a 5 percent reduction in the news division's $300 million budget. When NBC News president Larry Grossman publicly resisted the initiative, Wright brought in McKinsey.[27] "If a consultant is being used, does he realize it?" Hal Higdon asked in *The Business Healers*. "And if he realizes it, does he care, or does he accept it as part of the price he pays for his home in the suburbs?"[28]

McKinsey can also be hired when one executive needs "disinterested" support for an idea that might just also result in the removal of an internal rival. Lee Iacocca wrote in his autobiography that when Henry Ford wanted Iacocca out of the firm, he hired McKinsey to recommend a new organizational structure. Iacocca went to Chrysler, where he used Bain & Company instead of McKinsey.[29]

Finally, McKinsey does what all its competitors do, which is act as de facto industrial spies. The firm would surely take umbrage at the suggestion, but the whole notion of competitive benchmarking is just a fancy way of telling one client what other clients are up to, with the implicit—and somewhat dubious—promise that their most sensitive secrets will not be revealed. "The strategy boutiques have produced some of the more ruthless and effective approaches to industrial espionage," said Lewis Pinault, author of *Consulting Demons*.[30]

Teflon Dons

Considering that 85 percent of McKinsey's business comes from repeat clients, it's quite clear that the occasional disaster does not define the firm. And there's good reason for that. For one, there will always be value to an outside opinion, no matter who you are, and if McKinsey can bring the best minds to bear on a project, its consultants will be hired again, despite its ability to make mistakes.

Or its premium prices. "They pride themselves on being 2 percent above the market," said rival consultant Frederick Sturdivant. "What a lovely place to be. How do they get away with it? It used to be terribly frustrating as a competitor. It's one thing to be knocked off the block by a price competitor, but another thing entirely by someone who is charging a premium."[31]

Even so, critics have long marveled at McKinsey's ability to shrug off failed consulting engagements such as that of General Motors and to just keep marching forward, getting repeat work from the very same clients it has occasionally failed in the past—be they large banks like Citicorp or companies like AT&T.

One reason for this success is the firm's self-confidence. McKinsey is *all about* confidence. The McKinsey sales pitch is a simple one: "Whatever your problem is, we're the smart guys that can help you fix it." Is it a con? Maybe. The young MBAs the firm fields on its engagement teams learn on the job on the client's dime, and it's hard to argue that a McKinsey associate has anything to offer the clientele but long nights.

Marvin Bower told his protégés that the secret to success was to act successful. He wasn't just talking about McKinsey. He was talking about a specific kind of American confidence that allowed the country to conquer the economic globe to a degree that is only now being called into question, some fifty years later. The country has that confidence—or it used to—and McKinsey expressed that as totally and fully as any company the world has ever seen. So it made mistakes. It could fix them. And it did.

Another reason the firm has been so successful is that it has peopled the global business community with alumni and friends—all of which it treats very well. Like almost no other firm in existence, McKinsey becomes a part of its people's self-image. Years after leaving the firm, ex-consultants still use "we" when referring to McKinsey, even in the present tense.

One primary factor setting McKinsey apart from its competition—indeed, from most institutions—is that extraordinary alumni network—the McKinsey mafia. While the firm had been running alumni outreach for some time by this point, it wasn't until the turn of the century that the number of alumni became truly meaningful. By 2000, there were more than 19,000 living professional alumni of the firm.

More than seventy past and present CEOs of Fortune 500 companies are McKinsey alumni. A 2008 study by *USA Today* calculated that the odds of a McKinsey employee becoming a CEO at a public company were the best in the world, at 1 in 690. The closest rival was Deloitte & Touche, at 1 in 2,150. McKinsey is certainty the most *efficient* producer of CEOs the world has ever seen. In 2011 more than 150 McKinsey alumni were running companies with more than $1 billion in annual sales.

Perhaps the only alumni network with more reach and lifelong relevance to its members is that of Harvard University. And there's no small amount of overlap between the two.

7. REVENGE OF THE NERDS

A Guy Like Fred

Fred Gluck was not a born-and-bred McKinsey man. Born in 1935, he grew up in a one-bedroom apartment in a Roman Catholic neighborhood in Brooklyn with his mother, father, grandmother, and five siblings.[1] Few from his neighborhood ever made it to college. Gluck did that and more. After attending a Jesuit high school, he obtained a degree in electrical engineering from Manhattan College, then a PhD from Columbia in operations research. His first job was at the legendary Bell Labs, where he worked on antimissile systems. He was an actual rocket scientist. And this is why he is crucial to McKinsey's story—he shepherded the firm into the age of technology. In the process, he led it into its full realization as a truly global entity.

Gluck loved being a rocket scientist until the moment he abruptly lost interest in it. "When I was about thirty, I had a dream," recalled Gluck. "At the time, I was at Bell Labs and was the program manager for the Spartan missile, which was our long-range interceptor against ICBMs. And in the dream, I saw my tombstone. It said, 'Fred Gluck died. He worked for forty-five years designing antimissile systems.'"[2] He cast about for a new job, eventually hooking up with a recruiter in

New York City. A series of interviews with chemical giant Union Carbide went nowhere, and he decided he'd wait until Bell Labs fired its first missile in the interceptor program. Lo and behold, it worked. He then called his recruiter back and said he was ready for a change. The recruiter said he'd found the perfect job for Gluck: at McKinsey. Like many of the firm's eventual starts, Gluck had never heard of the place. But he interviewed anyway and took a job in 1967. He was thirty-one years old.

Gluck did not get off to a good start. And even though he had overseen a $300 million missile program, that did not qualify as business experience from a McKinsey point of view. Nor did he look the part: A short, bespectacled man, Gluck was hardly an Oxford crew team member like Rod Carnegie. He was an odd duck at McKinsey, and when executives considered him for staffing on a job, the typical response was: "No, he talks a different language. Plus he's a short little guy." But those who passed on the chance to make an ally of Gluck in those early days came to regret it.

When Gluck finally had his first assignment at the firm—on a study for specialty glassmaker Corning—the partner in charge was Carnegie himself. "He had shoulders about this wide," recalled Gluck with a laugh, "and one of the first things he said to me was, 'Oh, Gluck. You're the guy we hired from Bell Labs. The firm should have never hired a guy that was dumb enough to spend ten years in an R&D lab.'"[3] Carnegie reportedly forbade Gluck to make any contact with Corning executives, for fear of putting the McKinsey image at risk. Gluck was a show-not-tell sort, though, and before long his superior work habits and rigorous commitment to research had managers fighting over him. Soon enough, he was running projects himself, with a specific focus on electronics and telecommunications. (For his part, Carnegie doesn't quite recall what he actually said to Gluck that day, but does remember telling him that he had to go slow, especially with a proud client like Corning that might not take too kindly to a novice consultant breaking any glass on his first big project. "I told Fred to take it quietly until he understood the culture of their research effort," recalled Carnegie. "It was different from the one at Bell Labs, and he just needed to figure out how they did what they did before he could add any value to the process.")[4]

Gluck's work with Northern Electric, the predecessor to Northern Telecom and, subsequently, Nortel Networks, showed how McKinsey could bring novel thinking to routine problems. In an initial meeting with the chairman of the company—Vernon Marquez, who went by "Marq"—the consultants were told that the one thing they didn't need to look at was the telecom company's R&D program, which was working like a charm.

This had the unintended effect of making Gluck and his colleagues want to look at R&D *first*. What they found was, in fact, a system in desperate need of reform. Northern had recently changed the way it evaluated R&D proposals. Instead of focusing on the here and now, the company was asking managers to estimate the return on investment for each initiative and then basing the decision to proceed on that. Rosy projections abounded, so much so that in the few years since the change, no project had been turned down. "Think about that," said Gluck. "To calculate the return on investment of a project that's still in R&D means you're projecting sales way out into the future. You can project anything you want, which makes it a totally useless way of selecting projects. The way you *should* select R&D projects is based on what it does to your competitive position. Or whether it opens up a new market to you."[5]

Another simple but powerful piece of advice Gluck and his team gave Marq had to do with international expansion. At the time, Northern was a purely Canadian company with big dreams. Marq had a point man for his international plans named Ernie Kovats, who was Hungarian and had negotiated contracts with Hungary and Czechoslovakia with fractional market shares to manufacture switching equipment for rural telephone systems. What Kovats and his team had overlooked, though, was that while the rest of the world used so-called CCITT standards, the United States and Canada used the Bell protocol. Gluck and his team presented Marq with a simple pie chart showing that 53 percent of all the world's telephones were in the United States. The message was clear: Northern was chasing a very small market with protocols that would require substantial reengineering of its products. Marquez was no fool: Northern immediately shifted its focus—and engineering—to the United States and became the world's dominant maker of telephone hardware over the next few decades.

One person who took a shine to Gluck from the beginning was Ron Daniel. Which was surprising, in a way, because the two were an odd match. Daniel had graduated from Wesleyan—a small Ivy—and gave off the aura of a stately ocean liner parting the waves, large, impenetrable, and radiating gravitas. He was a picture of impeccably tailored elegance with just enough intentional discord—the man had great sideburns—to signify the ease with which he wielded power. Gluck, on the other hand, looked (and acted) a bit like a street fighter, with a devil-may-care grin and an irreverent sense of humor. What they shared was a deep understanding of how technology was revolutionizing the business world. While in the navy, Daniel had managed one of the country's earliest large-scale computer installations, and when he joined McKinsey in 1957 he was the firm's first computer expert.[6] He and Gluck were a couple of nerds.

Though many within McKinsey doubted that someone with Gluck's idiosyncratic background and skill set could ever lead the firm, Daniel had great, unwavering confidence in him, and he made it clear to all. It was one of Daniel's strengths, said his admirers, that he could see beyond the McKinsey personality clichés and identify quality people who didn't fit the mold. "Ron Daniel was one of the first to recognize the importance of delivering content-driven expertise into the client agenda," said McKinsey alumnus James Gorman. "McKinsey evolved from general advisers to 'knowledge bearing' advisers. Fred Gluck was at the forefront of that evolution and provided an intellectual spark to the firm in accelerating that change."[7]

Before long, Daniel put Gluck in charge of the strategy initiative that was the firm's response to the rise of BCG and Bain and thereby solidified his standing at McKinsey. Gluck was elected principal in 1972 and director in 1976, just nine years after joining the firm.

For all his support, Daniel did enjoy needling the younger man. He couldn't help reminding Gluck that he didn't quite measure up to historic McKinsey standards. "Ron used to do this terrible thing to Fred, who is his genetic opposite," recalled one colleague. "When Ron introduced Fred at any event, just after Fred stood up and was ready to start, Ron would say, 'Stand up, Fred.'"

By the time of the election for managing director in 1988, Gluck was one of two finalists for the position. The other was the immensely popular Jon Katzenbach, considered by many to be the soul of the firm in the post-Bower era. But Gluck's work on strategy had reinvigorated the partnership. Katz actually came within an inch of beating Gluck, but he didn't resign in a fit of pique. Indeed, he was so universally liked that his colleagues offered no resistance to his staying on six years past the mandatory retirement age of sixty.

Gluck's main credential for rising to the top of the firm, insofar as it was understood by the outside world, was his work on the strategy initiative, which helped redirect the firm. That, supposedly, was more than enough to offset the fact that he'd never run an office or helmed an industry practice. But Gluck, who worked on more than a hundred engagements for AT&T and Bell Labs, was also one of the great rainmakers of his day. Between 1989 and 1994, AT&T paid McKinsey $96 million in consulting fees, including $30 million in 1992 alone.[8]

It was later revealed that Monitor, a competitor founded by Harvard professor Michael Porter and five others with connections to Harvard Business School, actually made more from AT&T, billing $127 million between 1991 and 1994. "Gluck was elected managing partner because of his deep client relationship at AT&T," said one ex-McKinsey consultant. "And then we find out from a *BusinessWeek* cover story that Joe Fuller from Monitor was pulling in way more than Gluck was. Everyone looked at him and said, 'Hey! We thought *you* were the guy at AT&T!'"

BusinessWeek marked Gluck's ascension with a cover story titled "What's a Guy Like This Doing at McKinsey's Helm?"[9] One thing he was certainly doing was laying out plans for expansion. In his first speech as managing director, he predicted the firm would have 5,000 consultants, 8,000 employees, and 75 offices in 30 countries by the year 2000. "I thought the guy was nuts," recalled Nancy Killefer, who had been with the firm for nine years at that point. "He was describing a firm I could not conceive of."[10] She wasn't alone. In 1988 the firm employed just 1,671 consultants and 3,034 employees in 40 offices across 21 countries. Gluck wanted to double the firm's size in just twelve years.

In fact, he *underestimated* the firm's potential. Twelve years later, McKinsey employed 6,210 consultants and 11,264 employees in 86 offices across 47 countries. Killefer recalled running into Gluck at the firm's 2011 retired directors conference. "I said, 'Fred, I don't know if you've read that speech again, but you were right. And we are the firm you envisioned.'"

The Third Wave

According to historian Matthias Kipping, there are three waves in the history of consulting. The first wave ushered the industry into existence: the Taylorist focus on efficiency enhancement. The second was consulting top management on organization and strategy. And the third was advice on information technology (IT) based networking. By the late 1980s, it was no secret that a company's IT strategy could be the difference between staying in the game and permanently falling behind. The IT budgets of financial institutions had grown to be larger than their profits, and telecommunications and healthcare companies were nearly as deeply invested.

Whereas McKinsey could relate to competitors like Bruce Henderson and Bill Bain, in the 1980s the firm came under siege from those it had long disdained: the accountants. But the Big Five accounting firms—Arthur Andersen, Deloitte & Touche, Ernst & Young, KPMG, and Price Waterhouse (later PricewaterhouseCoopers)—had sensed more quickly the profound changes afoot, and they had fielded legions of lower-priced consultants in the new realm of "systems consulting" to help their clients make moves in IT.

Then the attacks went full frontal: Arthur Andersen launched Andersen Consulting (later renamed Accenture), Deloitte & Touche created Deloitte Consulting, and Ernst & Young and KPMG also had their own efforts. The newer business models were different—they needed fast growth and larger size to make up for their lower price structure—but all this extra competition was clouding McKinsey's future.

And that wasn't all. More tech-focused competitors such as French computer and software company Cap Gemini, Computer Sciences Corporation, Electronic Data Systems, and IBM were also outmaneuvering McKinsey in bake-offs for information-technology consulting business that clients believed increasingly crucial to the survival of their companies.

In an effort to downplay the competition, McKinsey spread the notion that Andersen was the army to McKinsey's marines, but that didn't take away from the fact that Andersen was fielding a much larger—and competitive—force of consultants. The new competition wasn't just temporary, either. By 1998 Andersen Consulting reported $8.3 billion in revenues, PricewaterhouseCoopers $6 billion, and Ernst & Young $4 billion. McKinsey? A relatively minuscule $2.5 billion.

Luckily, the firm had just the right man in the wings to confront the challenge: Fred Gluck. Just as his entry into McKinsey had been a rough one, however, Gluck's first big attempt to tackle the IT challenge was a bit of a misfire as well.

Fred's Folly

It wasn't as if Daniel and Gluck hadn't realized that technology strategy represented a paramount concern for clients. They saw it within their own business: McKinsey tested one of the first IBM personal computers in 1982 and, later on, beta-tested the fourth computer Compaq ever made. The firm test-drove one of the first releases of the spreadsheet Lotus 1-2-3—the son of VisiCalc and the father of Excel. But McKinsey was caught flat-footed by the whole new swath of competitors when it came to advising clients on the subject. And it did something uncharacteristic in response: It panicked, making the strategic blunder of acquiring Information Consulting Group, a technology-consulting venture, in 1990.

Gresham Brebach, the former head of consulting at accounting powerhouse Arthur Andersen, had founded ICG in 1988, bankrolled by a loan from advertising giant Saatchi & Saatchi. ICG's stated mission had been to provide information-technology consulting to its clients. Brebach found a better target, though: Fred Gluck. "Fred went skiing with Gresh and came back in love," recalled one of McKinsey's original technology experts. With the support of Carter Bales—who had found his way back into the good graces of the McKinsey leadership by taking a lead on all things technological—Gluck rammed the decision to buy ICG for a nominally small $10 million past a skeptical partnership.

Deep down, McKinsey consultants were worried that clients didn't view them as the answer to crucial technology questions. They were right, and that was the main reason Gluck and his executives pushed through the ICG deal. Given McKinsey's long-held emphasis on organic growth, it was deeply out of character and required some extra explaining. The firm tried to rationalize it by calling it recruitment instead of an acquisition. "What this is is a massive recruiting effort," Bill Matassoni told the *New York Times* when news of the impending transaction leaked out. "About a year and a half ago we felt we really needed to build capability in this area. ICG represents an unusual opportunity to accelerate this process."[11]

The transplant didn't take. While embracing technical expertise made sense for McKinsey, its elitist generalists couldn't help looking down on the plumbers of ICG. The merger brought in some major IT engagements, but the marriage was doomed from the start, with powerful McKinsey engagement managers refusing to staff their new geeky counterparts on major projects. Just over three years later, more than half of ICG's partner-level consultants had left.[12] Brebach himself left for Digital Equipment Corporation in 1993. "It wasn't a particularly big acquisition," recalled German office head Frank Mattern. "But it wasn't done well. It was a failure."[13] ICG eventually evaporated entirely inside the hothouse of McKinsey.

Even though the move proved a misfire, it was an understandable one, given the times. In the late 1980s, United Technology picked Ernst & Young over McKinsey for an IT project, and German home-appliance maker BSHG hired Arthur D. Little to help with office automation concepts. As part of a "Worldwide Competitor Review" of technology and systems consulting presented in Rome in September 1991, the consultants explored reasons they had lost consulting contracts for IT and concluded—not uncharacteristically—that those clients had made poor decisions. "Rightly or wrongly," the review stated, "outsiders sometimes take the position that other service organizations can add value equal to ours." The review also showcased a lingering denial about the technological changes afoot. "Frankly, [it's] not that important an issue for the senior executives I serve," an unnamed McKinsey consultant was quoted as saying.

In the late 1990s the firm made another run at the technology-consulting action, but this time it was from the ground up, launching a Business Technology Office. The goal wasn't to compete head-on with the accounting firms—McKinsey's relatively low associate-to-partner ratios wouldn't support such economics—but to advise the chief information officer on information-technology management, providing answers to questions like: How do you run your IT department? How do you prioritize projects? How do you keep IT costs down? "Because we're not actual vendors of technology like most IT consultants, we're sitting on the same side of the table as the CIO, not the opposite side," said Mattern. "That's an enormously powerful and valuable position to be in."[14]

This time it worked. And McKinsey succeeded in getting the upper hand once again. A McKinsey consultant didn't do mere systems integration. He told you *why* you wanted one system or another. In this move, the firm was going back to its familiar put-down of the competition. When Hal Higdon wrote in 1969 that accounting firms were making incursions into consulting, he referenced the idea of their built-in advantage to the McKinseys of the world, what with their already doing auditing work for pretty much any client McKinsey might approach. "We don't have to locate the bathroom," he quoted one accountant as saying. The McKinsey retort: An accountant who knows where the bathroom is located may be unable to recognize that the bathroom should be located elsewhere.[15] And there it was: McKinsey took the high ground of IT consulting away from the pretenders to its crown. By 2011 the BTO was the third-largest "office" in the entire firm, after the United States and Germany.

Not for Less Than $1 Million

By the end of the 1980s, McKinsey's struggles at the end of the Marvin Bower era were long forgotten. The firm had moved into a higher gear, with revenues almost doubling, from $350 million in 1985 to $635 million in 1989. Over the next three years they nearly doubled *again,* hitting $1.2 billion in 1992. The Gluck-era focus on embracing one's expertise was paying off in spades.

Remarkably, McKinsey was at that point demanding—and receiving—a substantial price premium over even its closest competitors. A "Competitive Assessment Review" from June 1989 showed just how powerful the brand had become. In a proposal for a large financial institution, Booz Allen Hamilton had offered to do the work in four to four and a half months, for $125,000 a month plus expenses, or about $675,000. McKinsey required more time—five to six months—and $175,000 per month plus expenses, a total of $1 million to $1.21 million. Despite its nearly double price tag, McKinsey won the assignment.

In 1982 McKinsey's revenues per professional had been $180,000; by 1988 they were $320,000; and by 1992 they were $387,000. Booz Allen Hamilton pulled in just $200,000. And even if Andersen Consulting was by that point larger than McKinsey, its own revenues per professional were less than a third of McKinsey's.[16] It had always been Marvin Bower's contention that McKinsey had no competition. As the years went on, the more right he became: If your direct competitors can bill at only 60 percent of your level, are they really even competing with you? On the other hand, deep down, McKinsey viewed some firms as threats. "Monitor, though only founded in 1983, is becoming a formidable competitor for the firm," read one internal report. Booz, on the other hand, "[does] not pose a great threat to McKinsey's overall preeminence in management consulting."

Occasionally McKinsey consultants wondered whether they were pushing a little *too far* on the fee front. Some of their clients told them that they were. In a letter consultant Tom Steiner wrote to his colleagues in the New York office in 1990, he related a conversation with Chase Manhattan executive Mike Urkowitz. "[In a discussion] . . . several weeks ago [he] got up and closed his door and said that among his banking peers at conferences and other gatherings McKinsey's prices were a subject of conversation," Steiner wrote. "He said, 'We all have the view that you won't do anything for less than $1 million. You have a problem.'"

Still, as recently as the late 1980s, McKinsey's fee arrangements with clients remained shockingly informal. The firm did not deign to explain to clients like Federated Department Stores how it arrived at a fee of $200,000 a month plus expenses—it was a take-it-or-leave-it proposition. In an interview with *Fortune,* Amsterdam office manager Mickey Huibregtsen said that the high fees were in the best interests of the company's clients as well as McKinsey, because "they protect us from not being taken seriously by the client and that protects the client from having the wrong studies done. It also protects the quality of the work. When you charge that much, the quality has to be there."[17]

Even as McKinsey preached the sanctity of high fees to its clients, internally the firm was downplaying individual partner revenues in annual evaluations. In 1990 it was made official: Client impact, people leadership, and knowledge development were now more important than client billings. Huibregsten was also front and center in this development. "Mickey was the first to articulate the idea that we'll have some people with poor economics, and some with very good economics," recalled Fred Gluck. "But most of the group was going to fall somewhere in the middle. And so we were going to forget about it, because no one could ever figure out who was behind this dollar of revenues or that one anyway."[18]

Bad Apples and the Return of Arrogance

By the middle of Fred Gluck's tenure as managing director, the brand was so powerful that rivals were reduced to competing for *second* place. Inevitably, the firm began articulating its sense of superiority in ways that beggared belief. The 1989 handbook for new client service staff stressed the necessity of delivering recommendations "that the client understands." In other words, "Keep it simple, boys. Not everybody went to Harvard Business School like us."

McKinsey was equally sure of its superiority to its competitors. One former partner recalled Jim Balloun, onetime head of the firm's Atlanta office, offering this line to the CEO of a client the firm had just begun to serve: "Let's say a client asks us what time it is," Balloun offered. "If you ask Booz Allen, their response will be 'What time do you want it to be?' If you ask A. D. Little, who are a little more technical, they will tell you that 'It's 9:45:20, Greenwich mean time.' But if you ask McKinsey, we will say, 'Why do you want to know? What decisions are you trying to make for which knowing the time would be helpful?'"

Clients clearly bought the image. When Tom Steiner and a few colleagues first left for A. T. Kearney and then later started their own firm, the Mitchell Madison Group, they found that having McKinsey on the résumé mattered little when they were competing against the mother ship. "It turned out to be much easier to sell work when we weren't competing directly against McKinsey than when we were," wrote Matthew Stewart in *The Management Myth*.[19] You might have McKinsey training, but if you couldn't bring the McKinsey machine to bear on a problem, clients weren't nearly as interested. That's a dirty little secret of McKinsey: Ask any outside recruiter and he will tell you most McKinsey partners could not sell nearly as effectively outside McKinsey. Tom Steiner was a notable exception, eventually building and selling a significant firm in its own right.

McKinsey had grown so sure of itself by the mid-1990s that, in contravention of its longtime policy against speaking about itself to the press, the firm cooperated with a substantial profile in *Fortune* by writer John Huey. What a blunder that turned out to be. "Laconic John Huey shows up," recalled a former consultant. "You can't help but like the guy. Fred Gluck insisted that John meet with the eighteen people on the shareholder committee. He met with everyone except for the Machiavellian Rajat Gupta."

In the 7,500-word story, Huey laid bare the firm's growing level of arrogance. He quoted partner Mickey Huibregtsen making the infamous claim that McKinsey's fees were high because such fees forced clients to take the firm seriously. Partner Pete Walker added this beauty: "It's almost never that we fail because we come up with the wrong answer. We fail because we don't properly bring along management. And if a company just doesn't have the horses, there are limits to what we can do."[20]

The article, which had been orchestrated by Gluck, was viewed *internally* as the epitome of arrogance and prompted healthy debate. McKinsey briefly contemplated severing all relations with *Fortune* as a result. It did so for a while but later rethought the notion. This was a whole new challenge for McKinsey—the idea of managing its *brand* as opposed to just its reputation.

The *Fortune* article demonstrated the extent to which the firm's arrogance had grown—to such a point that it treated even valuable clients with disdain. In the United States McKinsey reaped long-running fees from American Express, which had so many McKinsey teams going at once that it was essentially a training program subsidized by a client. "God, we were sucking off that teat for so long," said one New York–based employee of the firm. "McKinsey should be ashamed of themselves for that." Others closer to the American Express business were more pointed. "Good business leaders do not hire consultants," said a former partner of the firm. "Consultants feed off insecure megalomaniacs who are in fear of their own organization. [Amex CEO] Ken Chenault can't take a shit without calling a consultant. They're so deep over there, they're in the phone book." Daimler-Benz had a similar reputation as an easy mark. McKinsey performed a so-called "activity value analysis," or AVA, so many times at Daimler and elsewhere that young German consultants bemoaned being staffed on another OVA (the German office's version of the AVA).

Institutional arrogance occasionally led to blatantly unacceptable behavior. Suzanne Porter, a consultant in the firm's Dallas office, put an embarrassing spotlight on the firm when she filed a sexual discrimination complaint with the Equal Employment Opportunity Commission in 1993. Porter claimed she had been harassed by several of the firm's partners during her time there. McKinsey responded that she was disgruntled because she hadn't been made a principal. Two weeks after her husband, also an employee of the firm, gave a deposition in support of her claims, he was fired. McKinsey said that move was justified because he secretly recorded phone conversations with "various potential witnesses" in his wife's case.[21] A settlement was later reached with Porter.

One estimate in 1993 had McKinsey directors earning $2 million a year[22] in salary and bonuses, and another pegged Gluck's take-home at $3.5 million.[23] Even the youngsters were raking it in: Associates made more than $100,000 a year and principals made $250,000. A few years before he retired—in 1995—Marvin Bower told Jon Katzenbach that he was concerned about encroaching greed in the consulting industry. If it became *all* about the paycheck, he told Katzenbach, it wasn't going to work anymore. "Do our young professionals really need a lot of money? If we allow money to become the primary source of motivation for our people, greed will override our values. A great professional firm cannot allow greed to take hold," he told the younger consultant.[24]

It was the kind of success that allowed for team-building exercises that strain the imagination. When former senior partner George Feiger was put in charge of the professional portion of a partners conference in 1995 in Portugal, he split the assembled partners (and their spouses) into three groups and made each of them perform an opera. He'd had ex-opera singer David Pearl help him write a libretto, and also hired Barry Manilow's producer to help out, but the three groups were responsible for everything from assembling the stage to making costumes, learning the music, and performing. The mere transport of all the required materials across the English Channel and down to Portugal cost McKinsey 1.5 million pounds.

Still, despite the occasional team-building boondoggle, work at the office wasn't getting any easier: Only one in five associates became a principal, and only half of those who made principal became directors. McKinsey had built one brutally efficient meritocracy. But was it even that anymore? In the Ron Daniel era, the managing director's take-home pay was around eight to ten times that of associates. Reasonable McKinsey directors were asking themselves whether they were actually paying themselves too much. Was Fred Gluck really worth thirty-five times more than an associate? Was the typical director worth twenty to twenty-five? Most disappointed McKinsey alumni pinpoint the submission to avarice as a time during the tenure of Gluck's successor, Rajat Gupta. But others claim it started before that. "Fred had to prove he was a player," said one alumnus. "And in doing so, he sowed the seeds of greed at the firm."

The Safety Net

Though most McKinsey consultants would be loath to admit it, the firm's much-acclaimed risk-taking culture is actually one that offers great reward *without taking too much risk*. Want to go open an office in a new country? Unless you're a complete failure, you can always come back home. Want to spend six months trying to reel in a big client? If you don't succeed, just lean back on your old client list. Working for a firm that culls its ranks so ruthlessly is a form of risk taking, but if you've got the goods, it's a far safer bet than heading out on your own.

One associate admitted as much in the firm's internal magazine about his move to Hong Kong. He realized there was almost no risk in the decision. "The safety nets were all in place," he said.[25] McKinsey considers its culture an entrepreneurial one. But it's entrepreneurialism with a pillow waiting to soften any fall. Still, in its own insulated way, the firm allows an enviable spectrum of change-of-career options.

Stefan Matzinger, whom Herb Henzler sent to Brazil in the mid-1980s, said that the ability to feel entrepreneurial within the context of having a secure salary is one of *the best* things about working at McKinsey. "You are evaluated on a prudent use of firm resources," he explained. "We're not a budget-driven organization. The only question you need to be able to answer is, 'What's the right thing to do to build the practice?'"[26]

The key? You have to be able to bring the McKinsey network along with you. The power of McKinsey in its modern form is the number of people that can be brought into any particular client relationship. You can go to Brazil if you'd like, but you're going to need the rest of McKinsey's global partners on speed dial in order to make the office successful. This is one reason why the firm has found it difficult to make midcareer hires. Not only is there the indoctrination issue, but if you're new to the place at the principal or director level, you're not going to be able to bring the right people into your client relationships. One of the highest-profile lateral hires the firm ever made was luring famed media consultant Michael Wolf away from Booz & Company to be head of the firm's global media and entertainment practice in 2001. Wolf brought the client contacts, but he failed to put together a working internal network at McKinsey. He'd run into the buzz saw of personal profiles at McKinsey: The most successful McKinsey consultants are networkers of the highest order. Wolf was, well, a lone wolf. He left the firm after just three years.

Antiheroes

The biggest corporate buzzword of the early 1990s was reengineering—the idea of breaking down a company into its constituent parts and then rebuilding it into a more efficient machine. With almost two million copies sold, *Reengineering the Corporation,* by James Champy and Michael Hammer, became one of the biggest-selling business books since *In Search of Excellence*. Neither was a McKinsey man, but that didn't stop the firm from doing what it has done time and again—using someone else's idea to its own advantage. But it took some time to figure out just how it would do so.

Reengineering actually caused the firm a brief headache in the early 1990s, especially in Europe, where Cap Gemini, recently galvanized by its purchase of a bunch of "change management" firms, was running across the continent pushing what essentially was organizational transformation. Some partners, especially those in Scandinavia and the Netherlands, came up with their own versions of reengineering and wanted to brand their ideas. Gluck pushed back, arguing that the firm wasn't going to brand anything but that it would push McKinsey's established brand, which was built around long-term relationships and "transformational" work. His instincts were right: Reengineering faded out like a glowworm, but long-term clients kept reupping with McKinsey.

Rethinking the way one does business is a hallmark of the American success story. Despite the brutal implications at the individual level, one of the primary differentiators between American companies and their foreign competition is the ability to lay people off with relative impunity. From a cultural perspective, for example, Japanese and German companies both struggle far more with the Darwinian implications of mass layoffs than do their American counterparts. McKinsey, once again, found itself in the position to ease the process for its client executives, providing fact-based justification as well as a philosophical backdrop for downsizing.

McKinsey's advice to Frito-Lay in 1991 led to the dismissal of nearly a third of its headquarters staff. For the price of just $3 million, the consultants offered conglomerate ITT $90 million in savings, a large part of which came through layoffs.[27] A company in trouble has every reason to downsize. But just as McKinsey had taken the gospel of consulting from troubled companies to healthy ones, so it helped take the gospel of reengineering from the troubled to the healthy. In 1994 Procter & Gamble laid off 13,000 of 106,000 workers, while simultaneously claiming that it was in no way a sign of trouble at the firm. "That is definitely not our situation," said the firm's CEO at the time.[28]

There was one great side effect of the reengineering boom, at least as far as consultants were concerned. If, as a corporate CEO, you're going to rethink the entire way you do business, you're going to need to commit a large swath of your own staff to any consulting project. "By the late 1980s, virtually all the major consulting firms had begun to perfect the means to target client managers to do and sell the consultants' own work," wrote Lewis Pinault in *Consulting Demons*. If your goal is to make cumulative fixes in the way you do what you do—removing choke points, finding persistently high expense zones, or merely rethinking the route by which the mail boy walks through the building—you're going to need consultants who get really ingrained in your business.

The McKinsey Society

Whereas the occasional book has been written critiquing consulting as a whole—*The Witch Doctors, Dangerous Company,* and *Consulting Demons* were all published in a few short years at the turn of the twenty-first century—McKinsey has never been specifically and directly attacked in the United States, the world's largest consulting market as well as its largest publishing market. In Germany, however, several books have been published that attack McKinsey by name. There's a reason for it, too: Long after the reign of Herb Henzler, Germany remains, according to author Walter Kiechel, "pound for pound, the best market in the world for high-level consulting."[29]

He may be right, but it's of a very particular sort, the kind that resulted in McKinsey's earning the labels "job destroyers" and "axe wielders." McKinsey was so nearly omnipresent in Germany that immediately after unification, the firm was called in to sell all of the former East Germany's agricultural and industrial assets. (The firm later discovered that two McKinsey directors had been trading on the sales for their own accounts. Both were summarily fired.) German companies—if not German workers—had an inexhaustible appetite for McKinsey intervention.

McKinsey's success in Germany has been a double-edged sword, though. Nowhere else in the world—not even in the United States—has the sociocultural response to the "consultocracy" been as pointed and as persistent. Americans might work up a lather in the midst of a wave of layoffs in tough times, but their memories are as short as the economic cycle. Germans, on the other hand, for the better part of three decades and counting, have been launching sustained philosophical attacks on the whole idea of what has come to be known in Germany as "the McKinsey society." The attacks on McKinsey's particular brand of capitalism have intensified over the past decade.

In 2003 Dirk Kurjuweit wrote *Our Efficient Life: The Dictatorship of the Economy and Its Consequences,* about the ruthless obsession with corporate profits. He decried the simplistic and fundamentally inhumane notion of a society in which efficiency is the ultimate goal. "In the Middle Ages, the church influenced thought and conduct," he wrote. "Since the enlightenment, reason was regarded as the standard of all conduct. Today, the economy plays this role and marks our ideas of happiness, love and meaning of life."

McKinsey Is Coming, a play by Rolf Hochhuth, followed Kurjuweit's book. Hochhuth covered territory similar to Kurjuweit's, including unemployment, social justice, and the "right to work." He focused his audience on the question of whether Deutsche Bank had any right to lay off 11,000 employees in a year when it earned 9.4 billion euros—the most in its 130-year history. Hochhuth was criticized for advocating violence against corporate executives, which he denied.

McKinsey partners don't necessarily argue with the core premise of either work—that they stand for efficiency and rationality. What bothered them about Hochhuth's, though, was that even though his work wasn't about McKinsey per se, the firm was in the title of the play. "We stand for rationality and we stand for objectivity," proclaimed German office head Frank Mattern. "If you read the theater pages in Germany, some of them talk about 'the McKinsey society.' But that's ridiculous. There's no such thing. For better or worse, we stand for originality, for objectivity. We stand for doing what's right. It gives us a lot of clients and followers and friends. But you know, if you stand for *anything,* you're going to have critics."[30] Or possibly worse: Herb Henzler had become very concerned about his own safety after the Red Army Faction assassinated Deutsche Bank chief Alfred Herrhausen with a car bomb when Herrhausen was on his way to work in 1989. Henzler was also rumored to have received death threats in light of the massive job losses in German industry in the early to mid-1990s.

Journalist Thomas Leif wrote *Advised & Sold: McKinsey & Co—The Big Bluff of the Management Consultant* in 2006. The book caused momentary controversy but quickly faded from notice. Still, debate about the firm's true and enduring effect rarely reaches the level of public discourse, so it does say something that even Germany—a country celebrated in 2011–2012 for the ruthlessness of its economic discipline in the face of Continental profligacy—has never quite managed to reconcile the wider social costs and benefits of embracing McKinsey ideas.

The Jesuits of Capitalism

Fred Gluck's tenure at McKinsey was distinguished by his fixation on knowledge—amassing it, organizing it, and making it available to consultants and, ultimately, the firm's clients. "When I joined the firm, I was kind of surprised by the relative lack of knowledge," he recalled. "It wasn't all relationships, of course, but the analyses weren't based so much on knowledge as on the diagnostic guide, which said, 'Look at inventory, look at this, look at that.' It was kind of a menu approach."[31] Gluck had always had a different vision in mind: Jesuit-educated himself, he meant to turn McKinsey into the Jesuits of Capitalism. And he succeeded.

"In the early 1980s we were still a generalist firm," noted former partner Clay Deutsch. "There was a premium on free-association problem solving, and a sense that specific skills and knowledge were dirty and vocational. By the turn of the century, it was hard to succeed in the place without being a specialist of some sort. There's still some mythology that McKinsey consultants are all still generalists. Today's firm is incredibly specialized."[32] In other words, after fifty-plus years of experimenting with nonpartner-track associates, T-shaped consultants, and the 1990s variant—"spiky integrators"—the firm had finally been persuaded that expertise is good. It's not as if McKinsey was alone in fetishizing the notion of generalists, either. As recently as 2012, McKinsey client General Electric finally capitulated to the idea itself and reversed a longtime policy of rotating senior leaders through different divisions in favor of leaving them in place to deepen their understanding of a particular business unit.[33]

"[Today] McKinsey positions itself as the repository of all business information and theory worth knowing," wrote John Huey in his infamous story in *Fortune*.[34] The firm claimed to do more research on business issues than the business schools at Harvard, Stanford, and Wharton combined. With nearly two thousand consulting engagements a year, McKinsey considered its purview "an invaluable laboratory in which to observe and participate in real-time experiments in management."[35] That was Fred Gluck's legacy. Well, that, and planting those seeds of greed that would bloom during the tenure of McKinsey's next managing director, Rajat Gupta.

"We had a saying at Bell Labs that with just three phone calls, we could reach the expert in any technical subject, anywhere in the world," said Gluck. "And much of the time he or she would be at Bell Labs. My ambition for McKinsey was to be like that. That's what drove me."[36] A small army of McKinsey partners threw themselves into the task to help the firm reach that destination. Three were dedicated to the task full-time: Hans Dieter-Bluhm, Roger Ferguson, and Brook Manville. Three others spent an inordinate amount of their time on it: Partha Bose, Alan Kantrow, and Bill Matassoni. Others took it upon themselves to drive knowledge development within their individual industry and functional practices, including Nathaniel Foote of the massive organization-design practice and Tom Copeland, the firm's renowned corporate finance guru. But consultants had a hard time finding all these new ideas until Gluck asked Matassoni to create an effective way for the firm to share its knowledge. "Until we did that, if you wanted our best thinking on an issue, you would call the practice leader, who might be in Cleveland, get his secretary, and she would look in his files," explained Matassoni. "Fred wanted a real system put in place that delivered documents. But he didn't want it to replace conversation."[37]

And Gluck was willing to have this done at the expense of revenues. Other consulting firms talk a big game about knowledge building, but McKinsey might be the only one that has forsaken actual income to do it. "Other firms compile what they know in quiet times," said Alan Kantrow, who worked with Matassoni, "but McKinsey actually 'wastes' money doing it. They could make more by maximizing consultant utilization, but instead associates sit there after a project and catalog everything they learned for the next generation."[38]

"You have to give credit to Gluck for basically saying, 'Look, you should have as deep an intellectual understanding of your industry and the functional areas that support it,'" noted former McKinsey consultant Tom Steiner. "If you have those, you will serve your client well."[39] "I helped create a multiyear, $30 million knowledge effort in broadband," recalled another former partner. "That's way outside of investments that BCG or Bain would make."

"The pursuit of fresh content in the service of clients and in building a distinctive firm was paramount in the minds of leaders like Gluck," proclaimed Partha Bose. "I once flew London to Denver, picked up the Stanford economist Brian Arthur, and the two of us drove up to Beaver Creek for a two-hour meeting with Fred. Brian, one of the leading lights in 'increasing returns economics,' had published a paper in *Scientific American* that was all the talk in economics and technology circles. At the meeting, Fred grilled Brian for the entire two hours, repeatedly asking, 'So what would Lou do?'" He was referring to McKinsey alum Lou Gerstner, who was then CEO of IBM. "It was like watching an Ali-Frazier fight up close," continued Bose. "Neither was willing to concede an inch." At the end of the meeting, Arthur joked that he needed a stiff drink; Gluck said that he wanted to find a way to work with the economist. Over the next several years, a Dick Foster–led McKinsey team partnered with Arthur and the Santa Fe Institute in the study of complexity.

The search for content didn't stop at academic disciplines. During the First Gulf War, the head of the firm's operations practice, Graham Sharman, went to Saudi Arabia with Bose to spend a week with the U.S. generals leading the multinational forces against Saddam Hussein. The Pentagon had cleared them for complete access, and McKinsey was privy to observing big strategic and operational decisions being made on the front lines of a literal war. "We were there in the sands of Arabia connecting with a treasure trove of knowledge and experience that could only help our clients do better," explained Bose. "And you know what? I know the generals learned a lot from Sharman too. They said it."[40] Indeed, when one of the three-star generals wrote a book for Harvard Business Press on the management lessons learned in the Gulf War, *BusinessWeek* advised readers to skip the book and read the *McKinsey Quarterly* article by Bose and Sharman instead.

The shift to a knowledge culture that had begun under Daniel and picked up pace under Gluck was reflected in the nature of the firm's partner conferences. In 1980, long before the McKinsey consultants had truly understood the need for a radical change in perspective, the conference was in Vienna. McKinsey partners and their wives stayed at the most expensive hotel in the city and were taken in horse-drawn carriages to a private concert of the Vienna Boys' Choir. At the next conference, though, Daniel had redirected the partners' attention toward the matter at hand. At that year's conference, in Washington, D.C., the cocktail party to kick things off was at the National Air and Space Museum. "We had the whole place to ourselves," recalled one partner, "so it was still pretty clear that we were doing okay. But it sent a different message than 'Spend It If You've Got It.'"

Despite some missteps, Gluck also grasped that the firm had to do a better job publicizing its accomplishments. Under his direction, in 1990 the firm launched the McKinsey Global Institute (MGI), an independent research operation with the goal of developing "substantive points of view on the critical issues" faced by McKinsey clients.[41] Even in a world overflowing with economic think tanks, McKinsey brought a unique perspective to the table: The firm's understanding of actual company economics and industry structures gave specificity to its work. "What's different about MGI is the unique access we have to information that doesn't show up in statistics that we can use responsibly to inform research,"[42] said Diana Farrell, head of MGI from 2001 to 2008, when she left to join the Obama administration.

MGI has been successful in giving the firm a quasi-academic glow that's yet another in the long list of ways it is differentiated from the competition.[43] The institute's work on productivity in the early 1990s is widely regarded as groundbreaking in economic circles. Later work on global capital market developments, the U.S. healthcare system, and energy productivity continues to give McKinsey a voice in conversations to which its competitors are not invited. But it has also given an outlet to the firm's recurring eruptions of arrogance. When the institute paid significant sums to lure Nobel laureate Robert Solow and other leading economists to its board, then-chairman Ted Hall reportedly professed the belief that the institute itself was doing Nobel-quality work instead of merely buying Nobel-quality window dressing.

Marvin Bower instilled the firm's values system, Ron Daniel perfected its personnel processes and institutionalized the place, and Fred Gluck was the architect of the firm's knowledge culture. Gluck's was probably the most difficult task of the three. After all, he was the one who managed to convince as self-confident a group of people as the world has ever known to reconsider their way of doing business. What's more, he helped keep the firm on its steady trajectory upward: During his six years at the helm, revenues had doubled to $1.5 billion. In 1993 the firm received 50,000 résumés for just 550 new consultant spots.

In the course of his career, Gluck remade himself completely. He took to wearing Brioni suits and started going to Studio 54. (He was single at the time, and there were even rumors of his being seen with Hollywood actress Karen Black.) And while he can be quite rightly credited for focusing the firm on the need to know what it was talking about, he also deserves a share of credit for kick-starting the shift toward a more commercial—and greedier—McKinsey.

Today he lives with his third wife, Linda, in a sprawling mansion in Montecito, California, where, among others, Google chief Eric Schmidt, Al Gore, and Carol Burnett own homes. He calls it Casa Leo Linda, and when you enter the gigantic front door, you pass by the house's ceremonial guards—two statuary lions. Once inside, past a number of rooms where marble seems the main building material, you can cozy up in Gluck's library, where a waiter serves you coffee and croissants. In 2006 Gluck went toe to toe with the actor Rob Lowe, who bought a parcel of land next door for $8.5 million in hopes of building a 10,000-square-foot mansion.[44] Gluck complained that the 24-foot-high fence Lowe proposed for privacy would diminish his ocean views and said the house was disproportionately large, even though Gluck's own house was larger than town regulations allowed. The town's planning commission sided with Lowe;[45] McKinsey influence doesn't extend *everywhere*.

Gluck became vice chairman of the largest engineering firm in the United States—Bechtel Group—after leaving McKinsey. He still consults with the firm on occasion, but he's just as happy schmoozing with his old scientist pals on the West Coast, talking about spaceships and lasers. Or helping his McKinsey friend Kevin Sharer examine the future of new molecules from his board position at Amgen, of which Sharer is CEO. In that way, he is unlike many of his McKinsey peers, for whom McKinsey becomes more important than anything else they've ever done. Not so Gluck: McKinsey did not define him. He is Fred Gluck first and a McKinsey man second. The two intersected for a time, but Fred Gluck came out on the other side. For many others, that separation never happens. This is why, even after McKinsey people have been retired for a decade or more, a scandal at the firm can inflict mortal pain on them. And the next decade provided a few.

8. THE MONEY GRAB

Quantum Shift

Though McKinsey was, by the 1980s, a truly global firm, there was never any doubt about where the power still resided: in New York, in the hands of true-blue American men. That partly changed in 1994 when the partnership elected its first non-Westerner as managing director: Indian-born Rajat Kumar Gupta. He was a naturalized U.S. citizen and had run the Chicago office for four years, but most of his experience had been overseas, including a nine-year stint running Scandinavia. Gupta symbolized how the new McKinsey ethos had finally found its way to the very top—the one that measured its employees not on race, sex, or nationality, but on intellect, achievement, and ambition. (The change was only partial because New York still reigned supreme. Gupta didn't want to move from Chicago but ultimately brought his family east and began working out of 55 East 52nd Street in New York City.)

Gupta also stood for something else: continued expansion. When Fred Gluck handed over the reins, the firm was in twenty-four countries. Over the next nine years, Gupta planted the McKinsey flag in twenty more, including the vital emerging economies of India and mainland China. The firm had fifty-eight offices in 1993. By 2001, nearly the end of Gupta's third term, it was up to eighty-one. Staffing more than doubled, from 3,300 consultants and 425 partners in 1994 to 7,700 consultants and 891 partners in 2001. Revenues nearly *tripled,* from $1.2 billion to $3.4 billion. The alumni rolls swelled to 8,000 names. '"It's a less personal place than it used to be," Nancy Killefer, a senior partner in Washington, D.C., said in 2002. "In the old days, you knew everybody. That's not possible anymore."[1]

McKinsey's growth strategy was dictated, in part, by the diffusion of corporate power. In 1974 the top hundred industrial companies in the United States accounted for 35.8 percent of GDP. By 1998 that figure had fallen to 17.3 percent.[2] It's hard to be in a thousand boardrooms unless you have thousands of consultants. So the push was on to grow.

Gupta stood for one more thing: the end of the firm's ambivalence about making money. One result of that shift was an unrest in the ranks despite the good times. It's not that the firm's finances weren't strong when he took over. The problem, as far as some McKinsey partners were concerned, was that growth had leveled off. After nearly doubling between 1988 and 1992—from $620 million to $1.2 billion—revenues stalled in 1993, while costs continued to rise. For more than a decade, McKinsey's expenses had risen faster than revenues. This was tolerable so long as the latter kept rising. But when revenue growth stalled, something had to be done.

"Because of that flattening, there was a sense that we needed to rein in all the spending on 'knowledge building,'" said a former partner of the firm. A growing minority wondered whether the firm's voluminous databases would prove valuable to anyone in the end save the database companies themselves. And Gupta was clearly the man to put a halt to what he considered to be money-wasting research. In his twenty-one years at the firm, he had contributed a sum total of *zero* articles to McKinsey's knowledge-management system. "He may have said he respected our knowledge building," continued the partner, "but actions speak louder than words." So do the actions of others: Soon after Gupta's election, Alan Kantrow left the firm to join competitor Monitor as its chief knowledge officer. One by one, others involved in Gluck's knowledge-management push left the firm as the Gupta regime went into full swing by turning back the knowledge focus—Partha Bose, Tom Copeland, Roger Ferguson, Nathaniel Foote, Brook Manville, and Bill Matassoni. With what they had achieved, and McKinsey's now-recognized reputation in "knowledge," all were aggressively pursued by competitors, academia, and even government. Ferguson became deputy chairman of the Federal Reserve under Alan Greenspan.

"Normally to get elected, you have to write articles, develop an intellectual capital portfolio, and serve clients," said another former partner. "Gupta didn't do that. He was a bean counter. When it came time to reverse Gluck's $100 million investment in knowledge, he was the easy choice."

In a revealing 1993 piece called "The McKinsey Mystique," *BusinessWeek* writer John Byrne had predicted that the firm would elect its first non-American director, and then he suggested four possible victors: Christian Caspar in Scandinavia, Lukas Muhlemann in Switzerland, Norman Sanson in London, and Herb Henzler in Germany.[3] Don Waite, the godfather of the firm's financial institutions practice in the United States, also threw his hat in the ring. None made the final cut. "Everyone stayed except Sanson, who was one of the most 'values-focused' partners at McKinsey," recalled a former partner of the firm. "He was edged out by Gupta. The firm should have seen at which end of the values spectrum he sat from that move alone." (In a side job, Sanson refereed international rugby matches on BBC TV on the weekends. He is credited with helping put an end to bad behavior on the rugby field.)

"Unfortunately for Don, everyone knew it was time for a non-American," said another McKinsey partner. "And Gupta had the advantage of being both foreign *and* American. Sure, he was an Indian, but he'd been running Chicago. And he was very much like Barack Obama, in a sense. He'd had a lot of 'present' votes in his past—he was there, but not always there, and in that way didn't offend too many people. Did we vote for Gupta? It's more like we voted for the *idea* of Gupta. He also had the advantage of *not* being Herb Henzler."

Rajat Kumar Gupta was born December 2, 1948, in Calcutta, the second of four children. He and his family moved to Delhi in 1953. His father, a journalist fighting for Indian independence, had served time in prison under the British. His mother was the principal of a Montessori school. But both parents had died by the time Gupta was nineteen years old.

After studying mechanical engineering at the famed Indian Institute of Technology Delhi, he was accepted at Harvard Business School and graduated in 1973. Like many HBS graduates, he interviewed for a job at McKinsey—and was summarily rejected. But the resourceful Gupta prevailed on a Harvard professor with McKinsey connections to put in a good word. After a full day of further interviews, Gupta was invited to join McKinsey's New York office as an associate. In 1981 Ron Daniel made him head of the Scandinavia office. Nine years later Gluck made him head of Chicago. Considered by his peers a paragon of humility, Gupta typified the McKinsey ideal during much of his career with the firm—he was content to operate behind the scenes on behalf of clients that ranged from Kraft and Sara Lee to Procter & Gamble. Even though he was one of the most prominent Indian-born executives in the United States, he stayed largely out of public view.

In gaining the top job, Gupta had successfully nurtured an image of himself as a lead-from-behind, quiet type, more Ron Daniel than

Fred Gluck. He told a reporter from the *Chicago Tribune* that the two people he most admired were a nineteenth-century Hindu reformer, Swami Vivekenanda, and Mother Teresa.[4] He sprinkled his speeches with well-known verses from the Bhagavad Gita, the ancient Hindu text. The real differences were less prosaic: Ron Daniel was a well-read intellectual. Fred Gluck was just massive horsepower. Rajat Gupta had a cultivated anti-intellectualism about him that was neither Daniel nor Gluck.

Descriptions of him from partners were rife with cultural clichés. "Rajat has a very Eastern orientation," the late Chicago director Joel Bleeke told the *Tribune*. "He puts a very strong emphasis on wisdom, rather than pure intellect. He understands that wisdom includes intellect as well as other aspects of life. With his Asian background, he understands the softer, emotional sides of people better than Western leaders do."

Richard Ashley, a member of the shareholders committee at the time who followed Gupta as Chicago office head, compared him to the great man himself, at least in part due to what was widely viewed as Gupta's personal leadership style: nonconfrontational yet still grounded in conviction. "Rajat Gupta is the closest person in the firm, by reputation and deed, to Marvin Bower," he said. "Bower brought a steadfast approach that pushed belief in the values of James O. McKinsey. Rajat is the embodiment of the philosophy of Marvin Bower."[5]

That's not exactly how the story went.

Cubic Consulting

In his heyday, Marvin Bower liked to talk of how many of the top 100 companies in the United States McKinsey counted as clients. By the turn of the twenty-first century, the focus had shifted to the entire globe. In 2003 McKinsey claimed 100 of the largest 150 companies on the planet as clients.[6]

After a Firm Strategy Initiative in 1995, Rajat Gupta rolled out a new gimmick: "100 percent cubed." From that point forth, McKinsey endeavored to bring 100 percent of the firm, 100 percent of the time, to 100 percent of the world. It sounds like a vapid marketing spiel, but at the time it served as a useful competitive differentiator for the firm. The competition—be it Boston Consulting Group, Bain, or Monitor—could not make such a claim with a straight face. And clients were clamoring for it.

"The fact is, no company has as many of these smart people as McKinsey does," said Jim Fisher, who worked in the firm's Toronto office from 1968 to 1970. "And even if they did, they couldn't pull them out of the line and assemble them and have them work on this one problem. And even if they could do that, they could never separate the politics of the organization from the work done. The client would never feel like they have a totally dispassionate view. That's worth it. And even if McKinsey isn't always right, they will always be sure that they are right. Sometimes, even that is useful."[7]

By fits and starts, the firm had somehow found its way into an internationality all its own. "Its nerve center sits in New York," the *Sunday Times* wrote in 1997. "Its managing partner works in Chicago. Its Global Institute is in Washington. But its truest address is in the world's capital and industrial centers. It is a United Nations of consulting, with one crucial difference: It works."[8]

"McKinsey always had great conceptual frameworks for analyzing problems," added Fisher. "But what was better was that you could go to a place like Argentina and have market analysis done by people with familiarity with the market—Argentinians—but that had been American-trained. It's astounding to me that they can run a global firm the way that they do. All management consultants are prima donnas who want to solve things their own way with their own conclusions. But McKinsey has an impressive discipline across the globe around how they approach problems, as well as the rigor that they use."[9]

This is a sentiment repeated by many McKinsey consultants with a heritage in the recent past: The fruits of rigorous training and indoctrination meant that McKinsey could gather eight different consultants from eight different cities across the globe, and it would take them just five minutes to get organized around the needs of any project. "It's the equivalent of making machine parts that need no further finishing," explained former partner George Feiger, who went on to run global investment banking at SBC Warburg as well as onshore private banking for UBS. "It was really a miracle, and it took decades to get to that point."[10]

McKinsey was not the largest consulting firm on the planet. Andersen Consulting's nearly $5 billion in 1995 revenues was three times larger than McKinsey's. But McKinsey still occupied the high ground.

Enter the Dragon

No country provides a better showcase for the modern ambition of McKinsey than China. And no consultant better exemplifies that ambition than Gordon Orr. A slim, studious-looking Brit, Orr joined McKinsey in 1986 and was elected to the partnership in 1993. In search of a new challenge, he asked the firm for a transfer to Hong Kong. "My wife and I weren't there for much more than a year when we said, 'This is actually pretty exciting, but if we're serious about this, the great big thing is up there to the north of us. Why don't we think about moving to Beijing and opening the office up there?'"[11]

It's at this point that the admirable efficiency of McKinsey's form of governance came into play. All Orr needed to do was present a brief to the firm's shareholders committee: "Here's what we want to do, here's what we think the opportunity is, and here's how we would go about making it happen." McKinsey's overlords approved the idea, and Orr, along with colleagues Tony Perkins and Josh Cheng, started laying the groundwork for McKinsey's second China outpost. (Consultants Jonathan Woetzel, Ulrich Roeder, and Olivier Kayser had opened an office in Shanghai in 1994.)

As with most new country initiatives, McKinsey was patient with Orr as he went in search of clients. McKinsey purposely doesn't set financial targets for new offices, preferring to let the *reason* for doing something take precedence over short-term expense issues. The push into China was no exception. In 1993, the firm opened offices in Bombay, Cologne, New Delhi, Prague, St. Petersburg, and Warsaw. In 1994, Budapest, Dublin, and Shanghai. In 1995, Jakarta, Johannesburg, and Moscow. In Moscow, the firm used its usual modus operandi to gin up goodwill in the country, doing pro bono work for the Bolshoi Theater as well as the St. Petersburg Hermitage Museum.

By 1996 McKinsey was ready to begin recruiting local Chinese in Beijing. The firm scheduled a recruiting seminar at Tsinghua University. Orr expected twenty or thirty people to show up. The turnout was eight hundred. True to form, McKinsey hired just two of them, one of whom stayed with the firm for almost a decade before becoming CEO of South Beauty, the largest Chinese "restaurant entertainment" company. The other is still with McKinsey and might soon be the firm's first female mainland Chinese director.

Finding new clients wasn't as easy as it had been when the London office was being opened. Orr and his colleagues had to figure out not only which companies had issues that McKinsey could solve, but also those that were willing to be helped. The Chinese business culture wasn't accustomed to paying for anything that wasn't 100 percent tangible.

McKinsey had to make other adjustments in China. Throwing young Harvard MBAs into the fire by making them present to CEOs so soon after being hired wasn't prudent in a hierarchical society that values age and experience over youthful promise. This wasn't a new issue for the firm: In the 1980s, when he was managing director, Ron Daniel had one meeting with the parents of a prospective Japanese recruit in which he had to reassure them that their young son was not being sold into some sort of modern slavery. "Asians venerate age," he explained. "We tend not to."[12]

"Gordon called me up one day and said he wanted to publish the *McKinsey Quarterly* in Chinese," recalled Partha Bose, who was editor in chief of the publication at the time. "We didn't have any foreign-language editions, and I wondered if he was going to be able to sustain a pipeline of new articles. He told me he wanted to use *past articles* that explained the basics of management, so that he could build the practice on a strong foundation. Part of that foundation was going to be translating and making available the best management thinking in Chinese."[13] The conversation led to the launch of the Chinese *Quarterly*.

One of the first successes of the Beijing office was helping four Chinese rice farmers who had decided to get into the bottled-water industry. "They had just bought a bunch of machinery," Orr said. With McKinsey's guidance, the outfit eventually became the number-two bottled-water provider in China, worth $200 million. McKinsey also advised two companies—Ping An Insurance and Legend Computers—that went on to become global players.

McKinsey's success in China hasn't been linear. The firm has had to contend with counterfeit operations that offer "McKinsey Reports" for as low as a hundred dollars. And the early years were very lean. Orr recalled at least one stretch in 1997 when *one* client supported the entire fifty-plus-person Beijing office. Some competitors pulled out of

China when the times got tough—Booz-Allen left, only to return a few years later—but McKinsey hung in there, and its perseverance ultimately paid off. Within ten years, McKinsey had three hundred professionals in China. By 2011 it had eight hundred. The firm also built a Consumer Insights Center in China, to monitor the spending patterns of sixty thousand Chinese consumers and inform McKinsey research about the increasingly important economy, and in 2012 opened the McKinsey China Leadership Institute in Beijing.

A Walk down Wall Street

Back in the United States, McKinsey continued its intimate dealings with the rapidly growing financial sector. The firm's influence ran so deep that it could actually make good on its mandate to confront clients with uncomfortable truths. MacLain "Mac" Stewart, a key figure in McKinsey's financial services practice, had a particular knack for dispensing blunt, unflattering advice to even the most puffed up of Wall Street CEOs. After sitting through a terrible presentation given by Dick Fuld, then beginning his career as CEO of Lehman Brothers, Stewart looked Fuld in the eye and told him that if he wanted to be successful, he'd better hire a speech coach.

In another instance, Stewart dressed down Citicorp chief Sandy Weill, whose meeting style was to say his piece, and then, while others responded, compulsively watch Citi's stock price on his Quotron. In a meeting with Stewart, Weill did just this and then briefly left the office. While he was away, Stewart put a book in front of the screen. When Weill returned and noticed the book, he erupted, asking who had had the temerity to do such a thing. "You're wasting my time," Stewart told him. "That's sending the wrong message." Weill paused, then said, "No one ever told me that before." The engagement moved forward.

Former Federal Reserve chairman Paul Volcker once told a pro-McKinsey dinner companion that there are four signs of an impending bank failure: (1) The bank has "rebranded"; (2) it has built a new headquarters; (3) it has acquired a corporate jet; and (4) McKinsey has been in there. That might not be good news for the bank involved, but it was very good news for McKinsey. The firm had become the consultants of last resort.

McKinsey was pulled in to mediate the battle inside Lazard Frères between chairman Michel David-Weill and deputy chairman Steven Rattner over the question of how the boutique investment bank should govern itself, particularly in divvying power among its three primary offices in New York, London, and Paris. According to journalist William Cohan, in 1998 McKinsey interviewed forty-six of Lazard's partners and helped establish a power-sharing arrangement in the mergers and acquisitions department.[14] The engagement highlighted the respect with which McKinsey was by this point held by its Wall Street clientele—the struggle for control at Lazard was one of the investment world's most Machiavellian dramas, and the idea that McKinsey could help find a way for two of Wall Street's largest egos to find peace was a high compliment indeed. With a McKinsey-aided fix, Lazard went on to strengthen its niche as a boutique M&A advisory power.

There was some criticism of the work at the time, including the suggestion that McKinsey had produced a "camel"—a horse designed by a committee—instead of actually solving Lazard's power-sharing problems. "[We] ended up with this mishmash of a structure that wasn't any better than we already had, really," one Lazard employee told Cohan. Still, the firm helped stop Lazard from splitting at the seams, a real accomplishment for a boutique bank that had been on the verge of doing just that.

A big part of McKinsey's influence in the financial sector was due to its alumni network. In 1996 the firm had well-placed alumni in the management suites of SBC Warburg (George Feiger), Lehman Brothers (John Cecil), HSBC Capital (Steven Green), Swiss Re (Lukas Muhlemann), UBS (Peter Wuffli), Morgan Stanley Dean Witter (Phil Purcell), and Goldman Sachs (Larry Linden).[15] Hamid Biglari left McKinsey in 2001 to join Citicorp. Jay Mandelbaum, until 2012 one of Jamie Dimon's closest advisers at JPMorgan Chase, is an alumnus. Not all of them have had successful runs—Purcell's Morgan Stanley tenure ended in his being deposed in a coup, Muhlemann's post-McKinsey career was a decidedly mixed bag. But that didn't stop boards of directors from going back to the McKinsey talent well again and again.

The firm infiltrated private equity as well. Don Gogel left McKinsey to become CEO of private equity powerhouse Clayton Dubilier. Chuck Ames, also formerly of McKinsey, worked alongside him. Ex-McKinseyite Sir Ronald Cohen was an early player at Apax Partners, one of England's largest private equity shops.

One primary reason that McKinsey has made significant inroads into the financial sphere is that finance is all about the numbers; it takes no stretch of the imagination to conclude that financial problems can submit to McKinsey's style of fact-based analysis. What's more, both consulting and finance tend to attract similar personalities—think MBA Mitt Romney instead of free-ranging "intellectual" Newt Gingrich—and so the two populations find themselves speaking similar problem-solving languages. And once deregulation had all the CEOs in finance looking to acquire or be acquired, they lined up for McKinsey's help in understanding the brand-new competitive landscape. Gupta wasn't part of McKinsey's New York financial institutions mafia, but he, like his predecessors in the corner office, knew to leave it well enough alone—that extended from Lowell Bryan's iron grip on the banking practice to Pete Walker's in the insurance industry.

McKinsey wasn't just in finance, though; it was everywhere. By the late 1990s the CEOs of America West Airlines, American Express, Delta, Dun & Bradstreet, IBM, Levi Strauss, Morgan Stanley, Polaroid, and USG were former McKinseyites.[16] In 1999 *Fortune* ran a story titled "CEO Super Bowl." The story suggested that just as the University of North Carolina "manufactures" basketball stars, and the University of Michigan "cranks out" football stars, so too was there a CEO factory in the country—McKinsey. The network is without a doubt the most powerful the world has ever seen. "You don't realize it until you're gone," IBM chief Lou Gerstner later told another McKinsey partner.

The Value of Values

Gupta initially seemed to grasp the importance of the firm's culture and values. In his first year as boss, he commissioned an internal task force, which aimed to identify what was wrong in the life of the firm's junior partners and what could change. It had impact. Whereas in previous years, the firm's profit sharing was split in the directors' favor—as a group, they received two-thirds of the pool, to principals' third—the task force convinced the shareholders committee to merely divvy the profits proportionally. Gupta also oversaw EAGLE—Exciting Associates for Greater Long-Term Enrichment—proving that a firm addicted to acronyms will always find newer and sillier ones.

Another effort, the Firm Strategy Initiative (FSI) in 1997, showed quite clearly just how rigorous McKinsey consultants can be. The goal of FSI, which they called "the mother of all engagements," was nothing short of a reconsideration of the most basic questions about McKinsey's raison d'être: *To whom should we provide our consulting services? What scope of services should we provide? What kinds of delivery models and fee arrangements should we employ?* A management group of more than six hundred members attended two conferences; sixty partners served on the task force; fifty associates and analysts worked on the project; more than a thousand survey questions were asked; forty "vision" papers were written by partner teams; six progress reports were produced, a total of more than fifteen hundred pages; over a hundred videos were made; more than a hundred and fifty exhibit decks were prepared; and over two hundred speeches were delivered.

One of the main conclusions of FSI was that McKinsey must restrict client engagements to the very top rungs of management. If they allowed their work to slip down to the middle rungs, the consultants reasoned, the money they'd make would come at the expense of their hard-won reputation for being the confidants of CEOs. This was a demonstrative reinforcement of Boweresque values. The FSI also reiterated McKinsey's commitment to loose corporate governance, despite the firm's growing size. This was also true to the firm's tradition of giving consultants the freedom to exercise their entrepreneurial instincts.

At the margins, however, change was creeping in. Usually it had to do with money. One result of FSI was the establishment of new "fee mechanisms" to enable the consultants to work with small but fast-growing companies. In lieu of its customarily high rates, the firm started taking equity in clients, something Marvin Bower had considered unwise. But the dot-com boom was in full flower, and McKinsey wanted a piece of the action. FSI also concluded that the consultants should officially enter the M&A advisory business, where they would compete with investment banks.

Rajat Gupta didn't change the firm all by himself—he needed his partners' assent and he had it. Still, under his watch, McKinsey began to chase top billings in a way it never had before. More than half of the partners had told the FSI that about 20 percent of their work wasn't interesting. And if you're going to be bored, you might as well be making money. Everyone else was. "His first term was very good," said an expartner of the firm. "But I think he took counsel of the wrong people. If you couldn't invoice $1 million from a client by 1997, you were encouraged to drop that client. That was pretty much the minimum."

In the 1990s McKinsey's revenues grew almost four times while the partnership grew by only two and a half. Associate leverage—the measure of associates relative to partners in the firm—grew from two to one to four to one by the end of the decade. McKinsey's partners were wringing more profits from their hardworking associates than ever. And the associates were feeling the pain. Yves Smith, a former McKinsey consultant and prominent blogger, has suggested that McKinsey's turnover reached 30 percent annually in the heat of the boom. That was not only disruptive; it threatened to waste the not insubstantial cost of training young recruits. What good is a shared narrative if people don't stick around to share it?

McKinsey, which had blocked its ears to the siren song of the go-go years in the 1960s, couldn't resist getting caught up in the dot-com frenzy. The shift was at least partly a response to increased turnover at the level of principal. With so much money being made so quickly in Silicon Valley and on Wall Street, McKinsey had to not only raise salaries but also shorten the time to partnership. "Some partners wondered whether the firm was abandoning its value, 'Clients first, firm second, professionals third,'" noted a Harvard Business School study. Short answer: It was.

As for the tradition of working only for the most prestigious companies, well, that too went out the window. In 2003, for example, SHC, Inc., the parent of the dying Spalding sporting goods brand, paid the firm $569,000 for consulting services. A year later it was bankrupt. McKinsey, it seemed, would actually work for anyone with an open checkbook. And it had introduced those new fee mechanisms. In 2001 McKinsey traded its advice for a 12.5 percent stake in a satellite-based advertising company in the convenience-store industry called On-Vance. The firm was later sued for $1.6 million by the bankruptcy trustee of a busted OnVance under the logic that McKinsey wasn't a creditor but an insider. Billing rates came down as well: In 2001 an industry researcher made this claim:" You can hire McKinsey for what it would have cost you to hire A.T. Kearney a year ago."[17]

Despite Marvin Bower's hope that it wouldn't happen, the envy of corporate (and Wall Street) cash overtook McKinsey consultants in the thick of the late 1990s dot-com boom, a time during which CEO pay was skyrocketing. The facilitators of CEO-ism—the consultants, lawyers, and bankers—lost their willingness to be paid the way professionals had historically been paid. It's extremely difficult for doctors to make more than $1 million a year. But by generally targeting only the largest of corporations, consultants have figured out how to secure ever-larger paychecks for themselves. What's a $10 million fee to a corporation with $2 trillion in assets? At one point Citigroup had eight active teams from McKinsey running around inside its offices.

If McKinsey's professional idealism had been attractive to MBAs in previous years, its more aggressive commercial orientation hardly slowed the flow of job applications. "Never underestimate the lemming-express effect that obtains among students at 'top' business schools and colleagues," wrote author Walter Kiechel. "You compete to get into the most prestigious college. Then you compete to get into the top-ranked business school. After you've learned and displayed so much independence of mind, what's left but to compete to be hired by the employer all your peers were clamoring to join?"[18]

9. BAD ADVICE

Rajat Gupta achieved a lot as the eighth managing director of McKinsey. He successfully diversified the firm's hiring, more than doubling the number of elite schools from which the firm recruited, from seven to twenty, as well as broadening the kind of applicant, including continuing and expanding the push to bring in PhDs as well as MBAs. He helped McKinsey gain a step on most of the corporate world in the outsourcing boom, not only counseling its clients to take advantage of a networked world but doing so itself. The firm's own number-crunching Knowledge Center in New Delhi brought labor costs down while also serving as a model for outsourcing to its clients.[1] Gupta's protégé Anil Kumar headed the effort.

And even as the firm had lowered some of its standards in search of growth, it hadn't taken the final money-hungry leap—selling shares to the public—a decision that positioned it to correct course far more effectively than it might otherwise have done with angry shareholders breathing down its neck. "This is a knowledge-intensive business," Gupta said in 2005, "not a capital-intensive one."[2]

Still, by late 2002, the firm wasn't feeling very good about itself. The consultants wondered whether the Gupta-led expansion had cost them too much in terms of culture and values. Enough wondered so in interviews with *BusinessWeek* writer John Byrne in a wide-ranging 2002 feature on the firm that one of Gupta's last moves as managing director was to push the firm's head of marketing and public affairs, Javier Perez, out the door as a result of the picture of poor morale painted by Byrne.

Ron Daniel had once told a partners conference that he thought the firm could sustain maximum growth of about 10 percent a year while still being able to absorb its people effectively. Gupta threw that out the window and chased an even faster rate of expansion of nearly 20 percent. Many partners, though, pointed out that he did it with their acquiescence. "Rajat made us all rich," said one.

That's fine for those who had made the money but weak gruel for those who had already left but still felt that at least part of their reputation depended on McKinsey's. "The place evolved from a very elite professional services firm to kind of a large factory that produced consulting projects," said one senior partner who left during Gupta's tenure.

McKinsey is not a command-and-control organization. The managing director does not manage by diktat. He must persuade. That said, he does get to choose committee leaders, office managers, and more. And on the margin, Rajat Gupta chose people who were more economically driven than in years past. That's how you move a firm like McKinsey. If you are the managing director for nine years, which Gupta was, every single person who is a junior partner got elected on your watch, as well as more than 50 percent of the senior partners. That allows you to change the character of an organization, and that's what Rajat Gupta did. And the new character of McKinsey suddenly seemed one that was capable of making a number of seriously questionable decisions—about which clients it got close to and what it advised those clients to do.

Sleeping in Enron's Bed

The most infamous McKinsey client of the Gupta era was Enron, the natural-gas-trading powerhouse that, when it imploded in 2001, destroyed not only itself but also Arthur Andersen, one of the Big Six accounting firms. Miraculously, though McKinsey was earning some $10 million a year in fees from Enron at the peak, it emerged unscathed. The whole ordeal nevertheless revealed quite a bit about the less attractive elements of the consulting business.

Jeff Skilling, one of the chief Enron villains, was himself a McKinsey alum. He joined the consulting firm in 1979 and quickly earned a reputation for an oversize ego. "Skilling worked for me indirectly for a short period of time," recalled Tom Peters. "God knows, he was intellectually arrogant in a way that beggars the imagination."[3] If you didn't believe Peters, you could ask Skilling himself; he once told *BusinessWeek* that he had "never not been successful at work or business, ever."

He was a standout, to be sure. After starting his career in Dallas, he moved to the Houston office six months later, where he was just the third employee. In five years he made principal, and he was elected director five years after that. He'd certainly found his intellectual home. "It was difficult to disagree with Jeff because he would elevate the disagreement to an intellectual disagreement, and it was hard to outsmart him," a former McKinsey partner said.[4]

John Sawhill, who was head of the firm's energy practice at the time, asked Skilling to help McKinsey client Enron, the product of a merger between Houston Natural Gas and Omaha-based InterNorth, decide whether it ought to move its headquarters from Omaha to Houston. Skilling refused to work on the project, knowing that whatever he recommended would make him an enemy of one faction within the company. "How do you win this one, John? How do you decide this? I want nothing to do with it," he said.[5]

A typical young McKinseyite would never be able to get away with turning down an assignment. But Skilling was anything but typical. He was already a star at the firm, and Sawhill didn't make an issue of it, instead pushing the firm's Washington office to help Enron make the call. (Houston was the final answer.) And Skilling, who eventually took Sawhill's place as head of the firm's worldwide energy practice, continued to advise Enron; his work included an assignment in the late 1980s on how to use derivative contracts to "smooth" the energy company's earnings.[6]

The singular insight of Skilling's McKinsey career was the one that launched Enron into the stratosphere. As the natural gas industry grappled with deregulation and its attendant uncertainty, the largest players moved from predominantly long-term contracts to using the so-called spot market for 75 percent of gas trading. The change left both buyers and sellers vulnerable to rapid swings in the price of gas. Skilling suggested Enron step into the breach, creating a "gas bank" to buy gas from producers and sell it to customers, capturing the spread between the two. Before Skilling's revelation, Enron had been a humdrum operator of gas pipelines. With the gas bank, he had helped turn it into a financial wheeler-dealer.[7]

"The concept was pure intellectually," Skilling later said, sounding *very* McKinsey-like. When he presented the idea to Enron's top twenty-five executives in 1987, he used just a single slide—also *very* McKinsey-like.[8] In large part due to his success with Enron, Skilling was elected a director at McKinsey in the summer of 1989. That December, Enron president Rich Kinder asked him to join Enron. At first he demurred, but he later reconsidered. This was his chance to go big, to show he could *do,* and not just *tell*. He jumped ship and had soon replaced Kinder as president of Enron.

Enron chief financial officer Andy Fastow was flabbergasted at the move. "You walked away from McKinsey?" he asked Skilling. "I did," the latter replied. "Why?" "Hey," Skilling replied. "How often do you get a chance to change the world?"[9]

Skilling turned Enron into a new economy darling that darted from market to market with blazing speed. It became the most celebrated company in the country, with revenues topping $60 billion in 2000. As Bethany McLean and Peter Elkind pointed out in *The Smartest Guys in the Room,* Enron was beloved by all: "*Fortune* magazine named it 'America's most innovative company' six years running. Washington luminaries like Henry Kissinger and James Baker were on its lobbying payroll. Nobel Laureate Nelson Mandela came to Houston to receive the Enron Prize. The president of the United States called Enron chairman Kenneth Lay 'Kenny Boy.'"[10]

Skilling took the McKinsey ethos with him to Enron. A description of him by McLean and Elkind reads like that of a typical McKinseyite: "He could process information and conceptualize new ideas with blazing speed. He could instantly simplify highly complex issues into a sparkling, compelling image. And he presented his ideas with a certainty that bordered on arrogance and brooked no dissent. He used his brainpower not just to persuade, but to intimidate. . . . But he also had qualities that were disastrous for someone running a big company. For all his brilliance, Skilling had dangerous blind spots. His management skills were appalling, in large part because he didn't really understand people. He expected people to behave according to the imperatives of pure intellectual logic, but of course nobody does that. . . . He was often too slow—even unwilling—to recognize when the reality didn't match the theory. Over time his arrogance hardened, and he became so sure that he was the smartest guy in the room that anyone who disagreed with him was summarily dismissed as just not bright enough to 'get it.'"[11]

Skilling paid homage to his former employer on countless occasions, including one time when he decried Wall Street's value system to *BusinessWeek*. "Given the financial churning many investment banks do, I'm not sure I'd feel real good about it when I went home at night," he said. "[McKinsey] has its values in the right place. You feel like you're doing God's work when you're there."[12] He spoke of Enron in similarly reverential terms. "If you walk the halls here, people have a mission," he said. "The mission is we're on the side of angels. We're taking on the entrenched monopolies. In every business we've been in, we're the good guys."[13] He also took time out of an extremely busy schedule to have more than twenty meetings with McKinsey partners Ron Hulme and Suzanne Nimocks between May 2000 and December 2001—this while also sitting for nearly twenty photo shoots for publications as varied as *Industry Standard* and *Architectural Digest*.[14]

Skilling had spent twenty-one years at McKinsey. Like many who'd left before him, he kept the connection strong. He tried unsuccessfully to lure McKinsey consultant Ron Hulme to come join him as Enron's chief financial officer, though that hardly damaged his relationship with his old firm. Enron remained the Houston office's most important—and lucrative—client. Hulme, who took over Skilling's role heading the consulting firm's energy practice, became a star in his own right. "Despite his young age, [Hulme] had a tremendously high standing and power that derived from the Enron relationship," a former McKinseyite told *BusinessWeek* in 2002.[15] At one point, his name was bandied about as a potential successor to Gupta.

McKinsey didn't just cash Enron's checks; it fully believed in the cult and helped spread the gospel, celebrating the company's "petropreneurs." As John Byrne pointed out in *BusinessWeek*, McKinsey was knee-deep with Enron in pretty much everything that made the firm distinctive, "[stamping its] imprimatur on many of Enron's strategies and practices, helping to position the energy giant as a corporate innovator worthy of emulation."[16]

In just six years, the *McKinsey Quarterly* mentioned Enron 127 times. Here's how much McKinsey loved Enron.

One: The firm endorsed Enron's asset-light strategy. In a 1997 edition of the *Quarterly,* consultants wrote that "Enron was not distinctive at building and operating power stations, but it didn't matter; these skills could be contracted out. Rather, it was good at negotiating contracts, financing, and government guarantee—precisely the skills that distinguished successful players."

Two: The firm endorsed Enron's "loose-tight" culture. Or, more precisely, McKinsey endorsed Enron's use of a term that came straight out of *In Search of Excellence*. In a 1998 *Quarterly,* the consultants peripherally praised Enron's culture of "[allowing executives] to make decisions without seeking constant approval from above; a clear link between daily activities and business results (even if not a P&L); something new to work on as often as possible."

Three: The firm endorsed Enron's use of off–balance-sheet financing. In that same 1997 *Quarterly,* the consultants wrote that "the deployment of off–balance-sheet funds using institutional investment money fostered [Enron's] securitization skills and granted it access to capital at below the hurdle rates of major oil companies." McKinsey heavyweight Lowell Bryan—godfather of the firm's financial institutions practice—put it another way: "Securitization's potential is great because it removes capital and balance sheets as constraints on growth."

Four: The firm endorsed Enron's approach to "atomization." In a 2001 *Quarterly,* the consultants wrote: "Enron has built a reputation as one of the world's most innovative companies by attacking and atomizing traditional industry structures—first in natural gas and later in such diverse businesses as electric power, Internet bandwidth, and pulp and paper. In each case, Enron focused on the business sliver of intermediation while avoiding the incumbency problems created by a large asset base and vertical integration."

As critics of Enron emerged and started to question the firm's accounting methods, McKinsey issued ever more ringing endorsements. As far as McKinsey was concerned, "[deal-making] skills have become more important than scale or scope, and strategic insight and foresight more important than structural position."[17] It's a statement that is baffling in its implication—that what matters is not what you actually *are,* but what you *want to be*. At Enron, the concept had finally trumped reality. This was nothing short of a McKinsey consultant's dream result.

Nearly all of Enron's allegedly innovative approaches ended up playing a significant role in the firm's collapse. Being asset-light left Enron with unsustainable debts. Being loose-tight excused a laissez-faire culture in which executives acted without oversight. Off-balance-sheet financing turned out to be a way to deceive investors and the IRS.

Enron was a transformational player in the natural gas industry. It was successful because it was a first mover in the newly deregulated field of energy trading. When Enron tried to replicate that success in other markets—broadband, weather, even advertising—it failed utterly, despite cheerleading from McKinsey. (At one point the consultants predicted that Enron would control 50 percent of the video-on-demand market.)[18]

Enron used a technique similar to McKinsey's "'up-or-out"—except under Skilling it was "rank and yank." The churn of executives in the company left it with little of the accountability that comes with continuity. Skilling's McKinsey-like lack of interest in actual execution also meant that no one at the top was focused on whether the firm could actually pull off its grand visions as it lurched from one new business idea to the next. What's more, a 2004 survey of human resource professionals reported that "forced ranking" had resulted in "lower production, skepticism, damaged morale, and reduced collaboration." Up-or-out might work for McKinsey, but the implicit social Darwinism sowed chaos both at Enron and elsewhere.[19]

"It was a given, of course, that [Skilling] was brilliant and that he could get to the essence of an issue faster than anybody," wrote McLean and Elkind in *Smartest Guys*. "But once he felt he understood the strategy, he lost interest. Execution bored him. 'Just do it!' he'd tell his subordinates with a dismissive wave of his hand. 'Just get it done!' The details were irrelevant."

Under Skilling, Enron even departed from lessons McKinsey had itself taught other clients long before. For example, Enron followed the unwise practice of paying bonuses based on forecasted profits, not actual cash flows, a system that posed a problem remarkably similar to the R&D issues Gluck and his colleagues had solved at Northern Electric years earlier. In short: You can *forecast* anything. Delivering *actual* results is a different story. The emphasis on forecasts also neutralized Enron's so-called risk-management group, which became a shrinking violet in the face of ever more outrageous estimates. The utter failure of the risk managers stood as the most egregious of its type for nearly a decade, until Wall Street's own risk-management divisions showed their inadequacy in the face of the profits offered by the real estate boom—another crisis, it should be noted, that was in large part due to the obfuscations of off–balance-sheet financing and securitization.

One former McKinsey partner remembered attending a partners conference in Barcelona on October 11, 2000. Two things stuck out in his mind. The first was that ex-McKinseyite Lukas Muhlemann, who by that point was CEO of Credit Suisse, stayed only for cocktails before jetting out again. The idea that he was too important to eat dinner with his former colleagues enraged them. The other thing: Jeff Skilling's presentation on how he had turned an energy company into a financial company. "All anyone was talking about was how dazzling Skilling was," said the ex-partner. "The analytics he showed! Everyone was having little orgasms in the elevator!"

Enron's success was McKinsey's success. More precisely, *Skilling's* success was McKinsey's success. By the end, Enron was spending upwards of $750 million a year on a combination of consultants and other professional services.[20] It was as if the consultants had burrowed inside the place and were ripping its guts out. The shock came only at the very end, and it was revealed that there *were no guts left*. What had once been a powerful and real competitor in the natural gas business had been turned into little more than a facade.

Ultimately, it was Skilling's disavowal of hard assets in favor of trading that doomed the enterprise. "All that trading and marketing is wonderful," said a former Enron executive, "but if you're going to be in the energy business, sooner or later you need to be turning on a generator or producing gas or oil." What Skilling had created was a trading firm. And because his marketing had also been top-shelf, the pressures became immense. Goldman Sachs, the longtime darling of the financial services community, usually traded for sixteen or seventeen times earnings. At the height of its glory—and despite being in pretty much the same business as Goldman—Enron was trading for *sixty* times earnings. When the opportunities in gas trading ran out and the new endeavors in broadband and weather failed to pan out, there were two choices for Enron: Dial back the market's expectations or do something to keep the fiction going. Skilling and Enron CFO Andy Fastow chose the latter route and engaged in outright accounting fraud.

The end came swiftly and brutally. In early 2001 short-seller Jim Chanos started sounding the alarm that something was amiss with Enron's accounting. The *Wall Street Journal* was soon on the case. After years of praising the company, *Fortune* jumped in with its own skeptical analysis. Skilling suddenly retired that August. And then the roof fell in, as much of the company's financial success was revealed as nothing more than accounting fraud of the most basic kind. Using so-called special purpose vehicles, the company had pretended to be far less indebted than it actually was. Enron's balance sheet at the end showed debts of $13 billion. Add in the off-balance-sheet liabilities, though, and the total nearly tripled, to $38 billion. The collapse of the firm was the largest bankruptcy in U.S. history at the time. And McKinsey's Houston office saw its revenues fall off a cliff.

• • •

The whole episode raised three very important questions. First, did McKinsey stray from its core values by effectively hyping Enron during the fraudulent rise? Second, was the firm liable for any of Enron's misdeeds? And third, would other clients care? The short answers: Yes, No, and No.

"Did we push hard enough?" asked one former partner. "There is evidence from McKinsey partners saying, 'This is not going right.' Did McKinsey stop it? No. Writing memos is not enough. So it did damage us. On the other hand, the liquidation value of Enron was still $12 billion. It was a great business that just got out of hand."

BusinessWeek went so far as to suggest that McKinsey had deliberately turned a "blind eye to signs of trouble" in order to perpetuate the lucrative relationship.[21] It was also perpetuating McKinsey's self-image as the cutting-edge intellectuals of the corporate suite. McKinsey partner Richard Foster's 2001 book, *Creative Destruction,* was nothing short of a big wet kiss to Enron's way of doing business. It was also a mere repackaging of economist Joseph Schumpeter's own work on the strengths of capitalism a half century before, but with a crucial twist: It was celebrating the worst instincts of laissez-faire capitalism, not the best.

The War for Talent, a 2001 book by McKinsey consultants Ed

Michaels, Helen Handfield-Jones, and Beth Axelrod (now head of HR at eBay), might have been an even wetter kiss for Enron than *Creative Destruction*. The book set off a worldwide craze for a raft of flimsy ideas, many of which were based on simple observation of Skilling's management style and practices, a large part of which had come out of McKinsey itself. (This was indeed the snake eating its own tail.)

An important part of the whole talent mind-set was the dissemination of McKinsey's cutthroat personnel policy to any companies that wanted to claim they cared about winning. Its advice: Identify your bottom 10 percent or 25 percent or 33 percent, and get rid of them as soon as possible. This was up-or-out writ large, the extension of a philosophy that had worked well enough for McKinsey into other companies in which such a system might not be such a great idea. It also provided convenient cover for layoffs, as a ready-made explanation for massive turnover even in the best of times. It simultaneously provided a quasi-academic foundation for defending the absurd levels of compensation the top 1 percent was paying itself for doing the same thing it had been doing all along.

The War for Talent was perhaps the most dangerous book to come out of McKinsey other than *Race for the World*—by Lowell Bryan, Jane Fraser, Jeremy Oppenheim, and Wilheim Rall—a manifesto for deregulation and a celebration of the likes of Citigroup that helped usher in a large financial crisis. It also contained, as McKinsey had long been wont to propagate, a regurgitation of the firm's own internal structure recast as the business model of the future. Mimic McKinsey, the inevitable conclusion went, and you would be celebrated, just as Enron was.

During McKinsey's nearly eighteen-year relationship with Enron, the consultants worked on over twenty different projects, including formulating pricing and strategy for new products, advising on M&A, and doing preparatory work on entering new markets, including Enron's much-vaunted broadband trading platform.[22] One former Enron executive later remarked that the consultants were "all over the place." At any point, there were between five and twenty McKinsey consultants working out of Enron's offices, and Richard Foster, a director, had attended six of the company's board meetings in the year leading up to its collapse.[23] In those meetings, Andy Fastow had laid out the off–balance-sheet arrangements that eventually bankrupted Enron. That same executive claimed he was "ordered" to check with McKinsey when making an investment in a gas transmission business, but McKinsey denied any role in actual decision making or that it acted as a review body of any sort.[24]

"In all the work we did with Enron, we did not do anything that is related to financial structuring or disclosure or any of the issues that got them in trouble," Rajat Gupta told *BusinessWeek* in the wake of the scandal. That was not entirely true. Whether or not McKinsey actually worked on Enron's off–balance-sheet financings, the firm was nevertheless enthusiastically applauding such pracrices in its own writings.

"We stand by all the work we did," Gupta said. "Beyond that, we can only empathize with the trouble they are going through. It's a sad thing to see."[25] And then he delivered the age-old dodge: "[McKinsey only advises] clients on their strategy. *They* are responsible for what action they take."[26]

The courts (and plaintiffs in lawsuits) appeared to take that in stride. McKinsey was never named as a civil or criminal defendant, nor were any of its employees asked to testify in congressional hearings.[27] That shocked many industry observers. "I'm surprised that they haven't been subpoenaed as a witness, at least," Wayne E. Cooper, CEO of Kennedy Information, a research and publishing firm, told reporter John Byrne. "There was so much smoke coming out of the Andersen smoking gun that all the firefighters went after that one. McKinsey was lucky. They dodged a bullet."[28] Luck, though, may have had nothing to do with it: For a firm as large as it is, and with such extensive global business, McKinsey has been party to lawsuits a remarkably small number of times. The reason seems an obvious one: Sue McKinsey, and lose access to the firm. A few ex-employees and a few bankruptcy lawyers have sued the firm, but McKinsey has rarely found itself on the losing end of a scandalous or expensive lawsuit.

Despite the fact that Ron Hulme ran the Enron relationship, Rajat Gupta protected him. "Ron was his blue-eyed boy," said one former McKinsey partner. Dick Foster, on the other hand, was hung out to dry and shoved out of the firm after a highly successful and inspiring thirty-year career. Foster had built the firm's chemical practice as well as its pharmaceutical practice. He'd maintained Johnson & Johnson as a client for more than two decades. His 1986 book, *Innovation: The Attacker's Advantage,* is considered one of the most influential on the topic. But the New York mafia decided that he was to be the fall guy.

"We were adamant that we had nothing to do with any criminality," said a former partner. "The business model was successful and then it wasn't. That said, a lot of the mud did stick to McKinsey, and deservedly so. We may say publicly that we don't take credit for our work, but when our clients do well, we do take credit for it."

Enron was, briefly, a terrible experience for the firm. Both the technology practice and the Houston office suffered. Most of the partners involved left the firm. (Most, but not all. Enron broke in 2001; Suzanne Nimocks stayed on at McKinsey for almost a decade, despite playing an extremely intimate role in the Enron relationship, perhaps even more than did Hulme.)

But when McKinsey tries to argue that Enron was an isolated case, it is right. Even if Andersen suffered an immediate implosion due to criminal behavior on the part of some of its partners, there was no reason for the Enron work to taint the entire McKinsey enterprise—unless McKinsey had been associated with those crimes, and it wasn't.

The consultants were merely giving advice, the same thing they have always done.

In July 2002, *BusinessWeek* ran a scathing cover story by John Byrne about McKinsey and Enron. But aside from that, the biggest public relations problem was that the business media just ignored McKinsey for a while. In the two years leading up to Enron's collapse, McKinsey had been cited eighty-six times in the business press, and twenty-five of the citations were quotes from McKinsey experts. In the two years after the scandal, total citations fell to fifty-six, with just seventeen expert quotes. But even that was short-lived pain: By 2005 the number of McKinsey mentions in *BusinessWeek* had returned to pre-Enron levels.[29]

McKinsey consultants even showed defiance in the face of all the criticism. When they were offered a chance to remove any of their favorable Enron citations from the company's website, not a single consultant did so.[30] The most noticeable change in the McKinsey culture—possibly the only one—was a pronounced increase in papers and studies produced on the issue of effective corporate governance.[31]

"The major barrier to an Enron-like scandal damaging the reputation of the consulting industry at large is that the selection and management of consultants is seen, by clients, to be their responsibility," analyst Fiona Czerniawska wrote in her 2002 report, "Consulting on the Brink."[32] There was that "perfect business" thing again: You're right when you're right, and they're wrong when you're wrong. As far as the outside world was concerned, McKinsey could do no wrong. "Like children, they are not perceived to be ultimately responsible for their actions," wrote Lewis Pinault in *Consulting Demons*.[33]

The official McKinsey line of defense boiled down to this: that its consultants, along with everyone else, were just dupes. They had no idea what was *really* going on at one of their largest clients. They were not the smartest guys in *that* room.

A study by Swedish academic Lars Engwall showed that in the decade before the Enron collapse, the firm dispensed similar advice to Swedish banks.[34] Acting partly on guidance from their consultants, Swedish banks reduced the number of people engaged in auditing and review by 12 percent between 1983 and 1990, while increasing the number focused on marketing and selling by 65 percent. The emphasis, clearly, was on market share and growth instead of prudent balance-sheet control. By 1992, after an orgy of speculative investment—a large part of which was in real estate—the Swedish banking industry blew up, causing a full-scale financial crisis. Fortunately for the world, Sweden is a small country and there was no contagion. McKinsey too was unharmed. In fact, it was one of the firms called in to help the banks untangle themselves. And who was running McKinsey's Scandinavian operation at the time? Rajat Gupta.

The Enron debacle had a similar perverse result for McKinsey. Among other things, it helped spur the creation of the Sarbanes-Oxley Act, which put executives and boards of directors more squarely in the gun sights of prosecutors. Whom have those boards hired to help shield themselves from liability? Consultants, of course. McKinsey's failures at Enron contributed, in a roundabout way, to its continuing success.

More Missteps

Enron wasn't the only blowup of the Rajat Gupta era. In its quest for growth and profits, the firm not only took on clients it wouldn't have considered in decades past but also found itself on the defensive for giving fundamentally flawed advice.

McKinsey, for example, was one of the primary advocates of Swiss bank takeovers of American financial institutions, such as the acquisition by Credit Suisse of New York investment banks First Boston and Donaldson, Lukfin & Jenrette. "It was a particularly bad strategy," admitted one Swiss banking expert. "The Swiss banks lost a lot of money on those purchases. Interestingly, too, they started trying to make all the banks look the same. McKinsey only had one model for a bank, so it all started converging."

Lowell Bryan, the firm's financial institutions guru, had predicted that investment banking was due for a secular decline in the mid-1990s, and banks were rushing to consolidate—in richly priced deals—to prepare for the downturn. When investment banking remained buoyant, the Swiss companies found themselves at a disadvantage as they contended with expensive integrations of new properties they didn't need. Lukas Muhlemann, the former head of McKinsey's Swiss office, was running Credit Suisse when it bought DLJ. Ex-McKinseyite Peter Wuffli ran UBS during much of the same decade.

The firm's advice even bordered on the preposterous. In 1995 McKinsey advised JP Morgan that its competitive troubles could be solved by getting out of the lending business. The consultants said this *to a bank*. "It was like telling McDonald's to stop making hamburgers," said a former executive of the client. Yet the bank—headed at the time by Sandy Warner—at least partly followed the consultants' advice and dialed back on lending. Smelling opportunity, Chase Manhattan's Jimmy Lee cranked his own bank's corporate lending into high gear. When JP Morgan floundered, Chase Manhattan swooped in and bought it in 2000.

McKinsey was also on the scene when Time Warner completed its notorious merger with AOL that same year. "They traded half of Time Warner for a box of air," exclaimed a rival consultant. Just over a year later, the consultants earned $9 million as advisers to then–Hewlett-Packard CEO Carly Fiorina in her quixotic acquisition of

Compaq that eventually cost Fiorina her job and brought the technology firm to its knees. These were not merely bad judgment calls; they were two of the most disastrous deals of the era.

The firm served as an adviser to Kmart from 1994 through 2000, a period during which the once-iconic retailer got thoroughly waxed by Walmart. The consultants' big idea at the time was selling groceries. It wasn't necessarily stupid—Walmart eventually moved into groceries and did extremely well—but Kmart just didn't have the expertise to pull it off. Ex-CEO Joseph Antonini, who stepped down in 1995, has kept McKinsey's code of *omertà,* and he won't even talk about the consultants' advice. Antonini's successor, Charles Conway, worked with the consultants for a time: McKinsey played a large part in BlueLight.com, meant to be Kmart's triumphant Internet land grab, but a planned initial public offering never happened.[35] Conway eventually disagreed with the consultants over strategy, and they parted ways in 2000, shortly before the company weakened further.

McKinsey also played an intimate part in a deal that was eventually seen as one of the signature M&A blunders leading up to the 2008 financial panic. In 2006 the relatively conservative, healthy Wachovia Corporation paid a whopping $25.5 billion for Golden West Financial, a leading subprime lender. "McKinsey was Wachovia's house consultant," said a rival, who estimated that the firm made at least $50 million from the relationship. "[Wachovia CEO Ken] Thompson wouldn't have made a big move without McKinsey." And no wonder: Peter Sidebottom, the former head of McKinsey's Charlotte office, was at that point head of planning and strategic initiatives at Wachovia, then the nation's fourth-largest bank.

Edward Crutchfield, Thompson's predecessor at Wachovia, had once compared the mortgage business to crossing five lanes of traffic to pick up a nickel. Thompson thought otherwise. Four years later,

Wachovia collapsed under Golden West's toxic book of adjustable-rate mortgages and was forced to sell out to Wells Fargo. Does McKinsey bear responsibility? No. Thompson pulled the trigger. But McKinsey certainly didn't convince him not to make the deal.

Flying Blind and Driving Without a Net

In 1993, after a possible joint venture with Scandinavian Airline Systems (SAS), KLM Royal Dutch Airlines, and Austrian Airlines had fallen apart, Swissair found itself in a jam and sought out McKinsey to help come up with a new plan. The consultants offered two-pronged advice. First, they advised the Swiss company to expand vertically, by buying minority stakes in smaller European airlines. Second, the airline should expand horizontally into aviation services: food, maintenance, and the like.

McKinsey had predicted that in the future, airlines would fall into one of three categories—network managers, capacity providers, and service providers. The sweet spot was to be the network manager, the airline that controlled a hub, and could use marketing and cost management to wring profits not only out of its own operations, but also out of those of the capacity providers drawn to the hub.[36]

So in 1995 Swissair restructured into four new divisions—SAirLines, SAirLogistics, SAirServices, and SAirRelations. By 1997 the nonpassenger businesses accounted for 60 percent of group revenues of $7.6 billion, up from just 24 percent in 1990. That year, McKinsey proposed to Swissair a multipartnership plan known as the "hunter" strategy—a Swissair-led equity-based alliance with an ultimate goal of 20 percent market share in Europe. CEO Philippe Bruggisser began buying equity stakes in other carriers pell-mell, including Austrian

Airlines; AOM, Air Liberté, and Air Littoral of France; charter carrier LTU of Germany; LOT (Polish Airlines); and South African Airlines.

On paper, it all looked perfect. There was just one problem: The real world intervened. A spike in oil prices in 1999 and 2000 slaughtered the entire airline industry. McKinsey was brought in to estimate the costs of Swissair's financing commitments to its minority investments. The estimates: between SFr 3.25 billion and SFr 4.45 billion. The board abandoned the hunter strategy and fired Bruggisser. In March 2001, nine of the board's ten members announced that they too would resign. By midyear, the company's balance sheet was 5 percent equity and 95 percent debt; the total debt was a staggering SFr 17 billion. By October, the airline was bankrupt.

McKinsey has a compelling case when it suggests the failure was not of strategy but of execution. With the exception of LOT, none of the acquired stakes were in target markets identified by McKinsey.[37] What's more, the consultants had suggested equity stakes of 10 to 30 percent; but with one exception, every single investment made by Bruggisser had been in excess of 30 percent, all the way up to 49 percent. McKinsey had suggested a mere $194 million in investments in alliance partners; Bruggisser's shopping spree had totaled $3.4 billion. Without operating control of the more poorly performing airlines, Swissair had no ability to attempt any turnaround. In 2000 McKinsey made a presentation—code-named "Shield"—that was an effort to alert the board and management of Swissair that there was a crisis at hand. It was ignored.

The blame for destroying the extremely valuable Swissair brand that had taken decades to build belongs chiefly to Bruggisser and his management team, no doubt about it. But just as with Enron, nobody involved in such an epic destruction of value should be allowed to escape without some reputational damage. Regardless of Bruggisser's profligacy, the acquisitive strategy, for one, would have run into trouble. The Swiss media certainly weren't willing to let McKinsey off the hook. The firm was pilloried in the press, and the rest of McKinsey's business in Switzerland nose-dived. Swissair's assets were absorbed by Lufthansa in 2005 and a national icon ceased to be.

As the accusations mounted, McKinsey offered little or no public defense. "The Swissair experience was unfair to McKinsey," said former managing director Ian Davis. "That's where we learned that there are certain situations where if you don't talk about your clients and the work you did, you become the whipping boy for everyone. That is something we debate."[38]

McKinsey's historians have this to say about Swissair. "Fortunately, while the failure sent shockwaves through the [firm], the impact on clients outside Switzerland was negligible. Other European airlines continued to work with McKinsey. As with similar crises . . . in the years before, the reputational damage was contained within national borders."[39]

Still, the entire episode showed something of the McKinsey man's ruthlessness. Whereas Swissair had kept McKinsey on as an adviser through the depth of its troubles, when former McKinsey consultant Lukas Muhlemann took the reins at Credit Suisse, he essentially shut the struggling airline off from the bank's lifeline, despite his having been involved in the Swissair strategy from the get-go.

• • •

When you're in the business of predicting the future, it's not a crime to be wrong. McKinsey may have steered Swissair right into a storm, but such advice isn't shameful, it's merely bad advice. On the other hand, the work McKinsey did for the insurance giant Allstate in the mid-1990s stands among the most questionable it has ever done for a client.

Allstate management initially brought in McKinsey to help improve "efficiency," which basically meant reducing the amount it paid out in claims. The insurer, known by its slogan "You're in Good Hands with Allstate," began ratcheting down payments to policyholders in 1996. The results were dramatic: In 1987 the insurer had paid 71 percent of its premium income to claimants. In 2006 that proportion was just 48 percent. Operating income rose thirtyfold as a result, the stock more than quadrupled, and company executives paid themselves extravagantly. Edward Liddy, who was chief operating officer of Allstate and then later CEO, made a fortune as a result of Allstate's skyrocketing stock price, pulling down $54 million in compensation between 2001 and 2005 alone. (It's no wonder that when he was brought in as CEO of AIG in 2008, one of the first things he did was hire McKinsey. His successor, Robert Benmosche, showed the consultants the door.)

New Mexico attorney David Berardinelli sued Allstate on behalf of one of its policyholders and subsequently became embroiled in a multiyear lawsuit that forced Allstate to release what became known as "the McKinsey documents." One McKinsey slide advising Allstate to take a more combative stance with claimants had the title "From Good Hands to Boxing Gloves," a phrase Berardinelli later used as the title of a book. An industry that once prided itself on helping people in need had become just another executive money grab, aided and abetted by its fancy consultants.

Another slide produced in court proceedings against Allstate was called "Alligator One" and had the caption "Sit and Wait," which suggested that payments to claimants be stalled for as long as possible so that they might accept a lowball settlement. Another, titled "McKinsey Perspective on Claims," suggested that "the potential for economic improvement is substantial, typically 5 to 15 percent reduction in severities and 10 to 20 percent reduction in expenses." The basic idea: to pretty much *stop* paying Allstate's policyholders at all.

"What if you discovered a secret set of construction plans for the Mother's Peas factory, proving that the company designed the machines to under-fill every can of peas by 30 percent?" asked Berardinelli. "What if you also had proof that the Mother's Peas Company did this to generate windfall profits for their shareholders and huge bonuses for their executives? Then you'd probably think you were the victim of a fraud."[40]

A number of other states, as well as other insurers, also sued Allstate. "[Insurers] are systematically [underpaying] policyholders without adequately examining the validity of each individual claim," former Texas insurance commissioner Robert Hunter told a U.S. Senate committee in 2007. "If you don't accept their offer, which is a low ball, you end up in court. And that was the recommendation of McKinsey."[41]

What was McKinsey's response to the growing roster of disastrous engagements? Flat-out denial of responsibility. "In these turbulent times," Gupta told *BusinessWeek*, "with our serving more than half the *Fortune* 500 companies, there are bound to be some clients that get into trouble." Once again, McKinsey stuck to its long-held precept that it bore no ultimate responsibility for *anything* that went on at a client. All that mattered was whether there was any meaningful blowback on McKinsey. And as far as it could tell, there was not. "[McKinsey] is the beneficiary of the fact that it is able to dispose of its mistakes, hide its embarrassments and display a façade that seems almost golden," said the *Sunday Times* in 1997.[42]

The Kids in the Conference Room

Rajat Gupta's McKinsey looked quite different from its starchy past. It recruited the best and brightest from around the world, regardless of gender, race, or nationality—and the machine hummed more efficiently than ever. This was Gupta's great achievement. He institutionalized the firm's practices to such an extent that as it grew, both its external reputation and its internal culture gained power, right along with its profits. With the double draw of intellectual cachet and personal riches, it had an inside track on the smartest graduates from all over the world. In 2003 the firm even lured Bill Clinton's daughter, Chelsea, to its ranks.

But it also started to attract serious, and often unfavorable, attention. Books like *The Witch Doctors* (1996), *Dangerous Company* (1997), and *Consulting Demons* (2000) all took a very a dim view of the consulting industry and its undisputed leader. Christopher McKenna's 2006 book, *The World's Newest Profession,* while an academic treatise, also focused on whether Bower's aim of professionalism had been discarded for commercialism during the economic boom at the end of the century. Indeed, as the 1990s drew to a close, critics wondered whether the consulting industry had grown so large and powerful that it was helping itself far more than it was helping its clients, a charge also leveled at the financial industry. Like bankers, consultants no longer looked or acted like the servants of industry. They'd passed through the looking glass and were now calling the shots.

John Byrne of *BusinessWeek* took offense at *Dangerous Company*. He accused authors James O'Shea and Charles Madigan—both award-winning journalists at the *Chicago Tribune*—of writing "an ill-informed, anti-consultant screed filled with grievances that have been leveled at consultants for decades. The pair decry the industry's high fees, its recycling of old advice, its willingness to tell clients only what they want to hear, and its penchant for putting raw MBAs into key problem-solving roles. But this is hardly news to anyone who has been either a victim or a beneficiary of a consulting assignment. Meanwhile, they fail to describe how the business really works—and why it has been so successful. . . . So consumed are the authors with a few of consulting's well-known foibles that they fail to explain why companies willingly pay $50 billion a year to advice-givers."[43]

But Byrne was missing the point. The alarm was sounded not because people had suddenly realized the above. The alarm was being sounded because, by the end of the twentieth century, the explosive growth of consulting (and investment banking, to be fair) meant that *an alarming proportion* of the graduates of the country's elite MBA programs were being diverted into places like McKinsey. The question being raised wasn't whether consulting itself had merit; it was whether the opportunity cost of consulting's rise was greater than previously understood.

Americans had also begun asking themselves deeper questions about their particular brand of capitalism than they had in the past. What, in an increasingly services-heavy economy, was American capitalism anyway? What did the country make anymore? Could the world's most powerful economy really eschew the dirt and grime of the making of things in favor of merely financing and advising others on how to do the same? Enron was the culmination of a capitalism severed from real things. And the collapse of the Houston-based company kicked off a broad ideological argument that continues to this very day: What role should business play in society itself?

The origins of Wall Street, for example, are good in theory: helping connect holders of money to users of money. But by 2011 the perverted structure of international finance was widely viewed as a drag on the system, not a catalyst. The financial sector took real economies hostage and pushed the entire global economy into chaos. The origins of consulting, by comparison, are also good in theory: helping executives answer tough questions and provoking much-needed change. When the advice givers start to outnumber the advice takers, though, the system tilts in the wrong direction. What the authors of all of the above books were wondering was whether consulting as a whole (and

McKinsey, as its standard-bearer) had become more drag than game changer.

In a memorable 1999 *New Yorker* story titled "The Kids in the Conference Room," Nicholas Lemann posed the question of whether, by virtue of McKinsey's overwhelming recruiting success, the United States had decided, "in effect, to devote its top academic talents to the project of the streamlining of big business." The question was—and remains—poignant. If there is no longer any disrepute in working in the field of commerce—which McKinsey surely does, even if it proclaims itself a profession—why weren't more MBA graduates going into business *itself* as opposed to a support industry such as banking or consulting? Taken to its logical extreme, if everyone becomes a consultant, who will be left to consult?

Lemann also explored what he ultimately saw as the sham at the heart of the McKinsey method itself. "The McKinsey method isn't merely about business," he wrote; "it's about making the chaos of the world yield itself to the intelligent and disciplined mind. You've been trained and selected over and over for all your life, and this is the payoff: at last, you can do something. You have an omni-applicable power to figure out stuff and explain it to people. In truth, it is more a simulacrum of intellectual mastery than intellectual mastery itself, but what's more important is how it feels. It feels as if you'd been given a key that opens up everything."[44]

In July 2002, the *New Yorker* ran yet another piece that constituted a further assault on the latest illusions of the cult of the MBA and, by extension, the cult of McKinsey. Penned by cultural commentator Malcolm Gladwell, the story, titled "The Talent Myth," concluded that the McKinsey echo chamber had fooled itself into buying its own bullshit. "The consultants at McKinsey," wrote Gladwell, "were preaching at Enron what they believed about themselves."[45]

While he focused on Enron, Gladwell was concerned that the obsession with "talent" had extended well beyond the McKinsey-Enron axis. McKinsey's 1997 study, "The War for Talent," had caused a mad rush to add a new (and questionable) dimension to the traditional human resources function: the talent manager. The idea, in its simplest sense: Rapidly promote "talented" employees (whatever that meant), encourage them to think outside the box, and pay them more than they are worth. One Enron employee quoted in McKinsey consultant Richard Foster's book *Creative Destruction* made the following absurd remark: "We hire very smart people and we pay them more than they think they are worth." It was nothing short of theory gone mad in practice. As Gladwell wryly observed in reference to Enron, "It never occurred to them that, if everyone had to think outside the box, maybe it was the box that needed fixing."[46]

"What if smart people are overrated?" asked Gladwell. Alternatively, argued consultant and author Kevin Mellyn in his 2012 book, *Broken Markets,* an excessive worship of formal credentials (i.e., the MBA) instead of actual ability has surely had the unintended effect of depriving the economy—and, just as surely, McKinsey—of true top talent.

If clients weren't exactly asking the same questions about McKinsey, a growing legion of journalists was. At first the firm didn't care; outsiders had questioned its merits since the beginning, yet clients were still banging at the door. But then something happened: Its own people—specifically, its young people, the fuel for its engine—started asking tough questions as well.

Grading Gupta

If Gupta found himself distracted by the external public relations fallout from Enron and other botched engagements, he was soon confronted with an equal if not greater internal challenge. McKinsey had stared down many a competitive recruiting threat in its lifetime—from Boston Consulting Group and Bain to Wall Street—but it had never seen anything like the dot-com boom. No one had.

BCG had once promised greater intellectual satisfaction than working at McKinsey, but the firm had essentially negated that threat in the Gluck era. Wall Street had *always* promised more money than a life in consulting, but it came with more punishing hours, bigger risk, and (to be truthful) a far greater proportion of bosses with a tendency to be assholes. And if Microsoft was minting millionaires, well, so what? For every Microsoft millionaire there was a broke software entrepreneur who'd been steamrollered by the software giant. Working in Silicon Valley wasn't exactly riskless, and then there was the whole nerd thing to contend with.

But then, almost in the blink of an eye, any MBA with a business plan with a *.com* at the end of it and the chutzpah to sell his idea to an ever more credulous stock market could get rich *overnight,* with little risk to no risk at all. How could McKinsey compete with *that*? How could law firms? How could Wall Street? Every single establishment firm in America suddenly had the same problem: Each looked like the past.

By 2001 Silicon Valley employed 1.35 million people, three times the total twenty-five years earlier.[47] The old guard of technology—Microsoft, Intel, and Dell—was being roughly pushed aside by a new generation of Internet-related companies, from network equipment maker Cisco to pure Internet players like eBay and eventual dominant players including Amazon.com and Google. By 2000 about 25 percent of U.S. household wealth was invested in stocks—particularly technology stocks—up from only 10 percent during the 1990s.[48]

McKinsey consultants were unable to resist joining the exodus from the seemingly old to the fancy and new. Overall attrition at the firm rose from 16 percent to 22 percent during the bubble. That didn't present a gigantic challenge, but the firm did take some hard blows: McKinsey lost the heads of both its insurance and its technology practices,[49] while one-third of the firm's San Francisco office left seeking new opportunities in 1999.[50] So many people were leaving that the office soon became referred to internally as "the launching pad." McKinsey veterans joined startups like CarsDirect.com, Cyber Dialogue, and Pet Quarters.

It wasn't just dot-com startups that were alluring. A whole new class of consulting firm burst onto the scene, with hipper names—Razorfish, Scient, Viant, and Sapient—and sexier projects. The work they were doing seemed far more crucial than redrawing organizational charts. They were helping companies use the Internet to transform everything about the way they did business—from sourcing to distribution to how they treated and served their customers.

The loss of this consultant or that one was no mortal blow. What seemed to have the potential to be so? The change in the way McKinsey operated in response to the challenges. The firm that emerged from the dot-com frenzy was very different from the firm that had entered it: Led by Rajat Gupta, the consultants systematically gave up whatever was left of Bower's hallowed principles.

The first operational change: Historically, McKinsey had refused equity stakes in lieu of cash payment for its services. Taking equity, Bower had argued, would sow the seeds of conflict, leading to the possibility that the consultants might offer advice that would produce short-term equity gains at the expense of long-term client success. Under Gupta, that policy was jettisoned. As of 2002 the firm had taken equity stakes in more than 150 companies over the previous three years, including dubious enterprises such as Applied Digital Solutions, which advertised itself as a developer of "life-enhancing personal safeguard technologies."[51] McKinsey pointed out that equity participation accounted for just 2 percent of revenues, compared with

40 percent or more at other consultancies. Still, with 2001 billings of $3.4 billion, that was $70 million worth of equity, not a small number.

The second: Gupta also sanctioned the linking of pay to client performance. Bower and his contemporaries had been adamant that McKinsey's advice was what it was: advice. It was up to the client to carry it out. As with equity stakes, Bower saw contingency fees as a path to conflicted advice, because they would take consultants' eyes off delivering the best possible result in favor of delivering that which might produce the most attractive payoff. When the firm advised Spain's Telefónica on the spinoff of an Internet subsidiary, it earned a $6.8 million bonus.[52] That was all well and good, but the move also opened up the notion that McKinsey *could* be judged on the success of its clients, something Bower had long preached against.

The third: While the firm would never admit as much, under Gupta, McKinsey began working for just about anyone with a fat bank account and a checkbook. From the days of James O. McKinsey, the whole idea had been that McKinsey could secure its place at the top of the consulting pyramid by working *only* for companies at the top of the corporate pyramid. That policy went out the window when the likes of Pets.com and eB2B commerce—firms well below McKinsey's long-held standard of quality—came calling. The firm had a thousand e-commerce assignments at the height of the madness.

The fourth: The firm's cherished culture of dissent was smothered under an "everything is good" attitude engendered by the sheer amounts of money being made. In that environment, suppression of independent thought or behavior occasionally reached levels of absurdity. At a full partners conference in 1994, urged on by a few senior directors including Gupta and Henzler, all the assembled partners stood up, held hands, and swayed to the saccharine lyrics of "We Are The World." Many of those present were aghast, but they felt powerless to resist. Gupta's style (as well as that of a large number of his closest associates) was "You're either with me or against me," and the old value of fierce internal debates and arguments gave way to acquiescence followed by grumbling over drinks in private. The culture of open debate and the free flow of ideas—where only the content mattered and not the person expressing it—was replaced by a culture of "bag carriers" (a notable McKinsey insult) who did as they were told.

The fifth: Compensation of senior directors went so high that the historic tradition of voluntary retirement began to be ignored. Second homes and country club memberships gave way to ranch ownerships and art collections. Houses were renovated to *Architectural Digest* standards. Directors would invite young recruits carrying massive college debts to their homes for dinner with the unsaid proposition: "Someday you could live like this." To add insult to injury: The same directors would walk past the young recruit the next day in the corridor of the New York office with no sign of recognizing them.

As a private partnership, McKinsey doesn't divulge its finances, but estimates of Gupta's take as managing partner run to more than $5 million annually. At this point, the ratio of the most senior compensation to that of the juniors now approached forty to one. After becoming managing director, Gupta moved with his family into an $8 million mansion a stone's throw from Long Island Sound in Westport, Connecticut, that was once owned by the J.C. Penney clan. Gupta's winter getaway is a sprawling $4 million oceanfront house on Palm Island, a private resort on Florida's gulf coast. One estimate in 2012 pegged his wealth at $130 million.

• • •

In April 2001 the dot-com bubble burst. McKinsey's revenue bubble soon did the same: For the first time in recent memory, the firm's top line declined, from $3.4 billion in 2001 to $3.0 billion in 2002, a 12 percent drop. It took only three years to climb back to the 2001 levels—the firm claimed $3.8 billion in 2005 revenues—but at the time the decline caused great consternation at the firm. The *New York Times* even headlined an article in 2002, "Hurt by Slump, a Consulting Giant Looks Inward."

What was it looking at? First and foremost, the merits of Rajat Gupta's tenure. It had taken Gupta an unusual three ballots to get elected to his third term in 2000, and even though he had guided the firm to an unprecedented level of prosperity, he had also overseen sky-rocketing growth that left it exposed when the downturn came.

In June 2001 Gupta asked all 891 partners of the firm to contribute to McKinsey's capital base. Some senior partners gave as much as $200,000. Partner compensation also fell by one-third. In this instance, McKinsey wasn't paying partners anymore; they were paying McKinsey.

McKinsey's balance sheet problems weren't entirely surprising. Because consulting firms pay out all their profits at the end of each year, they are usually funded for about the next three months and nothing more. Their lines of credit smooth out blips in business, but there's a balancing act to be done, even if McKinsey claims it doesn't focus on the bottom line. "Remarkably, these places are only ninety days away from going out of business," said financial services consultant Chuck Neul.[53]

Gupta turned the firm's focus even more toward client development and even farther from knowledge building. "The pendulum does swing a little bit," Gupta told *BusinessWeek* in 2002. "I'd say that client development in the last year or two is more in the forefront, simply because that is the biggest need right now."[54] And, as Walter Kiechel pointed out in *The Lords of Strategy,* "When business falls off, partner interest in breaking new intellectual ground largely evaporates; the rallying cry becomes client development, maintaining current relationships, and hunting for fresh ones."

McKinsey also suddenly found itself overstaffed: MBA acceptance rates had been steadily dropping due to competing opportunities, but in 2000 the trend reversed itself. McKinsey had made 3,100 offers that year, expecting 2,000 acceptances. More than 2,700 people accepted. As dot-com ventures suddenly appeared risky again, the firm found itself in the middle of a flight to quality by MBAs now looking for stability again. Attrition at the same time plummeted to a mere 5 percent. As these factors were combined with falling demand, the result was that McKinsey was carrying too many employees—the firm calculated at one point that it was overstaffed to the tune of about two thousand consultants—and consultant utilization fell to its lowest level in thirty-two years: just 52 percent, versus some 64 percent a few years earlier.[55] In other words, half of the consultants were getting paid to do nothing.

"We honored every offer and didn't push people out," Gupta told *BusinessWeek*. "And we had no professional layoffs other than our traditional up-or-out stuff." That just wasn't true: In 2001, 9 percent of associates and analysts were "counseled out" of the firm, versus just 3 percent in 2000.[56] McKinsey shrunk considerably over the next few years, with the number of consultants falling from 7,631 in 2001 to 5,638 in 2004. The firm's North American staff declined by 40 percent, while Europe and Asia each fell 15 percent.

The experience revealed the downside of McKinsey's cherished ethos of hiring good people and just letting them do their thing. When you employ ten thousand people around the world, and you let local offices take care of their own hiring without any centralized oversight—or, equally important, without centralized financial planning—the entire institution can be put at real economic risk by a sudden external change. And that's what happened. The firm got ahead of itself, grew too quickly, and chased some clients it shouldn't have. At one point, associates were leaving with just a week's notice in the middle of studies. Partners were furious with them for not honoring their professional obligations. And then, when the downturn came, associates were angry about getting neither bonuses nor the kind of exposure to CEOs that McKinsey promises. If the contract between associates and partners wasn't broken, it was at least cracked.

Still, for all the consternation over the Gupta era at McKinsey, the downturn proved just a blip in the top line. Even before Gupta turned over the reins to Ian Davis, the business had turned a corner and begun to accelerate. From a trough of $3 billion in 2002 billings, the consultants *doubled* revenues, to $6 billion by 2008. Even in the immediate wake of Enron, clients were still lining up for advice. The British Ministry of Defense hired McKinsey in May 2002 to help streamline "performance" of its $6 billion Defense Logistics Organization.[57]

Last Rites—For the Man, and the Myth

Marvin Bower died on January 22, 2003, at the age of ninety-nine and a half. "I told him he'd lived to his hundredth year, and that it was time to let go," said his son Dick.[58] Bower had outlived by four years his second wife, Clothilde de Veze Stewart, whom he'd married three years after his first wife, Helen, had passed away.

Rajat Gupta delivered the last of five eulogies in the Reformed Church of Bronxville, New York. "[Marvin had] a vision of a profession that did not exist," he said. "[He] sensed the opportunity in our profession, defined our aspirations, formulated our values and led our firm. . . . In many ways, certainly in spirit and soul, Marvin continued to lead it after he retired, and he leads it still."

While obviously heartfelt, the words were laced with irony—because the McKinsey of 2003 was no longer Marvin Bower's McKinsey.

It was Rajat Gupta's. "Bower gave the firm its principles," said one McKinsey veteran. "Ron Daniel gave it class. Fred Gluck gave it intellectualism. And Rajat? Don't ask me, because I haven't a clue, except maybe Kremlinesque politics."

Bower had turned consulting from a business into a profession, and McKinsey into its standard-bearer. His final reward? He got to see Rajat Gupta and Gupta's cohort turn it back into a business. The institution survived, but the cherished values fell by the wayside. Rajat Gupta's McKinsey was a business—not a profession—and that's all there was to it. It was, of course, a remarkably successful business, and the charitable view of Gupta's tenure can hardly ignore the firm's continued growth and deepening influence across the globe, as well as the exponential change in the partnership's wealth.

Of course, half a decade later—when he'd already quietly left through the side door—Rajat Gupta did more damage to McKinsey than he'd ever done sitting in the corner office. In 2012 he was convicted of insider trading—at least some of which activity had taken place while he still had an office at McKinsey.

10. RETRENCHMENT

Doing a 180

In the 2000 election for managing partner of McKinsey, Rajat Gupta put back a surge—from Ian Davis, then head of the London office; and Michael Patsolos-Fox, who was head of New York—in order to win his third and final term. An affable, polite Brit who had been at McKinsey since 1979, Davis had stood—unequivocally—for a return to Boweresque values and a pullback from the more commercial tilt of the past decade. But Gupta won the challenge. It was 2000, after all, and the full report on the dot-com mirage had not yet been filed.

Three years later, with Gupta unable to run for a fourth term, Davis and Patsolos-Fox faced off again. On Friday, February 27, 2003, the *Economist* ran a story on the coming election that Sunday. "Do not be fooled by the polite, low-key tone," the magazine wrote. "Next week's announcement will mark a critical moment in the [firm's] history."

The magazine wrote that Davis "wears his ambition lightly but is deeply committed to the firm's traditional values, in particular the need to invest in long-term relationships with clients and to nurture the associates who represent the firm's future."[1] This was a gift-wrapped endorsement that had obviously been helped along by loose lips within the firm. The magazine didn't criticize Patsolos-Fox; it merely positioned him as more of a continuation of the Gupta era. At a time when the firm's 280 senior partners no longer knew each and every one of their colleagues, the article surely helped tilt the election in Davis's favor.

Patsolos-Fox didn't come out too badly: Davis made him head of the firm's American practice as a consolation. Likewise, when Don Waite lost out to Gupta, he'd been made the firm's chief financial officer. The majority of people who lose in McKinsey elections *don't* leave the firm in a fit of pique. "Where would they go, anyway?" asked a former partner. "If you've been at McKinsey for twenty-five years, you're making $3 million to $5 million a year. There are not a lot of places you are going to go to, unless someone is going to make you CEO of a major company."

Davis was touted as the "values partner." He was widely regarded for his forthrightness, as well as his ability to ground most conversations about McKinsey in an expression of some core value of the firm: client first; the need to take on sensitive issues directly; and the importance of keeping the firm's most valuable asset—its people—focused on the highest standards of truth, integrity, and trust. More concerned with shoring up the firm's internal morale than with challenges to its public image, he didn't give his first interview to the press until a year and a half had passed.

In electing Davis, McKinsey partners had signaled that they wanted a return to the leadership style of Ron Daniel—a steadying hand instead of one that was merely reaching for more. Not that Davis was a Daniel replica: While Daniel could appear aloof and a bit imperious, Davis was engaging. He could make people feel comfortable, taking a genuine personal interest in everyone around him. And while Davis was more sharp-edged than Daniel, he could also draw upon deep reservoirs of empathy. He was the living and breathing example of his own philosophy: that having a high IQ isn't enough—one must also develop one's CQ (capability quotient) and RQ (relationship quotient). As evidence of the RQ, Davis freely admitted that the firm had turned a corner even before he was elected, that Gupta had guided the firm through the worst. He told Gupta as much himself. Still, one of his first moves was to reissue Marvin Bower's book *Perspective on McKinsey* in 2004, as a clear repudiation of the excesses of the previous decade.

What Davis did in his six years as managing director was rebuild the firm's confidence. The partnership is an incredibly self-critical one, and McKinsey consultants don't like to get things wrong. "I spent time with partners talking about values," Davis explained. "Just trying to reaffirm our basic mission and purpose. I told them not to get too excited that client activity was picking up again, that we had to learn from the previous four years."[2] The main thrust of his message: McKinsey was supposed to focus on benefiting its clients above all else, without putting its own needs on par with those of the clientele. The subtle distinction had been a hard one to delineate since the days of Marvin Bower himself, but in the Gupta era this fundamental priority had clearly become inverted, and at great cost to the firm's culture, if not necessarily its pocketbook.

"Ian took the chair of managing director at a very difficult time," said Juan Hoyos, head of the firm's Spanish office from 1997 to 2003. "He focused us on values, innovation, and distinctiveness, and kept hammering away on all three. That percolated and helped us to regain the higher ground we had somehow lost."[3] Internally, Davis pushed the consultants to get to know each other again. Specifically, he encouraged partners—who had become faceless to their underlings—to reintroduce themselves to their associates and staff. He called this "personalizing" the firm.

Exerting Control

In professional services firms, especially those full of self-starters like McKinsey, the organization is always moving in one direction or another on the spectrum of central control versus self-governance. In good times, the reins are loosened, and consultants are left free to build their own business under the McKinsey aegis. In tougher times, the reins are yanked back in. When Ian Davis was elected, one of his first tasks was to yank.

The issues were obvious. The firm needed to centralize its balance-sheet control, cost control, communications, press relations, recruiting, and risk management. In the late 1990s, while McKinsey played catch-up with its more aggressive peers, especially regarding consulting about the Internet and general technology space, the firm had basically abdicated any notion of central planning. "McKinsey doesn't really make decisions as an institution," admitted former partner Carter Bales. "It's kind of like the crawling peg system of currency exchange rates. It adjusts as it goes along without making abrupt changes."[4]

There is a reason for that, rooted in the firm's cherished philosophy of the self-governing partnership. McKinsey has always been a decentralized organization held together by the one-firm focus on assimilation, norms, how people are elected, how they are paid, and how work is actually done. But the actual business of consulting had tended to be left to the consultants themselves. So too were local decisions like recruiting. And that's where it went wrong—a generally bullish mood about hiring was compounded by supercharged recruiting at the local level, and there were no internal controls that might flag an overall excess of enthusiasm.

The question, then: If new controls were needed, who would exercise them? "We spent the first few months trying to figure out who had decision rights," said Michelle Jarrard, Davis's longtime right hand. "Which we learned in fine McKinsey fashion by looking back with one of our own engagement teams."[5] One result of the introspection: a scaling back of growth from the near 20 percent of Gupta to a mere 6 to 8 percent under Davis.

It's not that McKinsey hadn't had its own politburo. Bower had his "executive group." Ron Daniel had his "executive committee." Rajat Gupta created "the office of the managing director." McKinsey has always had bureaucracy, salted with a certain amount of Kremlinesque intrigue in its centers of power. Whereas Warren Cannon had exercised power behind the scenes for both Bower and Daniel, and Jerome Vascellaro behind Gluck and Gupta, Davis had Michelle Jarrard.

From then on, Jarrard was a point person in enforcing the Davis regime. She described their objectives in the context of age-old McKinsey precepts. "We have our own language," she said. "Which includes firm values, mission, and guiding principles. These are not religious principles; they're not moral or good or bad. They are decision-making guideposts that merely reflect our intentions." One thing Jarrard helped carry out was an even further broadening of the firm's hiring preferences, which by mid-decade ran about 40 percent to 45 percent MBAs, 40 percent to 45 percent advanced degrees (JD, MD, PhD), and about 10 percent to 20 percent experienced hires. In 2011 the firm had two priests on the payroll.

Davis wasn't entirely successful in wresting control from local interests. The financial institutions group (FIG) in New York has been a long-term thorn in the side of McKinsey managing directors. The group brings in so much money that it tends to ignore the concerns of the rest of the firm. Davis put a senior partner in charge of "breaking the back" of FIG in New York, according to one consultant. Younger consultants also thought a handful of older partners, including Lowell Bryan and Pete Walker, were staying on in violation of one of the firm's key tenets—older partners agree to leave around the normal retirement age in order to make room for younger ones. "These guys flourished under Gupta," said one partner. "But they've been using the McKinsey brand as their own annuity. They are totally anti-Bower in that regard." But the effort failed: Davis's man left McKinsey after four months, and Bryan and Walker were both still with the firm in 2012.

Davis, like Gupta, wasn't prisoner to the notion of analytic glory that seduces so many McKinsey consultants. But he did value "knowledge" more than his predecessor. Gupta had eliminated Gluck's cherished practice bulletins in his drive for profits. Davis reinstituted them. By 2008, McKinsey was arguing that the ability to "efficiently create, share, retain and transfer knowledge assets is the only sustainable competitive advantage of a twenty-first-century firm." In a sense, this was McKinsey selling its own snake oil; the firm sold *nothing but* knowledge. On the other hand, it represented a recommitment to the Gluck era over that of Gupta.

Mercenaries, Not Missionaries

By 2004 or so, McKinsey had become that which it had always intended to be, even if it never admitted as much: a high-end mercenary force for high-impact corporate engagements. "They're great at tactical stuff for us," explained one partner at a major private equity firm. "We don't need them for strategy. But they will do anything you want them to do, including filling out spreadsheets. I use them at twenty cents on the dollar so I don't have to hire more associates. They generally cost me about a hundred thousand dollars a week."

By the mid-2000s, many of those spreadsheets were once again focused on helping executives make the case for one of McKinsey's best-selling products: a justification for corporate downsizing.

In 2003 the consultants advised Madison Square Garden (owned by Cablevision) to cut 3.5 percent of its workforce.[6]

In 2005 McKinsey recommended to financial sponsors Texas Pacific Group and Credit Suisse First Boston that they slash 3,000 of the 4,300 hundred employees at German bathroom-fixture maker Grohe, in response to the idea that with 80 percent of sales outside Germany, the company shouldn't be making 80 percent of its products in its high-cost homeland. The advice put McKinsey deeper in the hole it had already been digging for years with Germany's unions.[7]

In 2007 the firm advised Walmart that the cost of an "associate" with seven years of tenure was almost 55 percent more than the cost of one with just a single year of tenure, but there was no difference in their productivity.[8] Beyond the obvious offensiveness of suggesting Walmart lay off its experienced and loyal staff in favor of cheap new labor, this was up-or-out all over again. McKinsey could push its system even in a place like Walmart. (Although on the other hand, McKinsey seems to have met its paranoid match in the giant retailer. According to a former Walmart employee, the retailer at one point suspected the consultants of leaking confidential company memos and monitored their Internet activities as a result.)[9]

Glitzy magazine company Condé Nast hired McKinsey in 2009 to help the publisher of the *New Yorker, Vanity Fair,* and *Vogue* resize itself for a new post-real-estate-bubble advertising climate. Media outlets like nothing more than to write about themselves, and this was as juicy as it comes: When the idea leaked of buttoned-up McKinsey MBAs telling the likes of *Vogue*'s Anna Wintour or *Vanity Fair*'s Graydon Carter to cut down on their $250 lunches, journalists (including the author of this book) gave McKinsey a level of exposure it hadn't seen since Enron.

While the firm claims it detests such coverage, an article titled

"The Gilded Age of Condé Nast Is Over" in the *New York Observer* included remarks from Condé Nast CEO Charles Townsend that could only be music to McKinsey's ears: "I asked them to . . . take a top-down look at the way we do business," he said. "Our processes. The way we do business. The use of technology. The way we deploy our resources in the pursuit of revenues. The way we communicate. The way we market to the consumer."[10]

It sounded just like what McKinsey would say. "The purpose is to deliver impact," explained partner Dominic Casserley. "That's a generic phrase, but it covers cost cutting, revenue growth, strategy, and more. We change the way people in a company make decisions or act. That's what this profession is about—helping other people do some things differently."[11]

Of course, the main goal at Condé Nast was mere cost cutting. On McKinsey's recommendation, the company shuttered four titles: *Cookie, Elegant Bride, Gourmet,* and *Modern Bride.* Some 180 employees were axed. "McKinsey is going to look over our shoulder as we sort out . . . financial controls [and] expense controls," Townsend later told *Ad Age*. "Their support of this process has been invaluable."[12]

Some Condé Nast executives weren't so sure about that. "They stood out like a sore thumb here," said the publisher of one of the company's most successful magazines. "A pack of people with pleated pants and their notebooks. How much they understood about our business, I cannot tell you, even though publishing is pretty simple—you either write copy or you sell ads. But not a single person on their team had ever written copy or sold an ad.

"How the fuck can you coach a football team if you've never played football in your life?" he continued. "And I'm not talking pro. I'm talking at any level. They don't have a clue. I don't care how many hours they spent firing people at Time Inc. or Meredith Corporation. They had this stupid red/yellow/green system, which they explained to me like I was a five-year-old. I wanted to reach across the table, grab one of them, and throw him across the room. And you should have seen them when the press reports of their engagement started piling up. They were bug-eyed, like white-gloved society women who only want to be in the paper when they get married and when they die."

McKinsey was all the rage in publishing at the time. Dow Jones, owner of the *Wall Street Journal, Barron's,* and *Smart Money* magazine, also brought the consultants in—although the executives at Dow Jones *insisted* they were looking to grow, not cut[13]—and Time Warner hired McKinsey to help it cut a reported $100 million in costs at the entertainment company's publishing unit, Time Inc. The new CEO, Laura Lang, later hired McKinsey's rival Bain & Company to help her assess the struggling magazine company's options.[14, 15] True to form, however, McKinsey had made its way back into the building by late 2012.[16]

Happy consulting clients don't speak up much; they like to take the credit for themselves. But some do speak up. And McKinsey had scores of them during Ian Davis's tenure. Tim Flynn, the chairman and CEO of accounting and advisory firm KPMG, brought McKinsey in over an eighteen-month period in 2008 to help chart the global strategy for its umbrella firm, KPMG International, after the company's German and UK outfits decided to merge. Accounting firms had historically been constrained by national borders, and the move created some energy within KPMG to take a more global view of its business. The assignment started as many do—small—but soon increased in range as the KPMG executives saw that McKinsey could help them understand how to capitalize on global trends in professional services.

Clients liked McKinsey so much that the inexorable diaspora of McKinsey consultants into the CEO ranks of industry continued at full force. A *USA Today* article in 2008 concluded that the odds of a

McKinsey employee going on to run a $2 billion-plus company were the best of *any* company—besting perennial management breeding grounds General Electric and IBM.[17]

Back to the Beltway

Despite the firm's early success in Washington, McKinsey hightailed it out of town in the 1960s when margins came under pressure. The firm had largely steered clear of Beltway business for the next forty-plus years. That all changed in the new century, in two significant ways. First, the firm reestablished a public sector practice under the guidance of partner Nancy Killefer. Second, McKinsey infiltrated the Obama administration.

After working in the Clinton administration for three years as an assistant Treasury secretary between 1997 and 2000, Killefer had returned to the firm in 2000 and expressed a desire to continue working with the public sector, even if she was now on McKinsey's side of the table.

Though he became a champion of the practice later on, Ian Davis wasn't immediately supportive of Killefer's desire to reestablish a U.S.-based public sector practice. "He told me he didn't think it was such a great idea," recalled Killefer, an honors graduate of Vassar College (economics) who has an MBA from MIT's Sloan School of Management. "I had a bunch of consumer products clients, and he suggested that focusing on them would be the best use of my time. I said to him, 'I don't think you understand, Ian. I'm not asking for permission. I'm calling up to tell you what I'm going to do as a courtesy.'"

Not only did Davis think her abilities might be better used elsewhere, he also wondered whether McKinsey could serve governments around the world in the same way it served corporate clients—that is, by advising on best practices. "Ian believed that all politics is local," Killefer continued. "I argued that we could add value by connecting governments." Killefer was right, and Davis came to embrace the public sector practice. By 2010 it was one of the fastest growing in the firm, with work spanning the United States, Europe, Asia, and Africa.

Killefer and her team helped the post-9/11 FBI build a domestic intelligence capability, including rethinking how the agency ran not just operations but recruiting. In China, McKinsey lowered its usual sky-high fees in order to get a foothold; but when it came to U.S. government work, the firm held the line. According to public disclosures made as a result of McKinsey's government contracts, it cost taxpayers $164,165 a week for the services of one engagement manager and three associates.[18]

In typical McKinsey fashion, the firm argued that this was in the best interests of its government clients. "I didn't want it to be anything less than what we give our private sector clients," said Killefer. "I wanted the same commitment of the firm, the same caliber of people. I didn't want us to become a stepchild of the firm."[19] Remarkably, skinflint governments around the world decided McKinsey was worth the price.

That was true at the municipal level as well. New York Mayor Bloomberg used McKinsey repeatedly. McKinsey sometimes worked for free (troubleshooting the police and fire departments' responses to 9/11) and sometimes for pay (a report on how the city could stand its ground in high finance against London). The Department of Education has also used McKinsey consultants, and New York City's PlaNYC—an ambitious and wide-ranging effort to address population concerns, aging infrastructure, climate change, and an evolving economy—was based on McKinsey data crunching.[20]

When Barack Obama was elected president in 2008, he tried to lure Killefer back into the fold by nominating her to be his "chief performance officer," but she was ensnared in that classic Washington gotcha!—a failure to pay taxes on household help. In early 2009 she withdrew her nomination and decided to stay at McKinsey. But Killefer wasn't the only McKinseyite on the president's radar. Two members of his transition team were McKinsey alums—Michael Warren, cohead of the Treasury team; and Roger Ferguson, once a Federal Reserve governor, on his economics team. He named former McKinsey Global Institute chief Diana Farrell as deputy director of his National Economic Council, and McKinsey vet and venture capitalist Karen Mills became head of the Small Business Administration.

In noticing Obama's predilection for hiring McKinsey types, the *Economist* pointed out how it signaled a distinct change from the Bush administration's apparent love of former Goldman Sachs employees. "[The] national mood has changed," said the magazine's editors. "Under Mr. Bush, working for Goldman Sachs, the greatest of Wall Street's then-great investment banks, seemed in itself to be a qualification for high office. This, after all, was an era where what counted was understanding the financial markets and globalization, and having great connections all over the world. . . . The new era may place a higher value on finding practical ways to improve the workings of vast bureaucracies."[21] For their part, the Clintons had been favorable to Rhodes scholars.

The magazine had a point. If the previous ten years had been about growth for growth's sake, then the post-real-estate-bubble era was about how to fix everything that had been broken. Wall Street types are better suited for the cheerleading era. McKinsey people are fixers. Even presidential candidate Mitt Romney said, if elected, he'd consider bringing the firm in to "fix" the government.[22]

That said, the firm's closeness with the Obama administration was also another example of just how malleable McKinsey can be. The McKinsey Global Institute is a strong proponent of the idea of unfettered markets for both labor and capital. Barack Obama does not necessarily feel the same way—he not only supported the bailout of Wall Street but has supported the subsequent and extensive regulatory overhaul and has not let the national housing market find its natural bottom. It is, in some ways, intellectually disingenuous for McKinsey people to be so close with this president. But it's not that surprising, as power and influence have always trumped ideas at the firm, no matter what it might argue. And Harvard eggheads tend to seek each other out anyway—Obama holds a law degree from the college. "Consultants are nothing if not ingenious in getting their feet on the fender," the *Economist* later wrote. "The Obama administration [was] a perfect mark when it came to Washington . . . on a wave of hope and hype."[23]

In July 2009, MGI issued a research report on just how much the federal government could save from productivity gains over the course of a decade. Anywhere from $45 billion to $134 billion, the consultants decided. "Don't think about it as cost reduction, think about it as adding value. . . . It's a lot of money to go after," said Killefer at the time.[24] McKinsey went after it with full force, and not just in the United States: Work that the firm has done for no less than six Western defense ministries has resulted in a cumulative economic impact to clients of more than $15 billion.[25]

If McKinsey has succeeded in getting lucrative government business around the world, the one place where it has truly infiltrated government is in London, where it has had pretty much uninterrupted access to 10 Downing Street for decades. The head of Britain's Financial Services Authority since 2008 has been Lord Adair Turner, a McKinsey alum. Lord Blackwell ran Tony Blair's Policy Unit in 1995, the closest any McKinsey alumnus had come to the true center of political power before alum William Hague became British foreign secretary in 2010.

In early 2012 an expansive article in London's *Daily Mail* laid bare the degree of McKinsey's influence in the country's National Health Service. Revelations included allegations of egregious conflicts of interest, such as advising the government to revamp the way it handled health service contracts in ways that would benefit McKinsey's own corporate clients and then sharing those proposals with the private sector clients in advance.

The article also highlighted the means of achieving influence, including the consultants' spending lavishly on an NHS regulator—including business class flights to New York, a five-star hotel stay, and a lavish banquet. The regulator? David Bennett, a former McKinsey consultant himself. Several consultants have passed through the revolving door between McKinsey and NHS, including Tom Kibasi, who left the firm to become a policy adviser to NHS before eventually returning; and David Cox, who left McKinsey to become strategy manager for London NHS.[26]

Helping Inflate a New Bubble

If McKinsey was caught unawares by the dot-com boom, it was no laggard when it came to the surge in financial services at the turn of the century. In 2002 the firm served 80 of the world's top 120 financial services companies.[27] McKinsey had long earned gargantuan profits from banks and bankers, be it from Merrill Lynch and Citigroup in New York, or its near monopoly on providing advice to the giant Swiss banks. Its alumni also populated the executive suites of nearly every financial company of importance.

McKinsey felt comfortable enough about its financial expertise to engage in public displays of "big think"—a 1997 editorial in the *Wall Street Journal* by consultants Lenny Mendonca and Greg Wilson announced: "Financial Megaplayers' Time Is Here."

The McKinsey partners were precisely correct when they predicted that "five years from now the financial services industry will look nothing like it does today. . . . The financial services business will be . . . dominated by a handful of national and global giants that dwarf even the biggest players today." There is no better example than JPMorgan Chase, the product of twenty-plus years of consolidation by Bank One, Chase Manhattan, Chemical Bank, First Chicago, JP Morgan, Manufacturers Hanover, and the National Bank of Detroit.

But they were precisely wrong when they concluded that, "as in other consolidating industries, these megaplayers will be tightly run, highly productive, highly innovative, highly skilled at mergers and acquisitions . . . Shareholders, customers and society at large will all be better off as a result."[28] With Jamie Dimon at the helm of JPMorgan Chase, that bank was both tightly run and skilled at mergers and acquisitions—witness the bank's Hail Mary acquisitions of both Bear Stearns and Washington Mutual in 2008. But that was the exception. It was an exception in another way too—it was the only one of the large banks to make sparing use of McKinsey consultants. Nearly every other major financial institution—from Lehman Brothers to Merrill Lynch to Citigroup (all major users of McKinsey)—showed a distinct loss of both effective management and risk control at the peak of the boom. In the end, shareholders were not better off, nor were customers, nor was society at large.

The postmortem on the real estate bubble is pretty much in, and there's blame enough to go around: from unscrupulous bankers to shady mortgage brokers, misguided policy makers, inept regulators and central bankers, and greedy homeowners. But while McKinsey might advise the occasional mortgage broker and policy maker, its bread-and-butter customer is the bank. So what were its consultants telling clients at the time?

One thing they were endorsing was the notion of the "ability to influence [one's] regulator"—an idea more aptly described as "regulatory capture."[29] McKinsey was certainly not on the "more" side of the oversight debate. This worked to the detriment of not only the industry but also society itself when it turned out that regulators had turned a blind eye to the excesses of their charges.

Another: The consultants were telling banks the very same thing they had celebrated at Enron, that moving assets off one's balance sheet—by securitization or in some other manner—was the surest route to continued, unhampered growth. Much of this advice was based on historical analysis—the kind that showed that securitization was a wonderful thing—but it ultimately proved flawed in its backward-looking perspective when widespread bond failures resulted in the bottom falling out of the nation's real estate market. This reliance on models came directly from the theory of the McKinsey/Harvard axis that the past was a reliable indication of the future.

"What you get from Harvard Business School is a wonderful network of people who were there with you and a set of tools that you can then bamboozle people with for the rest of your life," Radio 4 business reporter Peter Day told London's *Sunday Times* in 2009. "It is a habit of thought—conventional responses to conventional situations. Harvard teaches on a case-study basis, so it is always telling people how to respond to things that happened in the past. No wonder that when something like the credit crunch comes along, huge numbers of highly skilled people in compartmentalized worlds are unable to respond to it."[30]

What's more, McKinsey and others wholly endorsed bankers' move farther out on the risk curve in search of higher returns. Specifically, they were pushing the concept of risk-adjusted return on capital, or RAROC, as well as a notion called "shareholder value added," or SVA. Both ideas were based on a simple premise. "In theory, if a bank took capital out of a business with low-risk adjusted returns and put it into a business with high-risk adjusted returns, its overall return on shareholder funds should be higher. So would its position in the banking food chain," explained Kevin Mellyn in *Financial Market Meltdown*. "It seemed like a good idea at the time."[31] It wasn't. McKinsey wasn't alone in pushing RAROC, of course. Smaller, more focused financial services consultants were selling similar ideas. But McKinsey's ability to take an idea and then "leverage" it up, using its brand and organizational effectiveness through an essentially industrial-style process made its consultants far and away the most effective disseminator of ideas via the consulting process.

The long road of McKinsey helping lead bankers astray had actually started years earlier. As Mellyn pointed out in his follow-up to *Financial Market Meltdown, Broken Markets,* McKinsey banking practice lion Lowell Bryan was the go-to consultant for bankers in the 1980s. At the time, Mellyn argued, McKinsey was urging an industrial competitive strategy model on what had become a cozy regulated utility.[32] The result, which *did* work for a time, ultimately led to a complex and costly bank model in which bankers were pushed to actually create demand for credit rather than merely providing it, with the result that, over time, they moved farther and farther into questionable credits. "It is hard to generate more demand for credit among creditworthy borrowers," observed Mellyn, "so as we have seen time and again in banking's roller-coaster history, lenders began to inch farther and farther out [along] the risk curve." The process continued for years until the collective risk taking blew up in the banks' faces.

This was McKinsey losing the forest of reality in the analytic glory of its trees—with the result that it had rubber-stamped a banking industry strategy that was strikingly similar to the one that had brought down Enron. Except this time, the consultants helped inflate a bubble not just in a single stock but also in the entire global economy. "The ways of lending money safely are simple, obvious, and admit no variation," wrote Mellyn.[33] And yet McKinsey was helping all its large banking customers depart from that principle—focusing them on sales and marketing above all else—with predictably disastrous results.

McKinsey also prodded its biggest customers along with a fear mongering reminiscent of its bogus idea of a "war for talent." This time around, it was "extreme competition." A 2005 paper published in the *McKinsey Quarterly* said that top companies in any industry faced a 20 to 30 percent chance of losing their leadership positions within a five-year period. This risk had apparently tripled in just a single generation.[34] The implied solution: get a consultant to show you the way forward.

Here was one way: make as many loans as possible, package them just as quickly, and sell them out the back door to credulous institutional investors. In the meantime, load your balance sheet with unprecedented amounts of leverage in order to juice returns. The U.S. investment banks, for example, jacked their leverage—defined as the ratio between financial assets and the difference between financial assets and liabilities—from just over twenty-five times in 2003 to nearly thirty-five times in 2008.

Interestingly, the McKinsey Global Institute was doing substantial research of its own on developments in the global financial markets during the boom years, and it had reached conclusions that stood in opposition to the strategies of the firm's largest financial clients. "Like the rest of the world, we failed to have a full grasp of what was happening in the lead-up to the financial crisis," said Diana Farrell, "but we were beginning to sound a drumbeat about the degree of leverage in the economy."[35] MGI created a unique global database and captured a concept called "financial deepening," which indicated that it wasn't enough to look at individual institutions; a true understanding could come only from a systemwide analysis. MGI noted that financial assets were equal to global GDP in 1980, rose to two times in 1990, and rose to three times in 2000. "We were probing and understood this was important and worth ringing the bell on," explained Farrell. "But we did not fully understand that it was unsustainable."

What was acceptable to McKinsey—and its competitors serving many of the same financial institutions at the time—was that the profits of the financial services sector were skyrocketing, from 15 percent of U.S. corporate profits in 1980 to 41 percent in 2007. And so what its consultants told their clients was not necessarily the same thing Farrell suggested had been concluded at MGI. According to the *New York Times,* in 2007, in an engagement meant to evaluate the risks in General Electric's finance unit, McKinsey told its client that money from countries with trade surpluses—such as China and Middle Eastern oil producers—would provide a buffer for the increased lending and leverage for the foreseeable future.[36] That advice could not have been more wrong.

Perhaps in karmic reward for its contribution to the bubble, McKinsey lost money on its own investments in the aftermath. The value of McKinsey's Supplemental Retirement Plan declined by 21 percent in 2008, shedding $780 million out of a total of $3.8 billion at the start of the year. When it came to investments, the firm's bust-era results could be as spotty as some of its advice. What's more, McKinsey could be as gullible as any other investor: The firm lost $193.5 million in the Petters Group Ponzi scheme. On the other hand, McKinsey did manage to benefit from investment banks' and hedge funds' rigging of the CDO game, as it had investments in the Magnetar hedge funds, creators of the now-infamous "Magnetar trade."

Swiss bank UBS hired McKinsey to help it decide whether or not to enter the leveraged buyout market for midsize companies in 2002. But McKinsey and UBS's own board dithered over the notion until 2006, when the best idea was to *exit* middle-market LBOs. "I looked at one of my colleagues and asked him, 'How do we stop this?'" related a former executive of UBS. "He told me that it would take me three years to do so. People thought UBS was risk-averse at the time. I'd say they were decision-averse. They couldn't pull the trigger without letting McKinsey study something for a year or more.

"What drove me crazy was that McKinsey *knew* how screwed up UBS was," continued the executive. "They knew it. But when I asked them why they didn't tell the CEO in Zurich or the board of directors, I already knew the answer: telling them would put McKinsey's job in jeopardy. And that would cut off the $8 million to $10 million they made from us on that single project." The complaint leads to an important question, which is whether or not Wall Street firms have any business hiring six-month consultants to tell them how to set strategy. If you're making cars or selling soup, you may have a longer lead time; but trading securities is not conducive to six-month analysis. This is arguably the reason Goldman Sachs has for so long set itself apart from the competition. The company has people who make decisions. They make calls that would have taken UBS two years to consider.

Since pretty much every bank of importance had hired McKinsey, you had fifty companies in the mid-1990s focused on the same thing—global strategy—at the exact same time.[37] The same was true ten years later, raising an interesting issue of systemic risk. While the firm's fingerprints were once again nowhere to be found in the detritus of the real estate collapse, its consultants had been advisers to many of the companies that both inflated the bubble and collapsed as a result of it. Whatever the specific advice to specific clients, McKinsey had once again failed to give them the best advice of all, which was to go in the direction of less, not more. That makes the value of the advice *it did give* incidental at best, and destructive at worst.

What was McKinsey's response to the crisis? In October 2008 it opened a Center for Managing Uncertainty, headed by Lowell Bryan. This was the same Lowell Bryan who had developed a formidable U.S. banking practice by recommending the same thing to one U.S. bank after another. There was a joke in the New York banking practice: "We will do branch bank network *rationalization* and keep doing it in bank after bank until the banks have cut too far and the pendulum swings the other way, at which point we will then do a bank branch network *expansion* study and look for ways for organic expansion, acquisitions, and so on, until the pendulum swings again. Rinse. Repeat." Repeat studies of the same kind are the consulting world's cash cows. You don't need to create selling documents or work documents. Just fill in the frameworks with the client's data and do the same thing you've done before, thereby reaping the benefits of the simplest of equations: Low Cost = High Margins.

In 2009 the consultants began urging governments to tackle "whole-government transformation"[38] to deal with the credit crunch, with the consultants as trail guides on that journey. Oliver Jenkyn, who headed McKinsey's retail banking practice during the moment of the industry's worst excesses—in both mortgage and credit card lending—was hired by Visa in August 2009 as its head of strategy and corporate development. Failure to advise properly once again proved no impediment to further engagement.

In 2009 Edward Liddy, CEO of flailing insurance giant AIG, hired McKinsey to help sort out its multibillion-dollar mess—perhaps because of the goodwill the firm earned while working for him at Allstate. AIG referred to the engagement as Project Destiny. But the consultants failed to gain their usual purchase on the company, a remarkable failure considering the utter crisis that AIG was experiencing at the time. "AIG had workout specialist AlixPartners and McKinsey," recalled a consultant who also spent time at the insurer. "The Alix guy kept telling management that McKinsey was working in a theoretical vacuum. Alix was the M*A*S*H hospital, McKinsey was the brain surgeon who had no business being in a M*A*S*H hospital." That made McKinsey expendable when AIG's situation became increasingly acute: Liddy's successor, Robert Benmosche, promptly canned the consultants upon taking over as CEO in mid-2009.

Victims of Their Own Success

Remarkably, McKinsey didn't see much of a falloff in its business as a result of the global economic downturn. Revenues, which had flatlined in 2003 at $3 billion, kept growing right on through the financial crisis, hitting $6 billion in 2008. By that point the firm had eighty-two offices around the world and more than fifteen thousand employees.

In 2007, at the firm's partners conference in Singapore, Davis and Michelle Jarrard presented the findings from an internal study of just how the firm had gotten sideswiped by the dot-com bubble. The dot-com boom and bust, which had affected just 5 percent or so of the world economy, hit McKinsey hard. Given the resultant financial squall in Silicon Valley, New York, London, and Scandinavia—McKinsey strongholds—that wasn't so much of a surprise. But the financial crisis, which hit some 60 percent of the world economy, barely left a scratch. That was due at least in part to Davis and Jarrard focusing the firm on internal controls as well as traditional client development.

McKinsey found itself facing new questions, though. And one, in particular, began showing up in a number of different guises. Was the firm now so successful—and so big—that it was running the risk of becoming what it had long warned clients against becoming themselves: a hidebound bureaucratic organization that had lost the spark of its youth?

In 2007 Google knocked McKinsey out of the number one spot on the Universum MBA student ranking of preferable employers, a spot the consulting firm had held for the previous twelve years. This was certainly due in part to Google's astounding success, but McKinsey had outlasted any number of pretenders to its throne over the previous decade.

In 2009 *Fortune* named McKinsey the fourth-best company in the United States for producing leaders, after IBM, Procter & Gamble, and General Mills. This was no small honor, but also a comedown from the era when McKinsey was viewed as the preeminent creator of leaders the world over. That same year, Google retained the top spot over McKinsey in the Universum survey, a position it maintained through 2012. Adding insult to injury, the annual Glassdoor list of best places to work in 2012—a ranking created entirely from employee reviews—had Bain & Company (number one) placing *ahead* of McKinsey (number two) for the fourth year in a row. Google is one thing, but such success by a *direct competitor* is another. According to the website Poets & Quants, in 2011 McKinsey was still the single largest recruiter of MBAs from top schools.[39] Whether quality has kept up with quantity is an open question.

By 2009 McKinsey was attracting a very different crowd, according to some. "It felt deadening," said one person who worked in a support role for the firm. "Of course, it might not have felt that way to all those MBAs, engrossed in their charts and their teams. They were people who went to good schools but who weren't very intellectual. They were very successful grinds.

"I think the fundamental problem at McKinsey is that they have no real product," she continued. "What do you do when there's nothing there? You commoditize things that other people consider part of life, like personality and intelligence. You turn them into 'units.' They objectify basic human ideas and force them into 'workflows' and 'dichotomies' and 'frameworks.' These are not intellectuals. They are institutional people. They are people who spent a lot of time in the library memorizing things. They may talk of their new 'framework,' but it's not like it's an electric car or something."

The firm tried to continue what was an increasingly transparent illusion of exclusivity. The annual corporate charity run sponsored by JPMorgan Chase requires a company logo on participants' T-shirts. In 2009 there was substantial (and preposterous) internal debate about whether or not McKinsey should decline because of the requirement.

More important, McKinsey was now large enough that the possibility of questionable behavior—by both current employees and alumni—began rising coincidentally. In 2007 Chinese police detained twenty-two people in a bribery investigation related to equipment orders that had made its way into McKinsey's own procurement division. Upon investigation, it turned out that two McKinsey employees had taken $250,000 in bribes from four equipment suppliers.[40] And in 2008 Deustche Post CEO and McKinsey alumnus Klaus Zumwinkel resigned in disgrace after getting caught evading some $1.5 million in taxes and appearing on television in handcuffs.

McKinsey has a long tradition of feigned ignorance of its own financials in favor of obsessing about client needs. Do good work, the saying went, and the numbers would always come through at the end of the year. But that kind of informality doesn't really work anymore when you're so big that any line item on your income statement runs in the hundreds of millions or more. In 2008, despite outwardly robust results, McKinsey rolled a third of its partners' bonuses over to 2009.[41]

The firm proceeded to slash some $440 million out of support services, including marketing, "reputation," risk, and IT support.

Ian Davis had done what he was elected to do, which was to steady McKinsey & Company after the turbulent Gupta years and impose some stringent internal controls. He not only did that; he oversaw continued robust growth. On July 1, 2009, the relatively low-key Dominic Barton, a Canadian who had spent much of his McKinsey career in Asia, succeeded him. Barton was the coauthor of a book titled *Dangerous Markets: Managing in Financial Crises.* It was an apt title for the era. But Barton soon found himself managing over another kind of crisis entirely.

11. BREAKING THE COMPACT

The Mild-Mannered Canadian

In 2009, Dominic Barton was elected just the eleventh managing director of McKinsey—following in the footsteps of James O. McKinsey, Crockett, Bower, Clee, Walton, McDonald, Daniel, Gluck, Gupta, and Davis. And he is surely the most understated in the firm's history. Despite his enormous influence in global affairs, he still carries around a bit of the small-town boy from Sardis, a farming community outside Vancouver, British Columbia. Press him, and he will even evince a certain amount of surprise at his being elected at all.

But he would be the only one to do so. Because once more, McKinsey seemed to have found the managing director fit for the times. On the surface, Barton represents a continuation of the more restrained leadership of Ian Davis. He had been mentored by Davis, after all. And this was clearly what the rank and file was looking for: In one industry survey, he was one of only six CEOs of the top fifty companies to receive a 100 percent approval rating from his employees.[1] But he is more than that. If Al McDonald was a dose of tough medicine in the 1970s, Fred Gluck a signal of the importance of expertise in the 1980s, and Rajat Gupta a celebration of global growth in the 1990s, the selection of

Dominic Barton showed that, like the rest of the world, McKinsey was turning its attention to the Far East, as a source not just of both clients and consultants, but of ideas about business itself. McKinsey was taking the long view again.

Our Man in Shanghai

Barton joined McKinsey in 1986, as part of what was still a relatively rare breed at the time—the new hire without an MBA. Not that he was too far outside the norm—the graduate of the University of British Columbia went on to win a Rhodes scholarship and obtain an MPhil in economics from Oxford. And he had what McKinsey values almost as much as academic degrees and good comportment: a restless curiosity as well as genuine and fruitful interactions with his colleagues. Two years before his election, Barton was the director cited by the most consultants as a mentor. Senior partner Larry Kanarek noticed it at the time but says he didn't realize he was looking at the 2009 election results twenty-four months in advance.

In a stark departure from past managing directorships, Barton gave a wide-ranging interview to Canada's *Globe and Mail* newspaper just two weeks after taking office. This was the new McKinsey, one that once again proactively maintained strong relationships with journalists, after several years of a much more defensive posture. In the interview, Barton told the reporter of being born and spending his early childhood in Uganda, where his parents—an Anglican missionary and a nurse—were scolded by an army officer for letting their son sneak aboard a Land Rover without permission. That officer: Idi Amin, the future tyrant.[2]

While the family did return to Canada—Barton spent the first eleven years of his McKinsey career in the Toronto office—the Ugandan experience had given him wanderlust, and Barton jumped at the chance to move first to Sydney, Australia, and then Seoul, South Korea, when the firm was having trouble finding partners to staff that office. Almost as soon as he arrived, the Asian financial crisis hit, dealing a severe blow to the Korean banking system. For Barton, though, the crisis was a bit of a godsend: With thirty-four of the country's banks insolvent, his first big project was to help Korea restructure its entire banking system. "The public sector work was exciting," he recalled. "And then when the entire region was on the move, it was totally enthralling."[3] Barton later ran the firm's Asian operations out of its Shanghai office before moving to London upon his election as managing director. (Like all McKinsey partners, he's done quite well financially and keeps homes in Shanghai, London, and Singapore, as well as a summer cottage in Canada's exclusive Muskoka region.)

Barton is the polar opposite of Rajat Gupta in terms of academic output. He has written more than eighty articles on Asia alone, and two years after his election he wrote a prescription for the mess that had been made of Western economies, "Capitalism for the Long-Term," published—where else?—in the *Harvard Business Review.* He is so academically inclined, in fact, that in his early years with the firm, the Toronto office partners informed him that while wearing tweed jackets with elbow patches might play well in the ivory tower, it was a no-no at the firm.

The paper was a clarion call for business leaders to take control of their own destiny by reforming "the system" before governments exerted control. It was also a reaffirmation of one of McKinsey's basic tenets: that business should be a force for good, and that it was incumbent on executives to fix the failures of "governance, decision-making, and leadership." In it, Barton espoused a move from what he called "quarterly capitalism" to "long-term capitalism."

"In my view, the most striking difference between East and West is the time frame leaders consider when making major decisions," he wrote, drawing on the twelve-plus years he'd spent in Asia. "In my discussions with the South Korean president Lee Myung-bak shortly after his election in 2008, he asked us to help come up with a *60-year* view of his country's future . . . [whereas] in the U.S. and Europe, nearsightedness is the norm."[4]

Barton cited McKinsey research that has found that 70 to 90 percent of a company's market value is related to cash flows expected three or more years into the future. "If the vast majority of most firms' value depends on results more than three years from now, but management is preoccupied with what's reportable three months from now, then capitalism has a problem," he wrote. He even dared touch the third rail of the corporate governance debate, excessive CEO pay, and suggested a number of changes to current approaches, including the idea of evaluating executives over rolling three- or five-year time frames.

As one part of his own long-term planning, Barton has nudged the firm toward investments in so-called proprietary knowledge that might not pay off for three, five, or even seven years. One example: the firm's Organizational Health Index (OHI), which allows clients to benchmark any number of elements of organizational effectiveness—such as employee satisfaction, innovation, or company direction—against a proprietary database of 600-plus clients and over 280,000 employees. This kind of information can be a gold mine for executives looking for continual improvement in the way they run their businesses, and the OHI quickly became a powerful addition to McKinsey's arsenal of client offerings.

Another: McKinsey now tracks what it calls "global profit pools" of the entire banking industry. If a client wants to know, for example, if the profitability of its installment loan business in Korea is up to scratch, McKinsey can tell it where it stands compared with the entire industry. "We're always going to be a client service firm, first and foremost," said German office head Frank Mattern. "And with Dominic championing investments in proprietary knowledge, we're moving much more in that direction."[5]

The Double-Edged Diaspora

As the number of McKinsey alumni continued to grow—the firm's alumni directory numbered 23,000 as of 2011—so too did the number of possible clients peopled with those loyal to the firm.

Not only do alumni prove a source of future engagements—Stephen Kaufman, a McKinsey alum who became CEO of Arrow Electronics, commissioned eight studies from the firm over a period of 10 years[6]—they also tend to hire from their old stomping grounds. Andrall Pearson hired more than a dozen McKinsey alumni at PepsiCo, including Michael Jordan, who went on to run Westinghouse Electric. Lou Gerstner hired more than fifteen at American Express.[7] "American Express was a McKinsey subsidiary in a lot of ways," said one former partner. "They didn't have the management timber they needed, so they would constantly be raiding us for it."

McKinsey alumnus Paul Chellgren, who went on to become president of Ashland Oil, explained the preference to *BusinessWeek* in 1993: "[Working at McKinsey provides] a cram course in business experience," he said. "It was a compressed opportunity to see a lot of companies, industries, and problems in a short period of time. You got your BS, your MBA, and your MCK."[8]

Gerstner later carved his name on the door of fame at IBM, where he guided one of the most startling turnarounds in modern business, after which he became chairman of the Carlyle Group. At IBM, though, he showed that the Mafia doesn't *always* help the mother ship.

After his arrival at IBM, Gerstner created a consulting group that was bringing in $11 billion annually in just four years, clearly a direct assault on McKinsey's own technology consulting business. This was taking money out of McKinsey's pocket, not putting it in.

Invariably, alumni who go on to prominent outside positions find they must make adjustments. First, they have to learn how to actually manage people, something they're rarely called on to do at McKinsey outside a project team of four to six people. "That might be the toughest transition," admitted one alumnus. "You find you need a lot more sensitivity than you need at McKinsey." Second, they need to adjust to the fact that most corporate environments are, by nature, more hierarchical than McKinsey. "Early on [at American Express] I discovered, to my dismay, that the open exchange of ideas—in a sense, the free-for-all of problem solving in the absence of hierarchy that I had learned at McKinsey—doesn't work so easily in a large, hierarchical-based organization," wrote Gerstner in his bestselling autobiography, *Who Says Elephants Can't Dance?*[9] Gerstner managed to bring some of that McKinsey magic to American Express—and even more of it to IBM, which he famously rejuvenated after the once proud computer maker had suffered a long and slow slide toward complacency.

Bill Matassoni explained that the network is a primary differentiating factor for the firm because it proves McKinsey is a "leadership factory." It says much that Matassoni, who went on to spend five years at BCG after leaving McKinsey, still considers himself a McKinsey man above all else. "BCG asked me how come their alumni aren't as happy as McKinsey's," he said. "I told them it was simple, that when a guy left BCG they shat all over him and considered him a failure. When people leave McKinsey, they are counseled out and are proud of their time there."[10] There is no McKinsey boneyard, in other words; you're still McKinsey, even after you've left.

Even those who lose turf battles and feel forced to leave eventually come around to warm and fuzzy feelings again. Tom Steiner, who lost a struggle to head the firm's banking practice with Lowell Bryan, and another to oversee its in-house technology efforts with Carter Bales, left to head A.T. Kearney's financial services practice in 1992, taking sixteen consultants with him. Yet he can speak with a near religious fervor of his time at the firm, even though he went on to make far more money than he had at McKinsey by founding and then selling his own consulting practice—Mitchell Madison—during the dot-com boom.

The ability of McKinsey alumni to land in positions of real influence continues unabated. In June 2009 C. Robert Kidder—McKinsey alumnus and former chairman of both Borden Chemical and Duracell—became chairman of Chrysler Group LLC. In May 2010 alum Ron O'Hanley, who left McKinsey to join Mellon Financial, was hired to share duties atop mutual fund powerhouse Fidelity Investments with Fidelity scion Abigail Johnson (which possibly positions O'Hanley to be the next head of the firm when Johnson's father relinquishes the post). In the span of four months in 2010, Ian Davis was named not only to the board of oil giant British Petroleum, but also to that of Johnson & Johnson as well as Apax Partners, the highly successful private equity fund co-founded by ex-McKinseyite Sir Ronald Cohen.

Not all McKinsey alumni immediately pick up the phone and hire their former colleagues. Those of more recent vintage, in particular, are well aware of the nearly insatiable need among principals and directors to generate new business. Even if McKinsey does have continually deepening connections in business and government, it is also sitting across the negotiating table from more and more people who know just what McKinsey is good for and what its efforts—and associated billings—are wasted on. The virtuous cycle, in other words, can be self-defeating as well.

One alumnus, now head of a major financial institution, explained that while he will use McKinsey for highly analytic and focused projects, he has no time whatsoever for the typical McKinsey schmooze fest. "Of people who have worked at McKinsey who are now clients," he said, "there are two types. There are people like me who understand the bullshit side of it and who aren't too smart. We don't get caught up in the intellectual masturbation. And then there are the more cerebral people who hire them because they want other McKinsey people around. They get into these companies and think, 'Oh my God! Everyone here is a dope. I want to start using the whiteboard with someone, to talk about the effect of the Internet on *x*, *y*, or *z*.' Those are the guys who never left McKinsey. They carry it around with them, and their organizations hate them for it." The best clients of McKinsey, in other words, are junkies who need their fix.

"I have two senior partners who come and see me every three months," this alumnus continued. "I tell them I only want one sheet of paper. But they come in, lean back in their chair, and say things like, 'What's going on? How are you feeling about progress?' And my response is something like, 'Why are we having this conversation?' I don't need therapy right now. It's like someone told them to listen to the CEO and ask open-ended questions. It's amateurish. I want them to tell me five ways to knock five basis points off the cost base of crucial lines of business. In those cases, when getting it right or wrong by a small amount is real money, I have no problem spending five million or ten million on consulting. But it's a rifle shot, not a shotgun."

Would McKinsey hire itself? It does every single day, said Michelle Jarrard. "And while some people say the firm is a big pain in the ass as a client—that it's not change ready—that's baloney. We move fast. There are multiple McKinsey teams working for McKinsey at any given moment, right down to having engagement managers and McKinsey billing."[11]

The diaspora brings with it increased scrutiny too, as investors and the media show an increased vigilance for any sign of cronyism. In June 2010 investors in financial services outfit Prudential responded with outrage when it was revealed that high-flying Prudential CEO Tidjane Thiam—himself a McKinsey alum—had paid the consultants three million pounds during a *failed* $35.5 billion bid to acquire AIA, AIG's Asian business.[12]

A Criminal Mind

Here's an amazing statistic: Until just a few years ago, McKinsey maintained that no partner or other employee had been charged with securities law violations in the eighty-plus-year history of the firm. (That's not to say no violations had occurred; it's just that no one had been charged with any.) That's a remarkable claim to be able to make, especially in light of McKinsey's philosophical proximity to Wall Street, home to nearly seasonal spasms of criminality. That all changed on October 16, 2009, when federal agents arrested McKinsey director Anil Kumar on charges of being part of the largest insider-trading ring in history.

Because Kumar fainted upon being arrested and had to be briefly hospitalized, several hours passed during which McKinsey was in the dark about the charges. The confusion was such that for a time, it wasn't even clear if the charges had to do with a "security" issue like terrorism or a "securities" issue like insider trading. Whatever it was, it wasn't good.

Barton moved into damage-control mode immediately, convening a group at McKinsey known as SORC, or the Special Operating Risk Committee, which included regional leaders; the firm's general counsel, Jean Molino; and Michael Stewart, who heads media relations.

The arrest had happened on a Thursday. By Saturday Barton had circulated a note to the staff alerting them to the news of Kumar's arrest. On Sunday a similar message went to the firm's alumni. Barton spent the rest of the weekend on the phone with a highly concerned clientele. By Monday morning Barton had almost nine hundred e-mails from distraught current and former partners of the firm asking for more information.

Upon hearing the news famous McKinsey alum Tom Peters voiced what was surely a universal notion, even among those who hadn't actually worked at the firm in decades. "McKinsey and I parted company due to strangeness on my part and our big tussle over the *In Search of Excellence* project," he said. "But having worked for the institution was still a source of unmitigated pride for me. The first thing I did when I heard was call Bob [Waterman] and say, 'What the fuck is going on? This isn't my McKinsey. I smell a rat.' Bob didn't disagree with me."[13]

This was a trial by fire for Barton, who had been on the job just three months, not even enough time to appoint his own kitchen cabinet. And it was a mortification for Ian Davis. "The arrest and everything happened after I left, but the crime itself happened on my watch," said Davis. "It was the worst thing that happened to me in my time as managing director."[14]

When it emerged that Kumar had indeed been charged with insider trading—selling client secrets to his Wharton classmate and hedge fund billionaire Raj Rajaratnam, who used them to generate profits for his $3 billion Galleon fund—the gravity of the situation became crystal clear. The basis of any client relationship with the firm is trust. Companies share their most competitive secrets with McKinsey with the understanding that confidentiality is paramount. McKinsey consultants aren't even supposed to tell their own spouses about their client work—and here was *a partner* of the firm selling client secrets out the back door for cold, hard cash.

If Kumar was acting as part of some sort of insider-trading ring within McKinsey, the likelihood of an Arthur Andersen–style collapse was high. Even if he'd acted alone, nervous clients could defect en masse. At the very least, those clients whose information Kumar had been selling—technology companies AMD, Business Objects, Samsung, and Spansion—seemed likely to sever relations with the firm.

Known as a quiet, careful, and even shy man, Anil Kumar was one of McKinsey's Silicon Valley experts. A protégé of Rajat Gupta—some say a "bag carrier"—he had as modest a profile as you could have at McKinsey and still be a senior partner. That was, those who knew him argued, at least in part due to his relationship with Gupta. "He was a Rajat follower," said a former partner of the firm. "But that's okay. The big dogs always had people they carried."

But Kumar *did* have an impressive résumé. After joining the firm in 1986, he'd moved to India in 1993 to help build the firm's local operations, as well as to launch the New Delhi–based McKinsey Knowledge Center, a research and analytics subsidiary that was an early pioneer in the coming wave of outsourcing that was about to wash over India.[15] In 1996 he and Rajat Gupta co-founded the Indian School of Business in Hyderabad in partnership with the Indian government. In 1999, the year the foundation stone was laid, he returned to the United States to work with technology clients out of McKinsey's Palo Alto office. After his return, the Confederation of Indian Industries, a lobbying organization, asked him to cochair the Indian American Council.[16]

Kumar quickly denied the charges through his high-profile veteran defense lawyer, Robert Morvillo, but it was merely a pro forma—

and almost comical—denial. The government had wiretap evidence clearly implicating him, including an August 2008 call during which he advised Rajaratnam to buy shares of AMD in advance of an announcement coming after Labor Day that the government of Abu Dhabi intended to invest $6 billion to $8 billion in the microprocessor maker.

McKinsey didn't wait for the wheels of justice to start turning. The firm placed Kumar on an indefinite leave of absence and asked two law firms—WilmerHale and Cravath, Swain & Moore—to conduct internal investigations to find out just how far the rot had spread. By December McKinsey had severed relations with Kumar entirely. In January 2010 he pleaded guilty to one count of securities fraud and one count of conspiracy to commit securities fraud. He also agreed to forfeit $2.6 million authorities said he'd been paid by Rajaratnam since 2003, including money deposited in a Swiss bank account Kumar had set up under his housekeeper's name and some placed in Kumar's accounts at Rajaratnam's Galleon hedge funds. In mid-2012, after testifying against both Rajaratnam and Gupta in their respective federal cases, Kumar managed to avoid jail time and received just two years probation for his crimes. His banishment from McKinsey, on the other hand, was permanent.

But here's the remarkable thing: Even as the McKinsey name was dragged through the mud of the Rajaratnam investigation and ensuing trial, McKinsey's billings didn't fall—or at least did not fall by much. *Forbes* estimated 2011 billings at $7 billion.[17]

Resilient billings aside, it was still a public relations nightmare—and a worsening one. In March 2010 the *Wall Street Journal* reported that none other than Rajat Gupta himself was ensnared in the investigation. The *Journal*'s revelations prompted two almost unthinkable questions: Had a *managing director* of McKinsey engaged in insider trading? And had he done so *while running the firm*?

Et Tu, Gupta?

Of all the managing directors in the firm's history, Rajat Gupta cultivated the highest public profile after he left McKinsey. Indeed, by the time he retired from the firm in 2007, he was already well on his way to a second career as a global citizen and philanthropist. In 2001 he helped raise $1 billion in relief funds after the Gujarat earthquake in India. He co-founded the American India Foundation with Bill Clinton. Gupta co-founded the Global Fund to Fight AIDS, Tuberculosis and Malaria. He took on roles with the United Nations and joined the board of the World Economic Forum. He chaired the India AIDS initiative of the Bill & Melinda Gates Foundation. He was, in effect, the de facto chairman of the international division of India, Inc.

He also stayed connected to the corporate realm, and his long career as a well-connected corporate consigliere made him highly coveted as a director. Between 2006 and 2009, Gupta picked up seats on the boards of five public companies—American Airlines' parent AMR, global outsourcer Genpact (of which he was also chairman), Goldman Sachs, audio equipment giant Harman International, and Procter & Gamble. He also joined the supervisory board of Sberbank, the largest bank in Russia and Eastern Europe by assets, and the board of the Qatar Financial Centre. All together, those positions paid him more than $3.2 million in 2009.

In 2008 Sberbank paid him $525,000, while the next-highest-paid director on the board earned only $110,000. The question of whether he could actually be independent while being paid $525,000 was serious enough that RiskMetrics, the corporate-governance watchdog based in Washington, D.C., advised minority shareholders to vote against his nomination in 2009. He was reelected anyway.

When Gupta joined the board of Goldman Sachs in November 2006, he seemed a perfect fit—the former top executive of one secretive, elite firm joining another. Less than two years later Gupta reportedly told Goldman CEO Lloyd Blankfein that he wanted to step down—he had spread himself too thin—only to be persuaded to stick around to avoid the public relations fallout of a director quitting in the midst of the financial crisis.

Gupta's extensive connections and status as one of the most prominent Indian businessmen on the planet made him a natural guest at President Barack Obama's first state dinner in November 2009, in honor of Manmohan Singh, the prime minister of India. But if he put on a good face in the halls of power, there's a good chance he was fretting on the inside. Kumar and Rajaratnam had been arrested just weeks before. The Feds had busted Kumar on the basis of several incriminating calls he had made to Rajaratnam in the summer and fall of 2008. During that same period, Gupta had made several intriguing calls to Rajaratnam himself.

• • •

Gupta had gotten to know Rajaratnam in 1999, when the Sri Lankan–born hedge fund manager made a substantial donation to the Indian School of Business. The two South Asian–born businessmen had nearly crossed paths before, notably in the late 1990s when both invested in venture capital firm TeleSoft Partners. (Gupta remained an adviser to the firm; Rajaratnam was no longer an investor.) But after Rajaratnam's donation, they became fast friends.

Before long they were in business together. In 2006, shortly before his formal retirement from McKinsey, Gupta and Rajaratnam joined private equity veteran Parag Saxena and Mark Schwartz, a former Goldman Sachs executive, to found Taj Capital, an investment firm focused on South Asia. A planned hedge fund never came to fruition, so Rajaratnam eventually had no role in the operations of what came to be known as New Silk Route. (He remained an investor, however.)

Schwartz ultimately dropped out. Gupta and Saxena went on to raise $1.4 billion through 2007 and 2008. Gupta also invested several million dollars in a Galleon investment vehicle, GB Voyager Multi-Strategy Fund. According to the *Wall Street Journal,* Gupta was a frequent visitor at the Galleon offices.

If Gupta breathed a sigh of relief at not being implicated in the insider-trading scandal in October 2009, he had only five months during which to relax. In a front-page article on April 15, 2010, the *Wall Street Journal* reported that the government was investigating whether Gupta had shared confidential information with Rajaratnam. A second front-page story in the *Journal,* citing an unnamed source, reported that Gupta had tipped off Rajaratnam about Warren Buffett's confidence-boosting $5 billion investment in Goldman Sachs in September 2008, during the depths of the market turmoil.

Gupta's lawyer offered a defiant statement of his client's innocence. "Rajat Gupta's record of ethical conduct and integrity in his professional as well as personal life is beyond reproach," said attorney Gary Naftalis. "He also has served with distinction and selflessness many philanthropic and civic causes around the world, including both the United States and India. Rajat has not violated any laws or regulations, nor has he done anything improper."

Gupta nevertheless left the Goldman board in May when his term expired rather than stand for reelection. (He was replaced with another corporate giant, H. Lee Scott Jr., the former CEO of Walmart.) In June fellow Goldman director Bill George, the former Medtronic CEO, told *Fortune* that the board would miss Gupta's presence. "On boards of directors, you find out who really matters during times of crises," said George. "And in the fall of 2008, Rajat was an extraordinarily valuable member of the board. I was very disappointed to learn of his decision to step down. And as for the issues with Mr. Rajaratnam, no one [on the board] knows anything. No one has been contacted."[18]

Despite the uncertainty, Gupta showed no signs of backing away from his public life. He maintained board seats at four public companies, including Procter & Gamble. Former Procter & Gamble chief A. G. Lafley—with whom Gupta had worked on the Gillette acquisition—even stuck his neck out for Gupta. "Rajat starts from purpose and values and ends up at strategies and principles," Lafley told *Fortune*. "He also brings an analytical and objective approach to the question at hand. I think of him like Thomas Aquinas. He wasn't just asking what we should do. He was helping us figure out the right thing to do."[19]

The International Chamber of Commerce made him chairman in June 2010. And as far as successful Indians are concerned, he was still in the club. "I find him of exceptionally good character," multibillionaire Indian industrialist Adi Godrej told *Fortune*. "He is extremely devoted to helping India's development and progress, things he doesn't have to spend his time and energy on." In 2012 support for Gupta went the modern route, with the launching of a website, www.friendsofrajat.com, complete with inspirational quotations on injustice, suffering, and endurance from Bishop Desmond Tutu, Mahatma Gandhi, and Elie Wiesel. An open letter on the site was signed by Indian luminaries including Mukesh Ambani, Sabeer Bhatia (co-founder of Hotmail), and Deepak Chopra, among others, as well as retired McKinsey directors Anjan Chatterjee, Atul Kanagat, Michael Obermeyer, and Ali Hanna.[20]

Not everyone was so sanguine. Back at McKinsey, there was a desperate search under way to find out whether the firm was an investor in Galleon—McKinsey manages billions of dollars of its consultants' retirement accounts through the McKinsey Investment Office. There was a palpable sense of dodging a bullet when it came to light that no, the firm had not invested with the hedge fund.

Still, there was an anxious desire on the part of McKinsey that the charges against Gupta prove unfounded. Throughout 2010, he had spoken to a number of his former colleagues and assured them that there was nothing to the allegations. And there was reason for optimism, as more than a year after the big bust, neither the Justice Department nor the Securities and Exchange Commission had filed a single charge against Gupta. "My sense of it is that he has been caught up in the 'Get Goldman' furor," one of the firm's senior partners said in December 2010. "The press and the SEC were out to get Goldman, and he was on the board, so he was an easy target. I have talked to Rajat, and I don't think there is anything there." Three months later the partner was proven utterly, incontrovertibly wrong.

• • •

On March 1, 2011, the SEC filed a civil administrative proceeding against Gupta, accusing him of leaking confidential information to Rajaratnam, from not just the board meetings of Goldman Sachs but also those of Procter & Gamble. The SEC alleged that Rajaratnam had made $18.2 million in trading profits from Gupta's tips alone.

The allegations were damning, if not as undeniable as the wiretaps of Rajaratnam and Kumar. On September 21, 2008, for example, Goldman Sachs CEO Lloyd Blankfein informed the Goldman board via teleconference that the company was exploring "strategic alternatives," including a possible investment by Warren Buffett. The next morning, Gupta and Rajaratnam "very likely" had a phone conversation, after which Rajaratnam bought 80,000 shares of Goldman Sachs; he had no previous position in the stock. The *next* morning, Rajaratnam phoned Gupta for a fourteen-minute conversation. A minute into the call, Galleon purchased 40,000 more shares of Goldman. At 3:15 that afternoon, the Goldman board approved a $5 billion preferred stock investment from Buffett by conference call. That call lasted until 3:53 p.m. Just *three minutes* after the call ended, Gupta called Rajaratnam. In the remaining minutes of the trading day, Rajaratnam bought 175,000 more shares of Goldman.

And that was just one example. The SEC also accused Gupta of giving Rajaratnam confidential information about Goldman's second- and fourth-quarter 2008 results, as well as Procter & Gamble's fourth-quarter numbers. In April 2012 prosecutors added a claim to this effect to their charges against Gupta. After learning that P&G was going to lower its sales forecasts, prosecutors claimed, Gupta had lunch with Rajaratnam. Immediately after that lunch, Rajaratnam ordered his traders to short the stock of the company.[21]

From the very beginning, Gupta's lawyer, Gary Naftalis, called the charges "baseless"—a patently absurd remark, given the circumstantial evidence—and he spent a large part of 2011 making it clear that Gupta had made no money as a result of any of the alleged phone calls to Rajaratnam, in direct payments or as an investment in Galleon, and that it was therefore inappropriate to charge him with insider trading. Naftalis continued through 2012 with that simple boilerplate defense every time a new charge was added by prosecutors.

Gupta's lawyer and public relations team had insisted since the scandal broke that Gupta's original investment with Rajaratnam had already tanked by 2008 and that he had lost his entire $10 million. But evidence presented during the Rajaratnam trial in 2011 seemed to suggest otherwise, listing his stake in the Voyager Fund in June 2008 at $16.4 million.[22] According to testimony and wiretaps, Gupta was also negotiating with Rajaratnam for a 10 to 15 percent stake in the Galleon International Fund and a possible role as the fund's chairman in exchange for making introductions to new investors.

Two weeks after the SEC filed its charges, McKinsey's 1,200 partners were in Washington for their annual get-together, located this time around at the Gaylord National Hotel and Convention Center. On that day, prosecutors in the Rajaratnam trial played a wiretapped phone conversation between Gupta and Rajaratnam, during which Gupta told Rajaratnam that Goldman was mulling an acquisition of Wachovia or AIG Group. Whether or not it was legally damning, it was a clear indication of a breach of confidentiality.

What's more, the tapes appeared to show that Gupta knew that Rajaratnam was paying Kumar for information. The wiretaps also revealed Rajaratnam telling Kumar that he thought Gupta had tired of being a "poor" consultant and desired to join the "billionaire circle" of which Rajaratnam himself was a part. Response to the tapes was high anger. "If he'd come within fifty miles of the place, there would have been a lynching," said one partner. "At a minimum, grotesque unprofessionalism," added Ian Davis. "At a maximum, illegality."[23]

The firm's Professional Standards Committee convened for what proved a very brief meeting. The verdict: Forget the justice system; the McKinsey partners knew a violation of their values when they saw one. The next week Dominic Barton called Rajat Gupta to tell him that he was persona non grata at the firm from that point forward.

One former director thinks McKinsey's response to the whole debacle smacked of the firm's own myopia. "That's what's funky about the place," he said. "They actually think that was a big call that Dom made. I would have done it by 9:05 a.m. on the day the wiretap came out. You become much tougher and edgier outside those walls. 'But he was our *managing director*!' they'll say. Well, fuck him."

A cornered Gupta lashed out in response to the SEC charges. On March 18, 2011, he filed a lawsuit against the SEC in the Southern District of New York challenging the proceedings. Five months later, on August 4, 2011, the SEC dismissed the charges, suggesting for a brief moment that Gupta had prevailed in civil court, if not in the court of his McKinsey partners or that of public opinion. But that illusion proved short-lived.

On October 13, 2011, Raj Rajaratnam was convicted of insider trading and sentenced to eleven years in prison. Less than two weeks later, on October 26, 2011, the SEC refiled its civil charges. More significantly, the Justice Department did what so many had been wondering had taken so long—it indicted Rajat Gupta on criminal charges.

In a wide-ranging interview in *Newsweek* two weeks after his conviction, Rajaratnam claimed that FBI agents had asked him to wear a wire to catch Gupta in the act of insider trading. Rajaratnam may have been a billionaire hedge fund guy, but Gupta was one of the most respected Indian business leaders in the United States, if not *the* most respected of all. Rajaratnam had refused to cooperate. In the same article he referred to Kumar as a *choot*—Hindi for "c*nt"—and said, "That word fits him."

He went on to explain why, despite intense pressure, he wouldn't turn rat himself. "They wanted me to plea-bargain," he told the magazine. "They [wanted] to get Rajat. I am not going to do what people did to me. Rajat has four daughters."[24] Neither did Kumar seem to offer authorities anything on Gupta. But that was less of a surprise. Rajaratnam was Sri Lankan. With Kumar caught dead to rights on the wiretap, he had little choice but to turn on his erstwhile friend. But to turn on Gupta? He would be ostracized by the entire Indian community. In the end, though, he did just that and testified against his former mentor in order to avoid jail time himself.

Seven months after Rajaratnam's sentencing, Gupta himself was convicted of insider trading, in part due to helpful testimony from Kumar. After a month-long trial, it took the jury just two days to find him guilty of leaking confidential information to Rajaratnam on three different occasions in 2008, as well as a conspiracy charge. "Having fallen from respected insider to convicted inside trader, Mr. Gupta has now exchanged the lofty boardroom for the prospect of a lowly jail cell," said Preet Bharara, the United States Attorney in Manhattan.[25]

While Gupta's lawyer, Gary Naftalis, continued to insist that his client had done nothing wrong, the evidence was so overwhelming that the jury managed to get by what some had thought Gupta's strongest defense—the fact that he didn't seem to have enjoyed explicit personal financial gains from the leaks. But Rajaratnam had, and it was enough. There was something vintage McKinsey in the whole debacle: Ever the behind-the-scenes player, Gupta had ceded the outright financial gain in return for whatever influence with Rajaratnam the illegal favors might have earned him. But under the harsh glare of federal prosecution, the McKinsey model—take no credit, but take no blame—collapsed on itself. In October 2012, he was sentenced to two years in prison and fined $5 million for his crimes. At his sentencing, he expressed remorse for the negative association McKinsey had suffered from his case despite his having retired from the firm. "I am extremely sorry for the negative comments from clients and the press that McKinsey has had to deal with," he said. "I take some comfort that, given the strength of the firm, I hope that it will not suffer any long-term reputational harm."

The soul-searching at the firm and among alumni went deeper than examining the moral and ethical failures of two men. "I think it goes back to what happened after Marvin left," says one longtime and now retired partner of the firm. "Ron Daniel didn't entirely take up the mantle of Marvin's value-driven approach. And that left the door open to start focusing more and more on measurement of results by financial returns. Which created an environment where someone who was very good at producing those returns could lead the firm without the checks and balances Marvin put in place. That led to two separate things. The first was Gupta. The second was the abandonment of our top-management approach."

He continued: "But again, it's much larger than Gupta himself. The revelation that someone who had led the firm for ten years could have so lost sight of the value systems that Marvin had built into the place made me aware of both how far the United States had moved in a money-is-all-that's-important direction as well as how far the financial community had lost sight of why it was set up in the first place, which was to help actual companies doing actual things. And there is no doubt that the modern McKinsey is part of that malaise. Of course, it's very hard to see something you gave fifteen years of your life to succumb to such a different set of values than the professional ones it once had. But to have the leading nation in the world lose its soul is a much bigger loss than the mortification of Rajat Gupta."

Still, there was no question that McKinsey was left to wonder how, just nine years after his death, the spirit of Marvin Bower had been so desecrated in such a short period of time. "Marvin Bower said they were greedy fucks at the end," said one client who knew the man. "He was old but lively." And at least in this case, it seems he was right.

Who Are We?

In the search for answers in the midst of the Kumar/Gupta scandal, McKinsey turned inward. And it didn't like what it saw, which was a firm that had deceived itself into thinking that the Gupta-era excesses had been left behind. It had merely papered over the problem and missed a fundamental—and permanent—change in the nature of the firm. At its current size, McKinsey could no longer assume that Marvin Bower's principles would endure.

"The stuff with Anil [Kumar] was noteworthy in the effect it had on people," said Michelle Jarrard, director of firm personnel. "It was a disappointment, and we can't pretend it's not. You might try to tell a silver-lining story about the fact that it caused us to increase our vigilance going forward, but it's fair to say that it hurt."[26]

One obvious issue raised by the Kumar incident, in particular, is that of the senior person too far out on the fringe of a large and growing company. Did he engage in illegal behavior purely out of greed? Or out of frustration at not being close enough to McKinsey's inner circle? In a sense, McKinsey might have been a victim of its own success. It was now so large that the chance of a partner's becoming disaffected had risen along with the company's top and bottom lines. In the 1980s, for example, about half the firm's directors were on either the shareholders committee or the directors committee. If you weren't one of these directors, you certainly knew many (or all) of them, so few partners could get lost in the wilderness. By 2011 that proportion had fallen to about 10 percent, and the odds of disenchantment had risen inversely.

"I've talked to Dominic about the issue," said Ian Davis. "Which is: How do you create a feeling of real leadership amongst directors who don't feel that they are leading the organization? That's one of the reasons you create committees and networks. The key is keeping older consultants feeling connected. My father once told me that the mistake we all make is thinking teenagers are problematic. It's really people in their late fifties and early sixties that are the problematic ones. That's where real frustration arises."[27]

The real regret, though, was not about Kumar. It was about Rajat Gupta and what many at the firm felt they should have known all along. The revelations have caused a stunning crisis of confidence among one of the world's most confident collections of people. "They always felt a little unsure about Rajat," admitted a former director. "He never quite embodied Marvin's values. He was a much more commercial animal. That's why it surprised no one that he joined Goldman's board in the first place. That's why the venom is so strong about him, because they could see it coming and they didn't stop themselves. They just printed money when he was there, and now they're all feeling guilty about it."

There were clear signs that seem to have been ignored. For one, he'd muscled his way through objections from some partners and joined Goldman's board before he'd officially resigned from the firm—a clear violation of Bower's founding principles. And then came the worst news of all: A superseding indictment filed by the United States attorney in late 2011 suggested that Gupta was feeding Rajaratnam information from Goldman board meetings in 2008 *when he was still working out of McKinsey's New York offices*. He had given up his partnership in 2007, but still retained an office at the firm.

If you'd asked a McKinsey partner in 2011 whether Kumar and Gupta had damaged the firm, you would have gotten a resounding "yes" in response. But here's the remarkable thing: Ask a client, and you would get a different answer entirely. For the most part, clients didn't seem to care, or they even felt sympathetic. Despite a slight drop-off in 2009 due to the global financial crisis, the business continued to hold up relatively well in the face of the scandal. Even Walmart, which for years disdained consultants, had brought McKinsey on board at the end of the decade.[28] McKinsey's revenues actually *grew* by 9 percent in 2010—second in the industry only to Pricewaterhouse-Coopers.[29] The firm hired two thousand people in 2010.

Loyal clients included companies that were clients of Anil Kumar himself. In 2009, for example, Tim Flynn, chairman and CEO of accounting and advisory firm KPMG, was in the midst of formalizing a project with McKinsey. On Wednesday, October 14, Kumar spoke to the board of KPMG. The next morning Flynn and Kumar had breakfast. And the next morning Kumar was arrested. But like many McKinsey clients, Flynn apparently subscribes to the "bad apples" theory: Every organization has them, and the thing that's important is that once they're discovered, you do your best to make sure there aren't any more. KPMG decided to go ahead and work with the firm despite the controversy.

Peter Grauer, chairman of Bloomberg LP, expressed a similar sentiment. He first encountered McKinsey around 2006, when he asked the consultants to help chart a future for the financial information provider's domestic television business. Bloomberg adopted a series of McKinsey's recommendations in 2008, including bringing in proven talent—like network television veteran Andy Lack.

McKinsey also helped Bloomberg assess its strategy for an expansion into legal information through a new product, Bloomberg Law. At the time, Bloomberg was selling access to its law product on its famous terminals, and the product was priced more expensively than its main competitors, such as Thomson Reuters, Westlaw, and Reed Elsevier. McKinsey nudged the company toward a web-based platform that allowed for much more competitive pricing. "They did a great job on that one," said Grauer.[30] The consultants then moved on to a similar project on Bloomberg Government. Neither effort had been a resounding success through 2012, but, once again, the client is reluctant to pin any shortcomings on McKinsey.

"We have seen the quality of their work," said Grauer. "It's been fruitful working with them. We do business with other management consulting firms, but it just so happened that we find the intellectual processes and quality of output of McKinsey superior enough that we engage them more than others." And then he added something that might put a smile back on Marvin Bower's face: "We pay them what we think is fair, and I think we get value for it."

The firm's intellectual output continued to win raves as well. In mid-2010 Dominic Barton was meeting with Francis Mer, former minister of finance in France and then-chairman of French conglomerate Safran. Mer had read McKinsey's January 2010 report, titled "Debt and Deleveraging: The Global Credit Bubble and Its Economic Consequences." Mer told Barton that it was the single best piece of research he'd read in five years.

"Can I give you some feedback?" he asked Barton. "You couldn't market yourself out of a paper bag. Why didn't you take this report around to every single finance minister in Europe and force them to read it?" This was ignoring the obvious reason for McKinsey's retreat from active outreach. Since the arrest of Kumar and the rumors about Gupta, the firm had leaned back on its most cherished of public relations strategies: It had closed ranks. It was still pitching to clients, but McKinsey wasn't in a chest-thumping mode in 2010.

Despite the media frenzy over the insider trading scandal, the actual damage to McKinsey's reputation remained unclear. In *Consulting* magazine's 2009 ranking of the best firms to work for, McKinsey slipped from the number one spot to second, behind Bain & Company. But the firm remained at the top of the Vault.com survey of the most prestigious consulting firms in 2011, a spot it had held for a decade.

McKinsey's Thursday night party at the Belvedere Hotel during the World Economic Forum in Davos is still considered the best event of the week. There is talk in WEF circles of when Klaus Schwab, the seventy-three-year-old founder of Davos, lets go of the reins that McKinsey will take over management of the Forum. McKinsey Man is Davos Man, after all.

In March 2012 McKinsey partners quietly reelected Dominic Barton to a second term as managing director. No one even bothered running against him, which wasn't surprising. Barton radiates calm, and he is thus suited to lead the ever-larger collection of insecure overachievers as they once again do a little soul-searching.

EPILOGUE: THE FUTURE OF McKINSEY

Even as the Anil Kumar and Rajat Gupta episodes begin to fade in the rearview mirror, McKinsey is on a stretch of road as existentially foreboding as any in its history. The profession that it largely invented is more hotly contested than it has ever been. Everybody is competing to be a consultant. And many of the new, hot companies that are driving the economy have shown little or no interest in engaging McKinsey.

McKinsey's main asset continues to be the trust its clients have in the firm, an unquantifiable, intangible thing that is constantly being tested. The consultants' secondary assets—their trust in each other and the internal culture of the place—have likewise come under stress. The more the organization grows, the harder it is to enforce a coherent set of values. Marvin Bower's little club of Harvard MBAs with their Anglo-Saxon mores is ancient history. McKinsey is now a truly global corporation. The place is so big that the presence of more rogues on the payroll is not a mere possibility but a near certainty.

If they are to be believed, they *do* continue to trust themselves. It's the reason McKinsey partners spend such a ridiculous amount of time each year evaluating one another. And while there will certainly be more bad behavior by foolish people at McKinsey, it has never been a place that attracted the truly greedy. People obsessed with wealth tend to go elsewhere: to investment banking, private equity, hedge funds, or venture capital.

Trust issues aside, McKinsey's greatest challenge is finding things to tell its clients that they don't already know. The business world is overflowing with MBAs these days, and McKinsey-like advice can be easily bought at low, un-McKinsey-like rates. What's more, McKinsey's vaunted "transformational relationship" isn't a priority for many clients embroiled in global economic turmoil; results are. Even the most trusting client can lose enthusiasm for his consultants if they're not helping him solve his immediate problems. Many companies today don't have the luxury of indulging in long-term strategizing. They need to win right now. That's never been McKinsey's strength.

McKinsey was a great partner to the industrial era. This was especially true in the years after World War II—the era of Peter Drucker and the "invention" of management—when America was a place of giant firms that were quite literally out of control, conglomerates so large that their managers had trouble getting their arms around them. Marvin Bower and his peers gave them new tools and techniques for how to manage. The firm helped reshape the corporate sector as well as the government, often using McKinsey's own internal designs as a template.

After being sideswiped by more aggressive competition once or twice, the firm was also a great partner to the first postindustrial era. McKinsey was an invaluable partner to CEOs in industries facing rapid change—from finance to pharmaceuticals. Indeed, McKinsey seems to have played a part in *every* big trend of the past century, from deregulation and loosened capital markets to the spread of new technologies and globalization.[1] Whatever the corporate problem, McKinsey has often been able to offer a fix.

But while the firm continues to grow, there's an argument to be made that its influence has not kept pace. Few of today's winners got where they are today because McKinsey told them how to get there—consider Apple or Google. McKinsey's signature winners are from the old school: American Express, AT&T, Citibank, General Motors, or Merrill Lynch. McKinsey didn't work for Microsoft until the software company was already huge. McKinsey, in a way, is the Microsoft of its own industry—never out ahead but with the resources to play catch-up occasionally when others advance first.

As McKinsey loses its vitality, it has become less alluring for young talent. The firm dominated the era of the MBA—the late 1980s and early 1990s—when all any business student wanted to do was get a job in consulting or banking. Nicholas Lemann wrote in the *New Yorker* in 1999 that McKinsey had effectively encapsulated the zeitgeist of the moment, much as the CIA had done in the 1950s, the Peace Corps in the 1960s, Ralph Nader in the 1970s, and First Boston in the 1980s.[2]

But that was thirteen years ago. Today, the crème de la crème flock to younger, more vibrant companies, in both entry-level and much higher positions. The brightest students tend to not want to work for large companies anymore, and McKinsey is a large company. In the 1970s every smart student received an offer from Arthur Andersen, then about ten thousand strong. The more adventurous went to McKinsey, which employed a paltry four hundred by comparison. Today Arthur Andersen is gone, and McKinsey has taken its place in the student imagination. And, as has always been the case, McKinsey consultants continue to leave for big positions elsewhere. Among others, Facebook chief operating officer Sheryl Sandberg is a McKinsey alumnus, as is Google chief financial officer Patrick Pichette. McKinsey may be a career firm for some, but it tends to lose its best people.

MBA students across the globe still clamor for an opportunity to interview with the consultants, and the firm claims that the acceptance rate for job offers hovers around 95 percent. But look a little more closely and you can see the lure of a job at the firm fraying at the edges. Recent acceptance rates at Harvard Business School, for example, are not what they once were. Whereas in 1973 the firm made offers to 5 percent of the MBA class and had acceptance of about 80 percent, in 2013 McKinsey made offers to 15 percent of the class and only enjoyed about 70 percent acceptance.

Though the firm still invests more in its people than does any of its rivals, McKinsey is at risk of becoming a mere pit stop for talent, a place that trains young people for more exciting careers elsewhere. That presents a shocking disparity with the McKinsey of half a century ago. "Are they in the swiftest stream or not?" asked former McKinsey consultant Bill MacCormack. "What are they learning? In our day, we got to work at the very highest levels. It was an intellectual high. Is it still?"[3]

Winners don't win forever, no matter who they are. Goldman Sachs, long the gold standard in finance, has been outmatched recently by its much larger and better-capitalized competitor, JPMorgan Chase. Microsoft, lazy and dull after decades of dominance, was utterly outflanked by Apple after the return of Steve Jobs. And McKinsey? The firm has been winning at the game so long that one can only wonder if it will realize when it's lost what made it a winner in the first place.

The firm's centrality in the management process is also more difficult to see with the abstraction of the economy. While many assume that the growth of consulting is a direct result of the benefits it provides, there is an alternative view. "The world does not owe consultancies a living," Stefan Stern wrote in the *Financial Times* in April 2010. "After all, there was a time, not so long ago, when people ran their business without the help of strategy consulting firms."[4] In many cases, that is also true today: McKinsey alumni may have infiltrated the ranks of Google or eBay, but the fleetest young companies that are changing the face of business today don't have the time for McKinsey to establish a "trust-based relationship."

McKinsey is now large enough that it tends to reflect the consulting cycle, which waxes and wanes with the global economy. As a result, McKinsey has not seen meaningful growth in the United States for many years and is seeing dramatically slower growth in Europe, where it prospered in the 1990s. Like the Roman army, McKinsey needs to keep moving just to forage for food to sustain itself. Chinese executives and bureaucrats, naturally, find themselves enjoying a disproportionate amount of attention from the consultants. Burgeoning demand in Asia for McKinsey's services is due at least in part to the firm's sterling brand reputation in the West. But that demand won't last long if all McKinsey does is try to sell old formulas in new packages.

The firm's business is also so global that the revenue breakdown generally mirrors that of world GDP. The United States, for example, which accounts for about 25 to 30 percent of global GDP, also represents 25 to 30 percent of McKinsey's revenues. Europe and Africa? About 30 percent combined. And Asia and Latin America make up the balance. If the debt crisis takes down the European economy, more than a quarter of McKinsey's revenues could be at risk.

McKinsey's shareholder committee—its de facto board of directors—now numbers thirty-one people spread across the world. Such a cumbersome governing body is not built for speed. The firm's size has also finally voided the long-held pretense that the consultants work only with the corner office. They are now forced to admit that they accept assignments to work throughout large organizations. That has increased the volume of business available to them, but it has also dented their reputation as the close confidants of the corporate elite.

McKinsey still manifests strengths that its competitors have not been able to replicate. McKinsey's one-firm ethos—in which the head of the German office doesn't care if one of his local consultants is working for Daimler or Detroit—has allowed it to sidestep debates about intracompany profit centers and bonus pools that have terrorized the staffs of rivals. Its self-governing partnership—as opposed to a command-and-control setup—has also helped the firm avoid the pitfalls of more autocratic leadership models.

Most impressive, perhaps, is its still unrivaled ability to attract an enormous pool of smart people and to mold them into *like-minded* smart people—an army of highly motivated, high-impact consultants. This is done by weeding out those who can't be molded; the most important jobs at McKinsey are those doing the molding at different levels of the firm. The winnowing can be brutal on young people who were the smartest in their class and then suddenly are shown the door by McKinsey after two years. But if you make it onto the partner track, it's a contented little club of survivors. In a sense, McKinsey has solved the same riddle as the army has in convincing people to go to war and get shot at—for the feeling of serving something greater than oneself. None of its rivals have come even close to creating a system like this. They don't quite hold hands and sing the Japanese national anthem at McKinsey, but it's close.

McKinsey is as likely to cripple itself as a competitor is to do so. Which brings the focus back to size. Within McKinsey, the debate over what is the right size for the firm is a never-ending one. One camp, generally older consultants, thinks the firm has grown too large and could afford to shrink in order to maintain the quality of its people and their work. The other camp, made up of younger and hungrier consultants, has no memory of those days when the firm was just four hundred or a thousand or even five thousand strong. To them, size is power, and they make an argument for continued growth.

With size, too, comes complexity—the kind McKinsey claims it is expert in solving for its clients. The firm now has so many internal networks or "cells"—of geography, industry, and function—that the primary challenge of the place has moved from bringing in new business to making sure the internal structures don't fold in on themselves. The firm, in effect, is made up of dozens of mini-McKinseys. The benefit of such smallness in the presence of bigness is that it's actually quite difficult to fail as an institution. The challenge, though, is one of leadership: Is it reasonable to think one can gather fifty mini-Bowers or mini-Bartons under one roof, especially in light of the fact that, by design, no one runs anything at McKinsey for much more than six years anyway? From the outside, it's unclear how the cell system works. From the inside, it is also unclear how it works. And that's a problem for a firm at which the connections among people are all that matters.

And is a model where senior partners spend several weeks a year reviewing one another as efficient as it needs to be in today's hypercompetitive market? Especially from the perspective of the client, who might have a year-long project to contend with? McKinsey has long been enamored with the way it does things—going so far as to tell clients they can take the culture or leave it—but in an era of cautious corporate spending, McKinsey's idiosyncrasies run the risk of not being tolerated anymore.

McKinsey will tell you that there really is no secret to its success—it is based on a relentless focus on recruiting and training, rigorous peer review, hard work, and emphasizing one's contributions to the firm rather than taking credit for client billings. The firm's recruiting process has been compared to that for astronauts. That has surely allowed McKinsey to weather the necessary decline in selectivity that comes from hiring twice as many people a year than it did just ten years ago, but the job of keeping up the quality is an increasingly challenging one.

Yet it is also one at which the firm seems to be succeeding. Clay Deutsch, who recently left the firm after thirty years, said the McKinsey he joined and the McKinsey he left are two profoundly different firms. "Can a firm evolve and end up in a radically different place while still having many of the same central characteristics?" he asked. "Characteristics that animate rather than retard it? I think so, as cosmic an idea as that may seem."[5]

They are making changes in response to evolving client needs, and have even shown an unusual sense of urgency about new competitive threats. Which is a good thing, because even if McKinsey is usually the one hired to help clients protect themselves against competitive disruption, the need for the firm to do so itself has never been more acute. In 2007, the firm made the fairly radical decision to allow clients to use software and analytics tools that take advantage of those investments in proprietary knowledge championed by its latest managing director, Dominic Barton, *without necessarily keeping a McKinsey engagement team on for further project work*. In a widely read 2013 article in the *Harvard Business Review*, HBS professor Clayton Christensen pointed out that it was the first time the firm had "unbundled" its "judgment-based and bespoke diagnoses" from its "hard knowledge assets."[6]

According to Christensen, the move is part of a broader industry-wide response to an ongoing "disaggregation" of consulting services by clients. Fewer clients need McKinsey "walking the halls" on effective retainer anymore, in part because so many would-be clients have their own hordes of MBAs walking their halls already. But one thing those clients are very much interested in as the Internet's information-gathering tentacles continue to spread is Big Data and Analytics. To that end, there is burgeoning interest in the ability to tap McKinsey's proprietary frameworks, analytics, and databases quickly and at will through subscription- or licensed-based pricing instead of having to go through all the rigmarole of hiring an engagement team again and bringing everybody up to speed.

It can never be argued that McKinsey has not served its own people quite well. Those who leave the firm have what remains one of the business world's most admired names on their résumé. Those who make a career of it have gotten extraordinarily wealthy and have found entrée into the halls of power around the world.

In the end, though, the value of a professional institution might be more appropriately measured by what it has done for others. On that count, the verdict is less clear.

It does remain an open question whether McKinsey has really transformed the way businesses are managed. Did it save General Motors, the great American icon, despite study after study for millions upon millions over the years? No. Did it foresee and push its clients to the front of the era of Internet-based business? No. Did it stop the wayward drift of the banking industry that led to the global financial crisis? Again, no.

Which raises another question: Just what *have* the consultants done? Ask McKinsey about the greatest piece of advice the firm ever gave—Did it tell Coca-Cola to green-light Diet Coke? Did it assure McDonald's that serving breakfast could work out? Or tell Chrysler to go for it with the Jeep?—and the answer will be wholly unsatisfying. There are no legendary consulting engagements at the firm. There are only legendary client relationships, the kind that keep money pouring in the door. (And it *is* still pouring in: recent estimates put 2013 revenue at $7 billion.) One need not look further than this to realize that it's all been about selling from the start. In short, it's not *what* McKinsey sold, it's *that* it sold. What's more, despite its emphatic insistence on its culture of "values," those values have often shown themselves to be conditional. They are applied when they are helpful. And they are not when they are not.

That said, through its objectivist, skeptical, fact-based, integrative, and analytical approach to solving its clients' problems, McKinsey has certainly made the world a more efficient, rational, and objective place than it might otherwise have been. In a world full of talkers and blowhards, the firm is supremely capable of bringing the focus back to the data and research, and usually to efficient effect. Management guru Gary Hamel referred to the "machinery of management" as "one of humanity's greatest inventions" in his 2007 book, *The Future of Management*.[7] If McKinsey hasn't actually invented many of the bold ideas of management since the death of James O. McKinsey himself, it has certainly helped clients understand them and carry them out.

The firm has also served as a powerful talisman for the terrified executive, a corporate shrink for the insecure CEO, and a rubber stamp for the domineering boss who wants to ram a decision down his company's throat. In other words, it plays the role its clients have scripted. That's why the focus on personal relationships has worked for so long. What executive *wouldn't* want a high-quality rapid-response team of well-dressed worker ants to satisfy his every need?

McKinsey has also been instrumental in enforcing the rules and customs of modern business—the modern company is no one's nanny, it is not a permanent employer, and it is playing in a ruthless game of winners and losers. In that regard, McKinsey has also contributed to the effects of modern business on the rest of society. By serving the interests of the corporate suite, the firm has played a part in the growth of income inequality—the chasm between compensation of the heads of companies and their employees is the widest in history.

McKinsey's continued focus on the problem to be solved, as opposed to all the ramifications of the proposed answer, remains perhaps its greatest weakness. The focus on the purity of that answer, as opposed to how easy or difficult it will be to get to where one wants to be, has never been the firm's strong suit. Laying off 10 percent of the people might cut 10 percent of the costs, but it also might make the remaining employees 50 percent angrier about their increased workload.

In their worst moments, McKinsey consultants congratulate each other on being what more than a few have referred to as the greatest collection of talent the world has ever seen. And in a way, they may be right—it's difficult to think of a comparable group of such smart, driven people working for the same organization anywhere in the world. But you can also look at it as McKinsey claiming to have won a game that no one else is playing. Most organizations—be they large multinational banks or entities like Facebook—don't actually *need* everyone on the payroll to be a smart overachiever.

• • •

Charlie Munger, Warren Buffett's longtime partner at Berkshire Hathaway, wrote in his book *Poor Charlie's Almanack: The Wit and Wisdom of Charles T. Munger* that he had never met a corporate leader who'd actually read a consulting report.

Pin executives down, and they will surely be able to tell you about the most important decisions of their career. In a large organization, though—the kind for which McKinsey works—the value of most decisions doesn't necessarily reside in the actual choice made; it resides in the very fact that the choice is being made in the first place. Leadership is about getting people to follow you, but before they can do that you need to choose the direction in which you're heading. There will always be demand for such a service, and that's precisely what McKinsey provides.

At the moment, McKinsey is looking east. Its early successes in Asia offer an opportunity to get as strong a grip on the corporate imagination there as it once had in the days of the preeminence of the old-boy WASP culture of America's northeast. Again: It is no coincidence that Dominic Barton, the current managing director of the firm, spent his formative years navigating the back rooms of corporate Asia. One of the greatest challenges facing any global business in the early twenty-first century will be understanding how to navigate the cross-currents of a rising Chinese economic power in the face of a stubbornly persistent American one. If McKinsey can manage to be seen as the holder of that key, the firm's continued prosperity is assured, at least in the short term.

Marvin Bower wanted McKinsey to be considered in the same light as the trusted local banker. But the firm of today resembles much more closely a national or global banking conglomerate than the friendly face from down the block. McKinsey is now a large—and aging—company, much like the giants it advised in the 1960s and 1970s. Its clients—whether they are corporations or executives—are far bigger. The consultants push for and help bring about change on a massive scale. At the same time, though, McKinsey now spends more and more time navigating the same bureaucracies it once disdained, and the firm is inside those systems more than it is outside them.

McKinsey's greatest challenge going forward—the true test of its genius—is no longer finding inspired solutions to its clients' problems. The test is managing the complications that have resulted from its own stupendous success. One of the firm's recently stated goals is helping to "[solve] the world's great problems."[8] But if it wants to achieve this, it's going to have to continue solving its own.

ACKNOWLEDGMENTS

When you finally put the pen down (figuratively speaking) after a project of this magnitude, the experience is an unusual one. Just a few months before, it felt like a boulder on your shoulders. And suddenly you feel as if you could fly. For that reason, it's a good idea to keep a running list of the people you need to thank for helping you get over the finish line. Because if you went by your emotions alone, you might just suffer from the delusion that you managed to get there all on your own. Maybe some people do. I am not one of those people.

Let me start by thanking my publisher, Simon & Schuster. This is the second book with which these good people have entrusted me, and I greatly appreciate the repeat endorsement. First among equals at S&S: my editor, Priscilla Painton. I could not have hoped for a better hand-holder along the way. Thanks, Priscilla. Next, of course, is the man who signs the checks, publisher Jonathan Karp. Thanks for taking a chance on this one, Jonathan. Thank you too, Colin Fox, for your championing of the project. Thanks also to Victoria Meyer, Tracey Guest, and the S&S marketing team, as well as Michael Szczerban and Sydney Tanigawa.

Thanks also to the man on my side of the negotiating table, my agent, David Kuhn, and all the good people at Kuhn Projects: Casey Baird, Jessie Borkan, Becky Sweren, Nicole Tourtelot, and Billy Kingsland.

Another person owed a serious debt of gratitude: my old friend and mentor, Hugo Lindgren, who took time out of one of the toughest jobs in town to touch this book with his magic. Thanks, Hugo, for your help on this project and much else.

And now, to McKinsey. I didn't expect the firm to cooperate with this book. The firm had never done so before, it didn't know me from Adam, and, well, this is not exactly the most forthcoming bunch when journalists come poking around. Thanks to Michael Stewart, who shepherded me through to approval. I hope you will still speak to me, Michael.

Thanks to the current and former managing directors who spoke to me: Dominic Barton, Ian Davis, Fred Gluck, Ron Daniel, and Al McDonald. (It seems Rajat Gupta was indisposed, but I thank him for enriching the narrative in any case.) While Marvin Bower passed away a while back, his sons, Dick and Jim, both did me the favor of reminiscing about the remarkable man.

And then there's a long list of current and former McKinsey people who took time to try and help me understand an institution that's not that easy to pin down. In alphabetical order: Mike Allen, Carter Bales, Partha Bose, Sylvia Mathews Burwell, Dominic Casserley, Logan Cheek, Yolande Daeninck, Clay Deutsch, Diana Farrell, Jim Fisher, Peter Foy, James Gorman, Ted Hall, Juan Hoyos, Michelle Jarrard, Larry Kanarek, Alan Kantrow, Jon Katzenbach, Nancy Killefer, Matt Kramer, James Kwak, Eric Labaye, Michael Lanning, Bill Matassoni, Frank Mattern, Stefan Matzinger, Jodie Neve, Gordon Orr, Tom Peters, Jeff Pundyk, David Robertson, Elizabeth Riordan, Will Riordan, Yves Smith, Tom Steiner, and Bob Waterman.

There are numerous others who will go unnamed. Most of them said something not so nice about McKinsey and didn't want to suffer the firm's wrath. Others said very nice things and . . . still didn't want to suffer the firm's wrath. In writing this book, I'm sure I'm going to suffer a little bit of it myself, but I do hope that current and former McKinseyites do not regret the time spent. I do think I painted a balanced portrait of the place.

Thanks to the handful of McKinsey clients and competitors who agreed to speak publicly about things they normally keep private: Frank Cahouet, Jim Coulter, Robert Dell, Tim Flynn, Joe Fuller, Peter Grauer, Chuck Neul, Richard Rakowski, Frederick Sturdivant, and Bill Weldon.

Outside McKinsey, I am grateful to the work of a number of academics who have spent far more time than I have studying this remarkable institution, whether I spoke to them in person or not: Amar Bhide, Robert David, Lars Engwall, Pankaj Ghemawhat, Matthias Kipping, Rakesh Khurana, Christopher McKenna, Henry Mintzberg, and Andrew Sturdy.

And then there are the journalists and authors who informed my work. First place: longtime *Bloomberg BusinessWeek* scribe John Byrne, who has written more magazine pages on McKinsey than any other. Others who enriched the story: David Berardinelli, William Cohan, Stuart Crainer, Peter Elkind, Malcolm Gladwell, Daniel Guttman, John Huey, Maryann Keller, Walter Kiechel, Martin Kihn, Nicholas Lemann, Bethany McLean, Kevin Mellyn, John Micklethwait, Dana Milbank, Lewis Pinault, Stefan Stern, Matthew Stewart, Barry Willner, and Adrian Wooldridge.

I am grateful to those who kept the money coming in the door during the project as well (the nanny needed to be paid, after all): Andy Serwer and Stephanie Mehta of *Fortune*, Graydon Carter and Dana Brown of *Vanity Fair,* Ryan D'Agostino of *Esquire,* Brad Wieners and Julian Sancton of *Bloomberg BusinessWeek,* Michael Hogan of *Huffington Post,* and my old pal Jeanhee Kim.

Special mention goes to Mo Cunniffe, an almost relative-by-former-marriage who convened a summit of vintage McKinsey men (and bought the lobster sandwiches) in Greenwich a few years back. Thanks to those who came that day: Doug Ayer, Bill MacCormack, Edward Massey, and Peter von Braun. Thanks too to Bill Stromsem, for being a dedicated copy editor.

Last, my family and friends.

Thanks, Mom, for all the notes you send me telling me I'm a wonderful writer. They make for bright lights on dark days. Thanks, Dad, for all that you were. I still think of you nearly every day. While you never met your granddaughter, I see echoes of your sly smile whenever I look at her happy face. I think she's got your sense of humor too, which will serve her well.

To my siblings, Steve McDonald and Jackie Pye, and Julie and Gareth Carter: Thanks for putting up with more Duff over these past few years than should reasonably have been expected. I have another sibling, but he comes with an interesting wrinkle. No matter who may have written this book, there would be a conflict of some sort, as McKinsey touches so many people in so many places. My own sin of connection is my brother Scott, who heads Oliver Wyman, a competitor of the firm. In the end, he didn't spend much time talking to me about McKinsey. But he made up for that crime in other ways. Thanks, brother.

Thanks, Chris Wahl, for your camera and your friendship. And finally, thanks to a very special group of people who provided invaluable support during this long endeavor: Will Arnett, Alan Baldachin, Lindsey Braun, Malcolm Fitch, David Foster, Peter Giles, Brendan Golden, John and Megan Grugan, Mike Guy, Michael Hawkins, Adolphus Holden, Peter and Karen Keating, Chris Kerr, Caroline McDonald, Matt McPherson, Christie Nicholson, Owen Osborne,

Gilda Riccardi, Maer Roshan, and especially Susan Duffy and Joe Schrank. Your friendship means the world to me. Thank you for being there when I needed you.

As always, to all who helped, I hope the results prove worth the time spent.

Duff McDonald
New York, March 2013

NOTES

INTRODUCTION: THE McKINSEY MYSTIQUE

1. Hal Higdon, *The Business Healers* (New York: Random House, 1970), 113.
2. Nicholas Lemann, "The Kids in the Conference Room," *New Yorker,* October 18, 1999.
3. Matthew Stewart, *The Management Myth: Why the Experts Keep Getting It Wrong* (New York: W.W. Norton, 2009), 178.

1. THE OZARK FARM BOY

1. William B. Wolf, *Management and Consulting: An Introduction to James O. McKinsey* (Ithaca, NY: Cornell University Press, 1978), 16.
2. Ibid., 1.
3. Marvin Bower, *Perspective on McKinsey* (New York: McKinsey & Company, Inc., 1979), 9.
4. George David Smith, John T. Seaman Jr., and Morgan Witzel, *A History of The Firm* (New York: McKinsey & Company, 2010), 18.
5. Hal Higdon, *The Business Healers* (New York: Random House, 1970), 13.
6. Ashish Nanda and Kelley Morrell, "McKinsey & Company: An Institution at a Crossroads," Harvard Business School, December 4, 2002.
7. Smith, Seaman, and Witzel, *A History of The Firm,* 35.
8. Wolf, *Management and Consulting,* 13.

9. Ibid., 42.
10. Alfred D. Chandler Jr., *Scale and Scope: The Dynamics of Industrial Capitalism* (Boston: Harvard University Press, 1994), 4.
11. Thomas K. McGraw, *American Business, 1920–2000: How It Worked* (Wheeling, IL: Harlan Davidson, 2000), 1.
12. Chandler, *Scale and Scope*, 71.
13. Jack Beatty, *Colossus: How the Corporation Changed America* (New York: Broadway Books, 2001), 178.
14. John Micklethwait and Adrian Wooldridge, *The Company: A Short History of a Revolutionary Idea* (New York: Modern Library, 2003), 66.
15. McGraw, *American Business,* 7.
16. Alfred D. Chandler Jr., *Strategy and Structure: Chapters in the History of the American Industrial Enterprise* (Cambridge, MA: MIT Press, 1962), 6.
17. Christopher D. McKenna, *The World's Newest Profession: Management Consulting in the Twentieth Century* (New York: Cambridge University Press, 2006), 20.
18. Chandler, *Strategy and Structure,* 36.
19. Pankaj Ghemawat, "Competition and Business Strategy in Historical Perspective," *Business History Review,* volume 76 (Spring 2002), 40.
20. James O. McKinsey, *Budgetary Control* (New York: Roland Press, 1922), 8.
21. Wolf, *Management and Consulting,* 5.
22. *McKinsey: A Scrapbook* (McKinsey & Company, 1997), 7.
23. Firm Training Manual (1937), 4.
24. John G. Neukom, *McKinsey Memoirs: A Personal Perspective* (Self-Published, 1975), 4.
25. Higdon, *The Business Healers*, 137.
26. Wolf, *Management and Consulting*, 45.
27. Matthew Stewart, *The Management Myth: Why the Experts Keep Getting It Wrong* (New York: W.W. Norton, 2009), 35.

28. Andrew Billen, "From Man Management to Mad Management," *Times*, March 9, 2009.
29. McKenna, *The World's Newest Profession*, 59.
30. Mathias Kipping, "Trapped in Their Wave: The Evolution of Management Consultancies," in Timothy Clark and Robin Fincham (eds.), *Critical Consulting: New Perspectives on the Management Advice Industry* (Oxford: Blackwell, 2002), 28–49.
31. Matthias Kipping, "Hollow from the Start? Image Professionalism in Management Consulting," *Current Sociology*, volume 59, issue 4 (July 2011), 530–550.
32. McKenna, *The World's Newest Profession*, 62.
33. Rakesh Khurana, *From Higher Aims to Hired Hands: The Social Transformation of American Business Schools and the Unfulfilled Promise of Management as a Profession* (Princeton: Princeton University Press, 2007), 92.
34. McKenna, *The World's Newest Profession*, 60.
35. Stewart, *The Management Myth*, 59.
36. Neukom, *McKinsey Memoirs*, 34.
37. McKenna, *The World's Newest Profession*, 48.
38. Smith, Seaman, and Witzel, *A History of The Firm*, 58.
39. Jack Sweeney, "The Last Lion: Marvin Bower and His Quest for Professional Independence," *Consulting Magazine*, February/March 2003.
40. Wolf, *Management and Consulting*, 10.
41. Ibid., 11.
42. Neukom, *McKinsey Memoirs*, 14.
43. Roger Lowenstein, *New York Times*, December 28, 2003.
44. Nanda and Morrell, "McKinsey & Company: An Institution at a Crossroads."
45. Marvin Bower, *Memoirs* (New York, Marvinstories, 2003), 44.
46. Bower, *Perspective on McKinsey*, 17.

47. Bower, *Memoirs*, 46.
48. Wolf, *Management and Consulting*, 11.
49. Bower, *Perspective on McKinsey*, 16.
50. Elizabeth Haas Edersheim, *McKinsey's Marvin Bower* (Hoboken, NJ: John Wiley & Sons, 2004), 57.
51. Bower, *Perspective on McKinsey*, 32.
52. Ibid., 18.
53. Ibid., 34.
54. Sweeney, "The Last Lion."

2. THE MAKING OF THE FIRM

1. James Gorman, interview by author, August 10, 2011.
2. Stuart Jeffries, "The Firm," *Guardian*, February 21, 2003.
3. John Huey, "How McKinsey Does It," *Fortune*, November 1, 1993.
4. Dick Bower, interview by author, April 5, 2011.
5. Christopher D. McKenna, *The World's Newest Profession: Management Consulting in the Twentieth Century* (New York: Cambridge University Press, 2006), 202.
6. Ibid., 201.
7. Marvin Bower, *The Will to Lead: Running a Business with a Network of Leaders* (Boston: Harvard Business School Press, 1997), 51.
8. Ron Daniel, interview by author, December 7, 2010.
9. Hal Higdon, *The Business Healers* (New York: Random House, 1970), 230.
10. Ibid., 232.
11. Marvin Bower, *Perspective on McKinsey* (New York: McKinsey & Company, 1979), 192.
12. Ibid., 114.
13. Ibid., 14
14. George MacDonald Fraser, *Flashman: A Novel* (New York: Plume, 1984), 30.

15. Mo Cunniffe, interview by author, May 7, 2010.
16. Elizabeth Haas Edersheim, *McKinsey's Marvin Bower* (Hoboken, NJ: John Wiley & Sons, 2004), 74.
17. Ibid., 71.
18. Harvard Business Study, "McKinsey and the Globalization of Consultancy," July 7, 2009.
19. *Investors Business Daily*, November 10, 2000.
20. Doug Ayer, interview by author, May 7, 2010.
21. Bower, *Perspective on McKinsey*, 37.
22. *McKinsey: A Scrapbook* (McKinsey & Company, 1997), 19.
23. Walter Kiechel III, *The Lords of Strategy* (Boston: Harvard Business Press, 2010), 25.
24. Pankaj Ghemawat, "Competition and Business Strategy in Historical Perspective," *Business History Review*, volume 76 (Spring 2002), 40.
25. Jack Sweeney, "The Last Lion: Marvin Bower and His Quest for Professional Independence," *Consulting Magazine*, February/March 2003.
26. Ibid.
27. Robert A. Caro, *The Power Broker* (New York: Vintage Books, 1974), 315.
28. George David Smith, John T. Seaman Jr., and Morgan Witzel, *A History of The Firm* (New York: McKinsey & Company, 2010), 113.

3. THE AGE OF INFLUENCE

1. Dick Bower, interview by author, April 15, 2011.
2. Robert A. Caro, *The Power Broker* (New York: Vintage Books, 1974), 688.
3. Elizabeth Haas Edersheim, *McKinsey's Marvin Bower* (Hoboken, NJ: John Wiley & Sons, 2004), 215.
4. Doug Ayer, interview by author, May 7, 2010.

5. John Micklethwait and Adrian Wooldridge, *The Company: A Short History of a Revolutionary Idea* (New York: Modern Library, 2003), 115.
6. Ibid., 117.
7. Rakesh Khurana, *From Higher Aims to Hired Hands: The Social Transformation of American Business Schools and the Unfulfilled Promise of Management as a Profession* (Princeton: Princeton University Press, 2007), 208.
8. Marvin Bower, *Perspective on McKinsey* (New York: McKinsey & Company, Inc., 1979), 120.
9. Edersheim, *McKinsey's Marvin Bower*, 28.
10. Christopher D. McKenna, *The World's Newest Profession: Management Consulting in the Twentieth Century* (New York: Cambridge University Press, 2006), 152.
11. William H. Whyte, *The Organization Man* (Philadelphia: University of Pennsylvania Press, 2002), 4.
12. Ibid., 276.
13. Khurana, *From Higher Aims to Hired Hands*, 200.
14. *New York Times*, November 30, 1996.
15. George David Smith, John T. Seaman Jr., and Morgan Witzel, *A History of The Firm* (New York: McKinsey & Company, 2010), 90.
16. Daniel Guttman and Barry Willner, *The Shadow Government: The Government's Multi-billion-dollar Giveaway of Its Decision-making Powers to Private Management Consultants, "Experts," and Think Tanks* (New York: Pantheon Books, 1976), 98.
17. Ibid.
18. Ibid.
19. *McKinsey: A Scrapbook* (McKinsey & Company, 1997), 26.
20. Guttman and Willner, *The Shadow Government*, 103.
21. McKenna, *The World's Newest Profession*, 98, 99.
22. Ibid., 105.
23. Ibid., 108.

24. Guttman and Willner, *The Shadow Government*, 111.
25. Ibid., 96.
26. Ibid., 275.
27. *New York Times*, July 3, 1970.
28. Carter Bales, interview by author, April 20, 2011.
29. Bower, *Perspective on McKinsey*, 72.
30. McKenna, *The World's Newest Profession*, 154.
31. Edersheim, *McKinsey's Marvin Bower*, 95.
32. Jon Katzenbach, interview by author, May 5, 2010.
33. Alfred D. Chandler Jr., *Scale and Scope: The Dynamics of Industrial Capitalism* (Boston: Harvard University Press, 1994), 613.
34. Bower, *Perspective on McKinsey*, 90.
35. Ibid., 95.
36. Ibid., 192.
37. Ibid.
38. Matthias Kipping, "American Management Consulting Companies in Western Europe, 1920 to 1990: Products, Reputation, and Relationships," *Business History Review*, volume 73 (Summer 1999), 190–220.
39. Hal Higdon, *The Business Healers* (New York: Random House, 1970), 15.
40. Mike Allen, interview by author, May 24, 2010.
41. McKenna, *The World's Newest Profession*, 174.
42. Doug Ayer, interview by author, May 7, 2010.
43. Stephen Aris, "Super managers." *Sunday Times*, September 1, 1968.
44. Edersheim, *McKinsey's Marvin Bower*, 106.
45. McKenna, *The World's Newest Profession*, 181.
46. Micklethwait and Wooldridge, *The Company*, 171.
47. Jean-Jacques Servan-Schreiber, *The American Challenge* (New York: Atheneum, 1968).
48. Walter Kiechel III, *The Lords of Strategy* (Boston: Harvard Business Press, 2010), 25.

49. Michael Useem, *The Leadership Moment: Nine True Stories of Triumph and Disaster and Their Lessons for Us All* (New York: Crown Books, 1999), 213.
50. Logan Cheek, interview by author, November 2011.
51. Kipping, "American Management Consulting Companies."
52. *McKinsey: A Scrapbook*, 21.
53. Smith, Seaman, and Witzel, *A History of The Firm*, 96.
54. Edersheim, *McKinsey's Marvin Bower*, 95.
55. Bethany McLean and Peter Elkind, *The Smartest Guys in the Room: The Amazing Rise and Scandalous Fall of Enron* (New York: Portfolio, 2003), 71.
56. James Kwak, interview by author, September 10, 2010.
57. Higdon, *The Business Healers*, 134.
58. Matthias Kipping, "Hollow from the Start? Image Professionalism in Management Consulting," *Current Sociology*, volume 59, issue 4 (July 2011), 530–550.
59. James O'Shea and Charles Madigan, *Dangerous Company: Management Consultants and the Businesses They Save and Ruin* (New York: Penguin Books, 1997), 283.
60. Matthew Stewart, *The Management Myth: Why the Experts Keep Getting It Wrong* (New York: W. W. Norton, 2009), 4.
61. Ibid., 125.
62. Ibid., 143.
63. Martin Kihn, *House of Lies: How Management Consultants Steal Your Watch and Then Tell You the Time* (New York: Warner Business Books, 2005), 11.
64. Lewis Pinault, *Consulting Demons: Inside the Unscrupulous World of Global Corporate Consulting* (New York: HarperBusiness, 2000), 13.
65. John Huey, *Fortune*, November 1, 1993.
66. Christopher McKenna, interview by author, 2009.

67. Higdon, *The Business Healers*, 181.
68. McKenna, *The World's Newest Profession*, 157.
69. Gordon Perchthold and Jenny Sutton, *Extract Value from Consultants* (Austin, TX: Greenleaf Book Group Press, 2010), 37.
70. Stewart, *The Management Myth*, 153.
71. Curt Schleler, "Consulting Innovator Marvin Bower: His Vision Made McKinsey & Co. a Pioneer," *Investors Business Daily*, November 9, 2000.
72. *McKinsey: A Scrapbook*, 41.
73. Walter Guzzardi Jr., "Consultants: The Men Who Came to Dinner," *Fortune*, February 1965.
74. Chandler, *Scale and Scope*, 622.
75. McKenna, *The World's Newest Profession*, 8.
76. Higdon, *The Business Healers*, 176.
77. Ibid., 84.
78. Ibid., 181.
79. Smith, Seaman, and Witzel, *A History of The Firm*, 185.
80. Jack Beatty, *Colossus: How the Corporation Changed America* (New York: Broadway Books, 2001), 267.
81. Bower, *Perspective on McKinsey*, 112.
82. Smith, Seaman, and Witzel, *A History of The Firm*, 114.
83. Stephen Aris, "Supermanagers," *Sunday Times*, September 1, 1968.

4. THE DECADE OF DOUBT

1. Alfred D. Chandler Jr., *Strategy and Structure: Chapters in the History of the American Industrial Enterprise* (Cambridge, MA: MIT Press, 1962), introduction.
2. Rakesh Khurana, *From Higher Aims to Hired Hands: The Social Transformation of American Business Schools and the Unfulfilled Promise of Management as a Profession* (Princeton: Princeton University Press, 2007), 208.

3. John Micklethwait and Adrian Wooldridge, *The Company: A Short History of a Revolutionary Idea* (New York: Modern Library, 2003), 121.
4. Chandler, *Strategy and Structure*, introduction.
5. "The New Shape of Management Consulting," *BusinessWeek*, May 21, 1979.
6. Thomas K. McGraw, *American Business, 1920–2000: How It Worked* (Wheeling, IL: Harlan Davidson, 2000), 157.
7. Christopher A. Bartlett, "McKinsey & Co.: Managing Knowledge and Learning," Harvard Business School, January 4, 2000.
8. *McKinsey: A Scrapbook* (New York: McKinsey & Company, 1997), 49.
9. Michael C. Jensen, "McKinsey & Co.: Big Brother to Big Business," *New York Times*, May 30, 1971.
10. Nancy Killefer, interview by author, July 6, 2011.
11. *McKinsey: A Scrapbook*, 47.
12. David J. Parker, "The Management Consulting Industry in Germany," Working Paper, Alfred P. Sloan School of Management, August 1974, 5.
13. Geoffrey Jones and Alexis Lefort, "McKinsey and the Globalization of Consultancy," Harvard Business School, July 7, 2009.
14. John Cable and Manfred J. Dirrheimer, "Hierarchies and Markets—An Empirical Test of the Multidivisional Hypothesis in West Germany," *International Journal of Industrial Organization*, volume 1 (March 1983), 43–62.
15. George David Smith, John T. Seaman Jr., and Morgan Witzel, *A History of The Firm* (New York: McKinsey & Company, 2010), 182.
16. Logan Cheek, interview by author, December 12, 2011.
17. Rod Carnegie, interview by author, October 4, 2012.
18. Walter Kiechel III, *The Lords of Strategy* (Boston: Harvard Business Press, 2010), 40.
19. Stuart Crainer, *The Tom Peters Phenomenon: Corporate Man to Corporate Skunk* (Oxford: Capstone Publishing Limited, 1997), 11.

20. Pankaj Ghemawat, "Competition and Business Strategy in Historical Perspective," *Business History Review*, volume 76 (Spring 2002), 45.
21. John Byrne, *BusinessWeek*, June 23, 1986.
22. Adrian Wooldridge, "Big Think in the Boardroom: How Business Moved from Affable Amateurism to Specialized, Intellectualized 'Models' and Expertise," *Wall Street Journal*, March 10, 2010.
23. Kiechel, *The Lords of Strategy*, 65.
24. Matthew Stewart, *The Management Myth: Why the Experts Keep Getting It Wrong* (New York: W. W. Norton, 2009), 194.
25. Henry Mintzberg, interview by author, April 7, 2010.
26. Ghemawat, "Competition and Business Strategy," 47.
27. Mike Allen, interview by author, May 24, 2010.
28. Kiechel, *The Lords of Strategy,* 72.
29. *McKinsey: A Scrapbook,* 55.
30. Smith, Seaman, and Witzel, *A History of The Firm,* 178.
31. Elizabeth Haas Edersheim, *McKinsey's Marvin Bower* (Hoboken, NJ: John Wiley & Sons, 2004), 113.
32. *Consulting News*, February 1973.
33. McGraw, *American Business*, 164.
34. Peter von Braun, interview by author, May 7, 2010.
35. Ed Massey, interview by author, May 7, 2010.
36. *BusinessWeek*, November 18, 1967.
37. Smith, Seaman, and Witzel, *A History of The Firm*, 166.
38. Christopher Bartlett, "McKinsey & Company: Managing Knowledge and Learning," Harvard Business School, January 4, 2000.
39. Smith, Seaman, and Witzel, *A History of The Firm*, 311.
40. Hal Higdon, *The Business Healers* (New York: Random House, 1970), 188.
41. Ashish Nanda and Kelley Morrell, "McKinsey & Company: An Institution at a Crossroads," Harvard Business School, December 4, 2002.

42. Frank Mattern, interview by author, July 6, 2011.
43. Partha Bose, interview by author, December 12, 2011.
44. Khurana, *From Higher Aims to Hired Hands,* 324.
45. Ibid., 2.
46. Al McDonald, interview by author, February 24, 2011.
47. Month by Month, "Life After Managing Director—Al McDonald: Dancing Between the Elephant's Toes" (McKinsey & Company), January/February 1998.
48. Ibid.
49. Al McDonald, interview by author, February 24, 2011.
50. Peter von Braun, interview by author, May 7, 2010.
51. Month by Month, "Life After Managing Director—Al McDonald."
52. Smith, Seaman, and Witzel, *A History of The Firm*, 214.

5. A RETURN TO FORM

1. Month by Month, "Life After Managing Director—Still Here. And Still Busy" (McKinsey & Company), July/August 1996.
2. John Byrne, *BusinessWeek*, June 23, 1986.
3. George David Smith, John T. Seaman Jr., and Morgan Witzel, *A History of The Firm* (New York: McKinsey & Company, 2010), 217.
4. Ibid., 225.
5. John A. Byrne, "Inside McKinsey," *BusinessWeek,* July 8, 2002.
6. Dana Milbank, "Critics Have Advice for McKinsey," *Globe and Mail,* October 12, 1993.
7. Partha Bose, interview by author, December 12, 2011.
8. *BusinessWeek,* May 21, 1979.
9. Matthias Kipping, interview by author, December 2, 2010.
10. Walter Kiechel III, *The Lords of Strategy* (Boston: Harvard Business Press, 2010), 104.
11. Ibid., 69.
12. Fred Gluck, interview by author, January 27, 2011.

13. Clay Deutsch, interview by author, April 2011.
14. Kiechel, *The Lords of Strategy*, 257.
15. Ashish Nanda and Kelley Morrell, "McKinsey & Company: An Institution at a Crossroads," Harvard Business School, December 4, 2002.
16. Partha Bose, interview by author, December 12, 2011.
17. Tom Peters, interview by author, July 27, 2010.
18. Bob Waterman, interview by author, 2010.
19. Stuart Crainer, *The Tom Peters Phenomenon: Corporate Man to Corporate Skunk* (Oxford: Capstone Publishing Limited, 1997), 12.
20. Ibid., 28.
21. Ibid., 27.
22. Tom Peters, interview by author, 2010.
23. Crainer, *The Tom Peters Phenomenon,* 41.
24. John Micklethwait and Adrian Wooldridge, *The Witch Doctors: Making Sense of the Management Gurus* (New York: Times Books, 1996), 46.
25. Tom Peters, interview by author, 2010.
26. Matthew Stewart, *The Management Myth: Why the Experts Keep Getting It Wrong* (New York: W. W. Norton, 2009), 247.
27. Bob Waterman, interview by author, 2010.
28. Ibid.
29. Tom Peters, interview by author, 2010.
30. Ibid.
31. McKinsey partner, interview by author, 2011.
32. Bob Waterman, interview by author, 2010.
33. John Huey, *Fortune,* November 1, 1993.
34. Bill Matassoni, interview by author, 2010.
35. Logan Cheek, interview by author, November 2011.
36. *McKinsey: A Scrapbook* (New York: McKinsey & Company, 1997), 68.
37. Smith, Seaman, and Witzel, *A History of The Firm,* 256.
38. Ian Davis, interview by author, June 16, 2011.

39. Smith, Seaman, and Witzel, *A History of The Firm,* 256.
40. Kiechel, *The Lords of Strategy,* 257.
41. Frank Mattern, interview by author, July 6, 2011.
42. Byrne, *BusinessWeek,* June 23, 1986.
43. Bill Matassoni, interview by author, September 3, 2010.
44. Smith, Seaman, and Witzel, *A History of The Firm,* 263.
45. Partha Bose, interview by author, December 12, 2011.
46. http://www.kohmae.com/book/index_e.html.
47. John Merwin, "We Don't Learn from Our Clients, We Learn from Each Other," *Forbes,* October 19, 1987.
48. Byrne, *BusinessWeek,* June 23, 1986.
49. Merwin, "We Don't Learn."
50. George Feiger, interview by author, January 9, 2012.
51. Crainer, *The Tom Peters Phenomenon,* 77.
52. Bill Matassoni, interview by author, September 3, 2010.
53. Gordon Perchthold and Jenny Sutton, *Extract Value from Consultants* (Austin, TX: Greenleaf Book Group Press, 2010), 51.
54. Jim Coulter, interview by author, 2011.
55. Robert Dell, interview by author, 2011.
56. John Huey, *Fortune,* November 1, 1993.
57. Byrne, *BusinessWeek,* June 23, 1986.
58. Huey, *Fortune,* November 1, 1993.

6. THE CRUCIAL QUESTION: ARE THEY WORTH IT OR NOT?

1. Stuart Crainer, *The Tom Peters Phenomenon: Corporate Man to Corporate Skunk* (Oxford: Capstone Publishing Limited, 1997), 167.
2. Dana Milbank, "Critics Have Advice for McKinsey," *Globe and Mail,* October 12, 1993.
3. Frank Cahouet, interview by author, August 30, 2010.
4. *McKinsey: A Scrapbook* (New York: McKinsey & Company, 1997), 67.
5. Ibid.

6. Matthew Stewart, *The Management Myth: Why the Experts Keep Getting It Wrong* (New York: W. W. Norton, 2009), 70.
7. Rakesh Khurana, *From Higher Aims to Hired Hands: The Social Transformation of American Business Schools and the Unfulfilled Promise of Management as a Profession* (Princeton: Princeton University Press, 2007), 326.
8. Martin Kihn, *House of Lies: How Management Consultants Steal Your Watch and Then Tell You the Time* (New York: Warner Business Books, 2005), 38.
9. Hal Higdon, *The Business Healers* (New York: Random House, 1970), 111.
10. James P. McCollom, *The Continental Affair: The Rise & Fall of the Continental Illinois Bank* (New York: Dodd, Mead, 1987), 231.
11. David Craig, *Rip-Off! The Scandalous Inside Story of the Management Consulting Money Machine* (London: Original Book Company, 2005), 170.
12. Ibid.
13. Michael Lanning, interview by author, April 27, 2010.
14. Tom Steiner, interview by author, 2010.
15. Milbank, "Critics Have Advice for McKinsey."
16. Maryann Keller, interview by author, 2009.
17. John Huey, *Fortune,* November 1, 1993.
18. Stewart, *The Management Myth,* 181.
19. John Merwin, "We Don't Learn from Our Clients, We Learn from Each Other," *Forbes,* October 19, 1987.
20. Alan Kantrow, interview by author, May 4, 2010.
21. Merwin, "We Don't Learn."
22. Stephen Aris, "Supermanagers," *Sunday Times,* September 1, 1968.
23. John Byrne, *BusinessWeek,* June 23, 1986.
24. Huey, *Fortune,* November 1, 1993.
25. Larry Kanarek, interview by author, 2010.
26. Merwin, "We Don't Learn."

27. Edwin Diamond, "News by the Numbers," *New York*, February 25, 1987.
28. Higdon, *The Business Healers,* 85.
29. Merwin, "We Don't Learn."
30. Lewis Pinault, *Consulting Demons: Inside the Unscrupulous World of Global Corporate Consulting* (New York: HarperBusiness, 2000), 47.
31. Fred Sturdivant, interview by author, April 22, 2010.

7. REVENGE OF THE NERDS

1. Walter Kiechel III, *The Lords of Strategy* (Boston: Harvard Business Press, 2010), 95.
2. Fred Gluck, interview by author, January 2011.
3. Ibid.
4. Rod Carnegie, interview by author, October 4, 2012.
5. Fred Gluck, interview by author, January 2011.
6. Month by Month, "Life After Managing Director—Still Here. And Still Busy" (McKinsey & Company), July/August 1996.
7. James Gorman, interview by author, August 10, 2011.
8. James O'Shea and Charles Madigan, *Dangerous Company: Management Consultants and the Businesses They Save and Ruin* (New York: Penguin Books, 1997), 6.
9. John A. Byrne, "What's a Guy Like This Doing at McKinsey's Helm?" *BusinessWeek,* June 13, 1988.
10. Nancy Killefer, interview by author, July 6, 2011.
11. Alison Leigh Cowan, "McKinsey May Buy Consultants," *New York Times*, October 2, 1989.
12. John A. Byrne, "The McKinsey Mystique," *BusinessWeek,* September 20, 1993.
13. Frank Mattern, interview by author, July 6, 2011.
14. Ibid.

15. Hal Higdon, *The Business Healers* (New York: Random House, 1970), 279.
16. Byrne, "The McKinsey Mystique."
17. John Huey, *Fortune,* November 1, 1993.
18. Fred Gluck, interview by author, January 2011.
19. Matthew Stewart, *The Management Myth: Why the Experts Keep Getting It Wrong* (New York: W. W. Norton, 2009), 171.
20. Huey, *Fortune,* November 1, 1993
21. John A. Byrne, "Sexual Harassment at McKinsey?" *BusinessWeek,* December 9, 1996.
22. Byrne, "The McKinsey Mystique."
23. Huey, *Fortune,* November 1, 1993.
24. Jon Katzenbach, interview by author, May 5, 2010.
25. *McKinsey: A Scrapbook* (New York: McKinsey & Company, 1997), 76.
26. Stefan Matzinger, interview by author, February 5, 2011.
27. Byrne, "The McKinsey Mystique."
28. John Micklethwait and Adrian Wooldridge, *The Witch Doctors: Making Sense of the Management Gurus* (New York: Times Books, 1996), 32.
29. Kiechel, *The Lords of Strategy,* 256.
30. Frank Mattern, interview by author, July 6, 2011.
31. Fred Gluck, interview by author, January 2011.
32. Clay Deutsch, interview by author, March 15, 2011.
33. Kate Linebaugh, "The New GE Way: Go Deep, Not Wide," *Wall Street Journal,* March 6, 2012.
34. Huey, *Fortune,* November 1, 1993.
35. McKinsey pamphlet, "A Career in Consulting."
36. Fred Gluck, interview by author, January 2011.
37. Bill Matassoni, interview by author, September 3, 2010.
38. Alan Kantrow, interview by author, May 4, 2010.
39. Tom Steiner, interview by author, October 28, 2010.
40. Partha Bose, interview by author, December 12, 2011.

41. Jay W. Lorsch and Katharina Pick, "McKinsey & Co.," Harvard Business School Case 402-014, August 16, 2001.
42. Diana Farrell, interview by author, 2011.
43. Micklethwait and Wooldridge, *The Witch Doctors,* 54.
44. http://www.planetizen.com/node/20477.
45. http://www.montecitojournal.net/archive/12/15/220/.

8. THE MONEY GRAB

1. John A. Byrne, "Inside McKinsey," *BusinessWeek,* July 8, 2002.
2. John Micklethwait and Adrian Wooldridge, *The Company: A Short History of a Revolutionary Idea* (New York: Modern Library, 2003), 129.
3. John Byrne, "The McKinsey Mystique," *BusinessWeek,* September 20, 1993.
4. Ronald E. Yates, "'The Firm' Myths Not So Firm," *Chicago Tribune,* July 10, 1994.
5. Ibid.
6. Stuart Jeffries, "The Firm," *Guardian,* February 21, 2003.
7. Jim Fisher, interview by author, March 19, 2010.
8. James O'Shea and Charles Madigan, "The Firm's Grip," *Sunday Times,* September 7, 1997.
9. Jim Fisher, interview by author, March 19, 2010.
10. George Feiger, interview by author, January 9, 2012.
11. Gordon Orr, interview by author, June 20, 2011.
12. Ron Daniel, interview by author, December 17, 2010.
13. Partha Bose, interview by author, December 12, 2011.
14. Bill Cohan, interview by author, October 21, 2010.
15. Michelle Celarier, "The Lowdown on McKinsey," *Euromoney,* July 1996.
16. Christopher D. McKenna, *The World's Newest Profession: Management Consulting in the Twentieth Century* (New York: Cambridge University Press, 2006), 3.

17. Ashish Nanda and Kelley Morrell, "McKinsey & Company: An Institution at a Crossroads," Harvard Business School, December 4, 2002.
18. Walter Kiechel III, *The Lords of Strategy* (Boston: Harvard Business Press, 2010), 48.

9. BAD ADVICE

1. Manjeet Kripalani, "India: The GE and McKinsey Club," *BusinessWeek,* February 23, 2006.
2. Ashish Nanda and Kelley Morrell, "McKinsey & Company: An Institution at a Crossroads," Harvard Business School, December 4, 2002.
3. Tom Peters, interview by author, July 27, 2010.
4. Bethany McLean and Peter Elkind, *The Smartest Guys in the Room: The Amazing Rise and Scandalous Fall of Enron* (New York: Portfolio, 2003), 31.
5. Kurt Eichenwald, *Conspiracy of Fools: A True Story* (New York: Broadway Books, 2005), 26.
6. Esther Maier, "Consulting Firms' Impact on Performance: A Case Study of Enron and McKinsey" (Independent Study, University of Western Ontario), April 29, 2007.
7. McLean and Elkind, *The Smartest Guys in the Room*, 31.
8. Ibid., 35.
9. Eichenwald, *Conspiracy of Fools,* 52.
10. McLean and Elkind, *The Smartest Guys in the Room,* xx.
11. Ibid., 28.
12. Michelle Celarier, "The Lowdown on McKinsey," *Euromoney,* July 1996.
13. Wendy Zellner, "Online Extra: Q&A with Enron's Skilling," *Business Week.com,* February 12, 2001.
14. http://www.justice.gov/enron/exhibit/04-17/BBC-0001/OCR/EXH059-00383.TXT.
15. John A. Byrne, "Inside McKinsey," *BusinessWeek*, July 8, 2002.

16. Ibid.
17. Maier, "A Case Study of Enron and McKinsey."
18. McLean and Elkind, *The Smartest Guys in the Room,* 295.
19. Andrew Billen, "From Man Management to Mad Management," *Times,* March 9, 2009.
20. McLean and Elkind, *The Smartest Guys in the Room,* 119.
21. Byrne, "Inside McKinsey."
22. Ibid.
23. Maier, "A Case Study of Enron and McKinsey."
24. Ibid.
25. Byrne, "Inside McKinsey."
26. Alex Grey, "Challenges to the Reputation of Consulting Firm: A Case Study of the Fallout from the Enron Demise" (Independent Study, University of Western Ontario), May 5, 2008.
27. Maier, "A Case Study of Enron and McKinsey."
28. Byrne, "Inside McKinsey."
29. Grey, "A Case Study of the Fallout from the Enron Demise."
30. Byrne, "Inside McKinsey."
31. Grey, "A Case Study of the Fallout from the Enron Demise."
32. Fiona Czerniawska, "Consulting on the Brink: The Implications of Enron for the Consulting Industry," *Arkimeda* (2002), 5.
33. Lewis Pinault, *Consulting Demons: Inside the Unscrupulous World of Global Corporate Consulting* (New York: HarperBusiness, 2000), 230.
34. Lars Engwall, "Bridge, Poker and Banking," Department of Business Studies, Uppsala University, 1995.
35. Byrne, "Inside McKinsey."
36. Stewart Hamilton and Alicia Micklethwait, *Greed and Corporate Failure* (Hampshire, England: Palgrave Macmillan, 2006), 118.
37. Ibid.
38. Ian Davis, interview by author, June 16, 2011.

39. George David Smith, John T. Seaman Jr., and Morgan Witzel, *A History of The Firm* (New York: McKinsey & Company, 2010), 419.
40. David Berardinelli, *From Good Hands to Boxing Gloves: The Dark Side of Insurance* (Portland, OR: Trial Guides, 2008), 31.
41. David Dietz and Darrell Preston, "The Insurance Hoax," *Bloomberg Markets*, September 2007.
42. James O'Shea and Charles Madigan, "The Firm's Grip," *Sunday Times,* September 7, 1997.
43. John Byrne, *BusinessWeek,* August 25, 1997.
44. Nicholas Lemann, "The Kids in the Conference Room," *New Yorker,* October 18, 1999.
45. Malcolm Gladwell, "The Talent Myth," *New Yorker*, July 20, 2002.
46. Ibid.
47. John Micklethwait and Adrian Wooldridge, *The Company: A Short History of a Revolutionary Idea* (New York: Modern Library, 2003), 144.
48. Thomas K. McGraw, *American Business, 1920–2000: How It Worked* (Wheeling, IL: Harlan Davidson, 2000), 36.
49. Nanda and Morrell, "McKinsey & Company: An Institution at a Crossroads."
50. Byrne, "Inside McKinsey."
51. Ibid.
52. Ibid.
53. Chuck Neul, interview by author, April 13, 2010.
54. Byrne, "Inside McKinsey."
55. Ibid.
56. Nanda and Morrell, "McKinsey & Company: An Institution at a Crossroads."
57. Heather Tomlinson, "After Enron, McKinsey Gets Call from the MoD," *Independent,* July 28, 2002.
58. Dick Bower, interview by author, April 15, 2011.

10. RETRENCHMENT

1. "McKinsey's Election Battle," *Economist,* February 27, 2003.
2. Ian Davis, interview by author, June 17, 2010.
3. Juan Hoyos, interview by author, March 17, 2011.
4. Carter Bales, interview by author, April 20, 2010.
5. Michelle Jarrard, interview by author, January 25, 2011.
6. "80 Layoffs at Madison Square Garden," *New York Times,* February 7, 2004.
7. Richard Milne, "'Locusts' of Private Equity Help Grohe," *Financial Times,* June 5, 2008.
8. Steven Greenhouse and Michael Barbaro, "Wal-Mart Memo Suggests Ways to Cut Employee Benefit Costs," *New York Times,* October 26, 2005.
9. Ann Zimmerman and Gary McWilliams, "Inside Wal-Mart's 'Threat Research' Operation," *Wall Street Journal,* April 4, 2007.
10. *New York Observer*, August 11, 2009.
11. Dominic Casserley, interview by author, January 14, 2011.
12. Nat Ives, "Conde Nast's Townsend on Why Gourmet Was Shut Down," *Ad Age,* October 5, 2009.
13. Dirk Smillie, "McKinsey Comes to the House of Murdoch," *Forbes .com,* November 13, 2009.
14. Ibid.
15. Amy Chozick, "Helping Hand for a Print Empire," *New York Times,* July 30, 2012.
16. Lucia Moses, "McKinsey's Back at Time Inc.," *AdWeek,* October 10, 2012.
17. Del Jones, "Some Firms' Fertile Soil Grows Crop of Future CEOs," *USA Today,* January 9, 2008.
18. Andrew Hill, "Inside McKinsey," *FT Magazine,* November 25, 2011.
19. Nancy Killefer, interview by author, July 6, 2011.
20. Duff McDonald, "The Answer Men," *New York Magazine,* July 26, 2009.

21. "Move Over, Goldman: It Is McKinsey's Turn to Try to Sort Out Uncle Sam," *Economist,* January 13, 2009.
22. Ibid.
23. "The Tale of Mr. Jackson: The Public Sector Has Had Its Fill of Management Consultants," *Economist,* January 23, 2010.
24. Gregg Carlstrom, "Report: What Measuring Productivity Could Yield," *Federal Times*, July 20, 2009.
25. http://www.McKinsey.com/Client_Service/Public_Sector.aspx#Defense_and_Security.
26. David Rose, "The Firm That Hijacked the NHS," *Daily Mail*, February 12, 2012.
27. Walter Kiechel III, *The Lords of Strategy* (Boston: Harvard Business Press, 2010), 304.
28. *Wall Street Journal,* September 29, 1997.
29. Kiechel, *The Lords of Strategy,* 306.
30. Andrew Billen, "Goodbye to Glib Gurus and Their Gobbledegook," *Sunday Times,* March 9, 2009.
31. Kevin Mellyn, *Financial Market Meltdown* (Santa Barbara, CA: Praeger, 2009), 71.
32. Kevin Mellyn, *Broken Markets* (New York: Apress, 2012), 153.
33. Mellyn, *Financial Market Meltdown,* 68.
34. http://www.nakedcapitalism.com/2009/05/guest-post-incredibly-uneven-recovery.html.
35. Diana Farrell, interview by author, 2011.
36. Steve Lohr, "GE Goes with What It Knows: Making Stuff," *New York Times,* December 4, 2010.
37. Michelle Celarier, "The Lowdown on McKinsey," *Euromoney,* July 1996.
38. Francois Bouvard, Thomas Fohrmann, and Nick Lovegrove, "The Case for Government Reform Now," *McKinsey Quarterly,* June 2009.

39. http://poetsandquants.com/2011/11/16/McKinsey-doubles-mba-hires-at-duke-haas/.
40. Jason Busch, "McKinsey Caught Up in China Procurement Bribe Scandal," *Spend Matters*, January 22, 2007.
41. Christine Seib, "Now Even Management Consultants Are Feeling the Squeeze," *Times* (London), February 19, 2009.

11. BREAKING THE COMPACT

1. http://www.glassdoor.com/Best-Places-to-Work-LST_KQ0,19.htm.
2. Gordon Pittso, "Dominic Barton's Global Challenge," *Globe and Mail,* August 17, 2009.
3. Dominic Barton, interview by author, June 23, 2011.
4. Dominic Barton, "Capitalism for the Long-Term," *Harvard Business Review,* March 2011.
5. Frank Mattern, interview by author, July 6, 2011.
6. Dana Milbank, "Critics Have Advice for McKinsey," *Globe and Mail,* October 12, 1993.
7. John Merwin, *Forbes*, October 19, 1987.
8. John A. Byrne, *BusinessWeek*, September 20, 1993.
9. Lou Gerstner, *Who Says Elephants Can't Dance? How I Turned Around IBM* (New York: HarperCollins, 2002), 3.
10. Bill Matassoni, interview by author, 2010.
11. Michelle Jarrard, interview by author, January 25, 2011.
12. Alistair Osborne, "Prudential's McKinsey Bill Annoys Investors," *Telegraph,* June 6, 2010.
13. Tom Peters, interview by author, July 27, 2010.
14. Ian Davis, interview by author, June 16, 2011.
15. Kunal N. Talgeri, "The McKinsey Way," *Outlook Business,* May 16, 2009.
16. Brooke Masters, James Fontanella-Khan, and Justin Baer, "McKinsey Partner's Arrest Casts Shadow," *Financial Times,* October 22, 2009.

17. http://www.forbes.com/lists/2011/21/private-companies-11_McKinsey-Company_IPPW.html.
18. Duff McDonald, "Rajat Gupta: Touched by Scandal," *Fortune,* October 1, 2010.
19. Ibid.
20. http://friendsofrajat.com/read-the-open-letter/.
21. http://dealbook.nytimes.com/2012/04/19/insider-trading-investigation--ensnares-goldman-sachs-executive/?nl=business&emc=edit_dlbkam_20120420.
22. Suzanna Andrews, "How Rajat Gupta Came Undone," *BusinessWeek,* May 19, 2011.
23. Ian Davis, interview by author, June 6, 2011.
24. Suketu Mehta, "The Outsider," *Newsweek,* October 23, 2011.
25. Peter Lattman and Azam Ahmed, "Rajat Gupta Convicted of Insider Trading," *New York Times,* June 15, 2012.
26. Michelle Jarrard, interview by author, January 25, 2011.
27. Ian Davis, interview by author, June 6, 2011.
28. Walter Kiechel III, *The Lords of Strategy* (Boston: Harvard Business Press, 2010), 11.
29. Andrew Hill, "Inside McKinsey," *FT Magazine,* November 25, 2011.
30. Peter Grauer, interview by author, July 26, 2011.

EPILOGUE: THE FUTURE OF McKINSEY

1. Walter Kiechel III, *The Lords of Strategy* (Boston: Harvard Business Press, 2010), 2.
2. Nicholas Lemann, "The Kids in the Conference Room," *New Yorker,* October 18, 1999.
3. Bill MacCormack, interview by author, May 7, 2010.
4. Stefan Stern, "Strategy Consultants Need Some New Ideas," *Financial Times*, April 5, 2010.
5. Clay Deutsch, interview by author, March 5, 2011.

6. Clayton M. Christensen, Dina Wang, and Derek van Bever, "Consulting on the Cusp of Disruption," *Harvard Business Review*, October 2013.
7. Gary Hamel, *The Future of Management* (Cambridge: Harvard Business School Press, 2007), 6.
8. George David Smith, John T. Seaman Jr., and Morgan Witzel, *A History of The Firm* (New York: McKinsey & Company, 2010), 444.

INDEX